Le Guin and Identity in Contemporary Fiction

Studies in Speculative Fiction, No. 16

Robert Scholes, Series Editor

Alumni/Alumnae Professor of English and
Chairman, Department of English
Brown University

Other Titles in This Series

Le Guin and Identity
in Contemporary Fiction

by
Bernard Selinger

UMI Research
Press

Ann Arbor / London

Copyright © 1988
Bernard George Selinger
All rights reserved

Produced and distributed by
UMI Research Press
an imprint of
University Microfilms Inc.
Ann Arbor, Michigan 48106

Library of Congress Cataloging in Publication Data

Selinger, Bernard, 1949-
Le Guin and identity in contemporary fiction.

(Studies in speculative fiction ; no. 16)
Bibliography: p.
Includes index.
1. Le Guin, Ursula K., 1929-   —Criticism and
interpretation.   2. Identity in literature.   3. Psycho-
analysis and literature.   I. Title.   II. Series.
PS3562.E42Z88   1988   813'.54   87-19215
ISBN 0-8357-1831-X (alk. paper)

British Library CIP data is available.

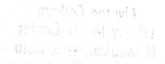

This book is for Frank and Mary

Contents

Preface

This study offers close, very detailed readings of Le Guin's major novels, readings which draw on contemporary theoretical—particularly psychoanalytic—concepts and issues. Theoretical tools are honed best through contact with literature; I would like to think that theory is sounder for having spent time with Le Guin and that Le Guin's works are richer because of their dialogue with theory. This exchange may also enhance our understanding of Le Guin's contemporaries. I wish this study to be regarded as an implicit counterbalance to (even a refutation of) the many Jungian readings of Le Guin's work. The tools that contemporary theory provides are much stronger and yet more delicate than those of the Jungians.

If this book, in any small way, helps the discourses of feminism, psychoanalysis, and Le Guin (along with her peers) to join hands and set each other in motion, then it may prove worth the tree or two it has destroyed. The different discourses that exist must move beyond the binary oppositions that they lock themselves into—oppositions that are ruining this ecosystem. Since our own sensibility is broadened when we take on the sensibility of an other, we need to work creatively in, and then attempt to transcend (as Le Guin attempts), the area of conflict between mass culture and high art, tradition and innovation, nonhuman and human, conservation and regeneration. The future, in this age, is no longer a given.

Acknowledgments

Acknowledgments always fall short and they tend to set up a hierarchy of who did what best for the author. The following have all been important to me—from academic influence to friendship, encouragement, and other kinds of assistance. My gratitude and best wishes go to Ray Mise, Norman N. Holland, Eli Mandel, Ian Sowton, Robert Scholes, Helen Weinzweig, Robert White, Ann Kniskern, Aydon Charlton, Darlene Owen, and the Saskatchewan Indian Federated College.

A version of chapter 8 of this book first appeared in *Canadian Woman Studies* 6:2 (Spring 1985): 48–51.

1

Autist, Artist, and Alternity

Can the gap between the entertainment and the serious art-form be bridged? Some say that science fiction will do it, though not the science fiction of pulp magazines. Therefore, post-Wellsian specialists in science fiction are serious intellectuals whose concern is with prophecy as well as with entertainment; the work of Isaac Asimov in America and Brian Aldiss in England are no easy fripperies for a loose-end evening; they demand concentration as Henry James demands it.

Anthony Burgess
The Novel Now

One of the main characteristics of life is discreteness. Unless a film of flesh envelopes us, we die. Man exists only in so far as he is separated from his surroundings. The cranium is a space-traveler's helmet. Stay inside or you perish . . . death is communion.

Vladimir Nabokov
Pnin

Every work, every novel, tells through its fabric of events the story of its own creation, its own history . . . the meaning of a work lies in its telling itself, its speaking of its own existence.

Tzvetan Todorov
Littérature et signification

I feel sometimes that I am not writing, but describing the struggles with writing, the struggles of birth.

Antonin Artaud
Artaud and After

When I first came across Ursula K. Le Guin's novels in the science fiction section of a bookstore several years ago, I had not read a great deal in the area of science fiction, so the memories and associations that I did have with that form were the usual space ships, bug-eyed monsters, robots, and mad scientists. After reading Le Guin, I found myself thinking, "So *this* is what science fiction is all about." This was a naive thought (especially when further explorations in the field revealed that science fiction, like everything else, is 95 percent trash); it would have been like reading, say, Thomas Pynchon's work and thinking, "So this is what contemporary fiction is all about." After all, Pynchon is as different from John Barth as Le Guin is from Stanislaw Lem. Because some of our finest writers, such as Le Guin, Samuel Delany, and Lem, invent worlds and times with which we are unfamiliar, their work is immediately designated science fiction by their publishers, and thereby its status as literature is reduced. Our most critically acclaimed contemporary fictionalists, such as Nabokov, Barth, Barthelme, Vonnegut, Butor, and Handke also invent worlds, worlds usually as unfamiliar to us as those of Le Guin. What is the essential difference between "mainstream" fiction and "fantasy" or "science fiction"? The answer to this question, if there is one, is complicated by the fact that over the last several years there has been a blurring of the distinction between science fiction and mainstream fiction (Durrell, Lessing, Burgess, Vonnegut, and, to some extent, Pynchon, most readily come to mind as examples of this crossover). Indeed, although Le Guin is generally regarded as a science fiction writer, one who receives both popular and critical acclaim, John Updike has written that "only recently has her reputation, passing through the same cultural space-warp utilized by Ray Bradbury and Kurt Vonnegut, entered what is hailed from the other side as 'mainstream fiction.'" Updike later adds that Le Guin's writing has had "a mainstream tact, color, and intelligence," and that the "social sciences inform her fantasies with far more earthy substance than the usual imaginary space-flight, and her hypothetical futures have a strong flavor of familiar history."[1] But then there are writers like Borges, Calvino, and Cortazar who are often referred to as "fantasists"—to which category do they belong? Ways out of this dilemma are provided by Le Guin:

> All fiction is metaphor. Science fiction is metaphor. What sets it apart from older forms of fiction seems to be its use of new metaphors, drawn from certain great dominants of our contemporary life.
>
> Essentially I am using the scientific element, not as an end in itself, but as a metaphor or symbol, a means of saying something not otherwise expressible.[2]

Whatever the case, when fiction reaches a certain high quality, as Le Guin's does, it defies and transcends limiting and distorting (although sometimes convenient) generic categorization. Mainstream fiction and science fiction or fantasy are essentially labels for the opposite ends of a continuous spectrum of strategies for portraying human relations—and each ignores the other to its own detriment. If these writers are at opposite ends of the spectrum or, rather, if they settle at different points along it, there is, nevertheless, much that they have in common. First of all, they are all postrealist (assuming, of course, that we could come to some agreement as to what constitutes realism); as Le Guin put it, "Realism is perhaps the least adequate means of understanding or portraying the incredible realities of our existence."[3] Secondly, all these fictionalists have a tendency to repeat certain concerns and devices: for instance, the origins of the creative process and the role of the artist, the nature of characterization and the question of the author-character distinction, the problem of illusion and reality, the inadequacy of language to convey experience, and the dilemma of identity, particularly the identity of the artist. But there are persistent, haunting questions which override and perhaps encompass all the other concerns: Who are we and why do we write? Why do we feel compelled to do what we do with tools that are inadequate either to express what we feel or to express the absurdity of our existence? Artists, of course, have traditionally questioned the tools of their trade, but this questioning has never been as intense and pervasive as in these postmodern times.

Language, the creative writer's tool, his pain and his pleasure, has been brilliantly investigated by George Steiner in *After Babel*. He contends that *"Language is the main instrument of man's refusal to accept the world as it is."*[4] The language he is speaking of here is the language of "counter-factuality, contradiction" or "alternity"—the language of the poet. *Established* language is the enemy, and the writer finds it "sordid with lies." A purely public, common speech "severely impairs our sense of self." In reaction to this, writers such as Pinter and Handke have strung together clichés and tags of commercial, journalistic idiom, to produce a discourse which shows no "roughage" of personal reference: "These satiric exercises have a direct bearing on the theory of language. The ego, with its urgent but vulnerable claims to self-definition, withers among hollow, blank phrases. Dead speech creates a vacuum in the psyche."[5] The rift that Steiner discerns and elucidates is between a public, standardizing language and an intuitive, private, and exploratory vision which can help to make language new, and without which there can be "no progress in letters." The public-private dichotomy is one that is experienced by all of us, but it is particularly acute for the child and for the artist:

> There can hardly be an awakened human being who has not, at some moment, been exasperated by the "publicity" of language, who has not experienced an almost bodily discomfort at the disparity between the uniqueness, the novelty of his own emotions and the worn coinage of words. It is almost intolerable that needs, affections, hatreds, introspections which we feel to be overwhelmingly our own, which shape our awareness of identity and the world, should have to be voiced . . . in the vulgate. . . . One can only conjecture as to the blow which this discovery must be to the child's psyche. What abandonments of autonomous, radical vision occur when the

maturing sensibility apprehends that the deepest instrumentalities of personal being are cast in a ready public mould? . . . It may be that the poet and philosopher are those in whom such outrage remains most acute and precisely remembered; . . . witness Sartre's study of himself in *Le Mots* and his analysis of Flaubert's "infantile" refusal to enter the matrix of authorized speech. . . . No word is adequate . . . to articulate a child's discovery of his own unreplicable self.[6]

Steiner further deduces that the uses of alternity, the instrumentalities of fiction, are "bound up with the slowly evolving, hazardous definition of self." So the real crux is "of identity, the perilous gift a man makes when he gives his true name into the keeping of another." To falsify or withhold one's "real name" is to guard one's life while "to pretend to be another, to oneself or at large, is to employ the 'alternative' powers of language in the most thorough, ontologically liberating way."[7] Consequently, and somewhat paradoxically, through the "'make-up' of language, man is able, in part at least, to exit from his own skin and, where the compulsion to 'otherness' becomes pathological, to splinter his own identity into unrelated or contrastive voices. The speech of schizophrenia is that of extreme 'alternity.'"[8] Autism is the earliest manifestation of schizophrenia; the "autistic child breaks off verbal contact. He seems to choose silence to shield his identity."[9]

These are important and revealing statements about the nature of language. They are particularly pertinent to modern and postmodern times because since Mallarmé and Rimbaud, nearly all poetry and prose that seem most vital have been moving audaciously against the current of normal speech—moving, in fact, toward silence or a kind of autism. For Steiner—and for Le Guin, as well as others—the public-private polarity, naming, childhood, the artist, schizophrenia, and identity are all intermingled in this distrust of reality; reality is represented by established language, within which is a hidden component that is compelled to posit otherness. The obvious question, it would seem, is when and how did human beings, artists in particular, grasp the power to "alternate" on reality, to "say otherwise"? And why do some of us appear to possess this private, almost anarchic, core of alternity while others do not? How does one begin to investigate what the poet intuits? We can start by asking the artists themselves.

Brewster Ghiselin's *The Creative Process* is a symposium in which many creative artists reveal what goes on in their minds as they begin and complete their work. Ghiselin's summary remarks are enlightening:

Creation begins typically with a vague, even a confused excitement, some sort of yearning, hunch, or other preverbal intimation of approaching or potential resolution. . . . Often it defines itself as no more than a sense of self surrender to an inward necessity inherent in something larger than the ego and taking precedence over the established order.[10]

This preverbal condition in which the artist experiences an inward necessity (that often generates a lonely and "trance-like state") works against the established order represented by language. This is borne out with remarkable regularity by various artists' statements. Stephen Spender, for example, says, "sometimes when I am writing, the music of the words I am trying to shape takes me far beyond the words, I am aware of a rhythm, a dance, a fury, which is as yet empty of words."[11] Le Guin has said that "the artist deals with what cannot be said in words" and that one of the functions of her writing is to create "metaphors for what our language has no words for as yet."[12] Picasso makes an interesting variation on the strength of the preverbal image:

> It would be very interesting to record photographically, not the stages of a painting, but its metamorphoses. One would see perhaps by what course a mind finds its way towards the crystallization of its dream. But what is really very curious is to see that the picture does not change basically, that the initial vision remains intact in spite of appearance.[13]

This image is persistent. It is the genesis of the work and it is also a microcosm of it—or at least it bears a synedochical relation to the whole.

Another constant in the creative process is the importance of childhood. In addition to noting that in the creation of fantasy worlds, "the role of the child seems central," and that "fantasists are childish, childlike," Le Guin points out that "fiction is made out of the writer's experience, his whole life from infancy on."[14] Spender suspects that "every writer is secretly writing for *someone,* probably for a parent or a teacher who did not believe in him in childhood." Max Ernst's creations often came by recalling a childhood incident, as when the sight of something like a panel opposite his childhood bed "induced one of those dreams between sleeping and waking."[15] T. S. Eliot said that "only a part of an author's imagery comes from his reading. It comes from the whole of his sensitive life since early childhood."[16] And Graham Greene contends that the "creative writer perceives his world once and for all in childhood and early adolescence, and his whole career is an attempt to illustrate his private world in terms of the great public world we all share."[17]

A crucial part of creativity, therefore, is an ability to become open to experiencing very early ego states. Ghiselin's book discloses evidence that creativity may involve such a phase of regression, even to primitive ego states of oneness with the totality of the environment, which can manifest itself, as he says, in a surrender of the self to "something larger." Ernst, for instance, confesses, "I have become the amazed lover of what I have seen, wanting to identify myself with it."[18] This is similar to Antonin Artaud's attempt to reconcile external phenomena with internal life and his preoccupation with finding correspondences between the inner and outer worlds. Georges Braque often said that he did not believe in things, only in the relationships that can potentially unite them. These notions are also articulated by D. H. Lawrence: "Art is a form of supremely delicate awareness and atonement—meaning atoneness, the state of being at one with the object."[19] And Le Guin says, "To reach the other, the artist goes into himself. Using reason, he deliberately enters the irrational. The farther he goes into himself, the closer he comes to the other."[20] At a basic level, one could argue, art is a reshaping of the world as it is absorbed into the psyche. Since none of the above artists has ever really attained the kind of relationship and/or union they seek, one might conclude that one of the mysteries art celebrates is the failure to achieve this union. Yet there is a great beauty in the endeavor and in the courage needed to undertake it.

The attempt for at-oneness with the early human and nonhuman environment is a positive and necessary element of creativity, but it is fraught with dangers. One may lose the boundaries of self completely, and this can lead to "insanity," or the schizophrenia that Steiner regards as the extreme alternity. That the artist is prone to what society terms insanity is a commonplace. Zola, Baudelaire, Rimbaud, Verlaine, and Artaud, to name a few, found strength in their physical and mental illness and pain. And theirs was the language of extreme alternity. Walker Percy has recently written about the problem of what he terms "reentry"—the artist having to continuously reenter the outside world from the inside and vice versa:

> But the most spectacular problems of reentry seem to be experienced by artists and writers. They, especially the latter, seem subject more than most people to estrangement from society around them, to neurosis, psychosis, alcoholism, drug addiction, epilepsy, florid sexual behaviour, solitariness, depression, violence, and suicide.[21]

These are all no doubt occupational hazards, the results of having to splinter one's identity into unrelated or contrastive voices, as Steiner would put it. Certainly there are no qualitative but only quantitative differences between the "neurotic" or "psychotic" individual on the one hand, and the "healthy" individual on the other. The poets are just like us, only more so. "What marks the artist," writes Lionel Trilling, "is his power to shape the material of pain [and, I would add, pleasure] we all have."[22] The tendency to valorize the relationship between "insanity" and art is also exemplified by Le Guin: "Fantasy is nearer to poetry, to mysticism, and to insanity than naturalistic fiction is." (She later adds, in typical fairness, "while we read a novel, we are insane—bonkers.")[23] And in her novel *The Left Hand of Darkness,* Genly Ai asks why the schizophrenic "foretellers" could not be cured. The reply is, "Would you cure a singer of his voice?"[24]

Schizophrenia is an extreme disturbance in identity, and the original manifestation of it is autism. Any artist, I think, would admit to retreating into an isolated, autistic state in order to create—to create something which is, paradoxically, a reaching out, an attempt at communion. Le Guin writes in a tiny room, "once a nursery," behind a closed door. After explaining how she writes, she concludes: "And all of this, every time, you do alone—absolutely alone."[25] Thomas Wolfe, speaking about his various peaks of creative activity, says that during "this time I reached that state of naked need and utter isolation which every artist has got to meet and conquer if he is to survive at all."[26] Ray Bradbury admits that "every single day for 50 years, if I can get to my typewriter by 9 o'clock, by

10:30 I'm protected against the world."[27] And Percy explains that "writers like Joyce, Faulkner, Proust are able to write about the market-place and society only in the degree that they distance themselves from it—whether by exile, alcohol, or withdrawal to a cork-lined room."[28]

What I wish to contend is that the creative state of mind is, among other things, at least a temporary regression to preverbal days, when (as I will later document) one's identity "theme" is "imprinted." This regression is not necessarily a defensive one, but an essential, recurrent phase in the development of a creative relation to the world—the autistic phase (which is a correlative of the symbiotic phase of childhood) is a crucial element of this relation. The artist, as witnessed by the above statements, seems to have a particularly broad range of ego-reality relation; it is an ego that integrates reality in such a fashion that the earlier and deeper levels of ego-reality (self/other) integration remain alive as dynamic sources of higher integration. This central aspect of the creative process, during which one is compelled to relive and attempt to express the feeling, the intimations, produced by the preverbal image—which is allied with one's identity theme and is the earliest possible sense of self as other—is nicely intimated by dancer Mary Wigman:

> Charged as I frequently am with "freeing" the dance from the music, the question often arises, what can be the source and basic structure of my own dancing. I cannot define its principles more clearly than to say that the fundamental idea of any creation arises in me or, rather, out of me as a completely independent dance theme. This theme, however primitive or obscure at first, already contains its own development and alone dictates its singular and logical sequence. What I feel as the germinal source of any dance may be compared perhaps to the melodic or rhythmic "subject" as it is first conceived by a composer, or to the compelling image that haunts a poet.[29]

The artist is someone with no strong sense of identity and hence must constantly create and recreate variations on the rudimentary identity theme which was established in the earliest days of her existence; these variations work against and tend to undermine the established order. John Keats insisted that "that which is creative must create itself" and looked on identity as a barrier to creative work—this is linked in with his notion of Negative Capability.[30] At one point he writes:

> As to the poetic Character itself—it is not itself—it has no self—it is everything and nothing. It has no character—it enjoys light and hate; it loves in gusto, be it foul or fair, high or low—It has as much delight in conceiving Iago as an Imogen. What shocks the virtuous philosopher delights the camelion Poet—A Poet is the most unpoetical of anything in existence; because he has no identity—Not one word I ever utter can be taken as an opinion growing out of my identical nature—the identity of everyone begins to press upon me.[31]

Not always confident about *who* she is, the poet's ego ventures out to meet its objects, seeking union with them, trying to become them. But the writer also requires periods of isolation or autism in order to create a language of alternity and in order to "shield" her self against the "pressing" or absorbing outside world. This is the paradoxical nature of identity; it is inherent in the word itself: it means both sameness and distinctiveness.

The central concern of Le Guin's work is with this puzzle of identity, especially as it is formed, or not formed, by or against language. This concern is also a preoccupation of the majority of our best contemporary writers. Tony Tanner writes:

> The kind of paradox suggested by Walt Whitman when he celebrated both the idea of an American society in which everyone would flow together in a loving "ensemble," and also the "principle of individuality, the pride and centripetal isolation of a human being in himself—identity— personalism," still confronts the American writer in various forms. We may say that a central concern for the hero of many recent American novels is this: can he still find freedom which is not a jelly, and can he establish an identity which is not a prison? . . . the dilemma and quest of the hero are often analogous to those of the author. Can he find a *stylistic* freedom which is not simply a meaningless incoherence, and can he find a stylistic form which will not trap him inside the existing forms of previous literature?[32]

The dilemma and quest of Le Guin's protagonists are, as we shall see, analogous to hers; and, similarly, the dilemma and quest registered by the work of Le Guin are congruous with those of her contemporaries. Le Guin's project has been located around the paradox articulated by Whitman: how to balance sameness and distinctiveness, or symbiosis and separateness/autism. On the deepest level, the artist Le Guin confronts the origins of her existence, the dilemma of identity, and the tension between private and public language, which is allied with naming. Our most enduring writers have been able to capture and put into words many of the secrets of their own creative ability and, by extension, the creative process in general. Accordingly, any light we can shed on the work of Le Guin will shed light on her contemporaries as well, no matter in what part of the spectrum they dwell.

2

Correspondences

No thinker can pass Freud, Marx, or Nietzsche unconcerned: he must find something in the mind of men like these that is more sublime than what their mind destroyed. It is not modishness but necessity that impels us to struggle with them, as Blake did with Milton, or the Biblical interpreter with the devastating and corrosive evidence of historical experience.

Geoffrey Hartman
"Literary Criticism and Its Discontents"

But underlying the literary and ideological games is the archetypal modern problem: the problem of individual identity. For, though there is nothing modern in the question, who am I?, *characteristically modern is the lack of* sense *of identity, the feeling of* I am no one—*of which the feeling,* I am more than one person *is a variant. "I am someone, no one, and a hundred thousand people," as one of Pirandello's titles (almost) reads.*

Eric Bentley
"Brecht and the Rule of Force"

This chapter, which is an attempt at formulating a methodology or a strategy, is constructed on borrowings from, and is an attempted synthesis of, works which have contributed to my efforts to come to terms with Le Guin and her major concern with identity, with which naming and language are tightly bound. Although the writers I have chosen are for the most part psychoanalytic, I have selected them because each has contributed to a growing understanding of the epigenesis of the self. I am aware of the limitations of psychoanalytic theory, or of any theory. We must, however, be patient of theory. Terry Eagleton, among others, has pointed out that those of us who dislike theory or claim to get along better without it are simply in the grip of an older theory. Thus hostility to "theory usually means an opposition to other people's theories and an oblivion of one's own."[1]

More so than other theories, psychoanalytic theory raises the ire of literary critics. There are several reasons for this. The most common complaint is that it is "reductive." To which, at times, I want to reply, "So what?" Surely any work of art worth its salt can undergo and transcend criticism that is apt to "reduce" it. But reduce it to what? What does reduction really mean? (Its archaic definition, interestingly enough, is "a restoration to righteousness.") Does it ultimately mean that literary studies are *not* about society, or sexuality, or psychic forces, or interpersonal and interfamilial relationships, but about masterpieces that are in need of frequent adulation? Admittedly, in its attempts to systematize and verify our own psychological insights, psychoanalytic literary theory does frequently imply that there is some fundamental "discourse" which it knows, but with which the text or writer is not yet sufficiently acquainted. In other words, the psychoanalytic critic is finding in the literary text what the Freudian or Lacanian orthodoxy has groomed him to find there, and continually returns the text to preexistent psychoanalytic models. Perhaps the worst tendency of psychoanalytic discourse is to be apolitical and to pay little or no attention to the historical context of the work. But isn't it an obvious critical dictum that no critical method will exhaust a text, and each will privilege certain things to the detriment of others? This points up the need for complementary approaches and is why Catherine Belsey, in *Critical Practice,* argues that to have a truly enlightened and radical criticism we need to combine or reconcile the Marxian project with the psychoanalytic one. This is no mean task (I cannot profess to be up to it), and it is one that some of our finest minds—for example, Roland Barthes, some members of the Frankfurt School, Fredric Jameson, Julia Kristeva (the early one)—have struggled with.

Whatever the case, since I am taking the psychoanalytic route to the mysterious heart of Le Guin (the Marxian way has been pursued most admirably by Darko Suvin and, to a degree, Fredric Jameson), I would like to end this prolegomenon or apologia by pointing out some of the positive qualities of psychoanalytic criticism. First, while one weakness of psychoanalysis is its tendency (in some hands at any rate) to be apolitical, the equivalent weakness in political approaches is to ignore the origins of desire, subjectivity, and the relatively independent play of unconscious psychic phenomena. By investigating these phenomena, the good psychoanalytic critic reads the work with a sense of its ambiguous and latent meanings, and thus can find new meanings and relations that will increase the importance of the work. Because writers tell us what is going on inside them (Le Guin is adamant about this fact), they are unusually available to psychoanalytic investigation and explanation. Although the state of an artist's mind may resemble that of the psychotic's, the crucial difference is that the artist is in command of his psychosis (at least while writing). Therefore his text will constantly lead to outer reality by taking account of it, as opposed to the psychotic, who is trapped inside his own fantasy world. Lionel Trilling makes a crucial point when he says that "the Freudian psychology is the one which makes poetry indigenous to the very constitution of the mind. Indeed the mind, as Freud sees it, is in the greater part of its tendency exactly a poetry-making organ."[2] Therefore some knowledge of the poetic process can lead to a greater understanding of the mind. An understanding of the mind, its inner drives and psychic forces, and how it relates to other minds, can lead to the emancipation of people from what frustrates their self-actualization and well-being.

Most of all, perhaps, psychoanalysis, like fiction writing, can serve to undermine many of our crippling and confining illusions. It constantly reminds us that we are neither as free nor as "adult" as we like to think. It makes us realize once again that we have mothers and fathers (for better or for worse), and what it means to be born. Edward Said reminds us that the "universalizing habit by which a system of thought is believed to account for everything too quickly slides into quasi-religious synthesis."[3] This habit, it seems to me, is one that psychoanalysis may help us break out of. Julia Kristeva is positing something like this when she writes:

> The psychoanalytic intervention within Western knowledge has a fundamentally deceptive effect. Psychoanalysis, critical and dissolvant, cuts through political illusions, fantasies, and beliefs to the extent that they consist in providing only one meaning, an uncriticizable ultimate Meaning, to human behaviour. If such a situation can lead to despair in the polis, we must not forget that it is also a source of lucidity and ethics. The psychoanalytic intervention is, from this point of view, a counterweight, an antidote, to political discourse which, without it, is free to become our modern religion: the final explanation.[4]

We should applaud any attempt to break out of departmental divisions (or compartments) and what Said calls "the proliferating orthodoxy of separate fields," which lead to such statements as "I'm sorry I can't understand this—I'm a literary critic, not a sociologist."[5] With all this in mind, I will attempt to illustrate (in as nonprocrustean a manner as possible) the existence, or potential existence, of a dialogue between the work of Le Guin and an important stream of contemporary psychoanalytic thought. As John Fekete says regarding the present criticism on Le Guin, we need a "juxtaposition of literary discourse with other modes of discourse for their mutual illumination."[6]

Le Guin's preoccupation with names and imaginative use of them is one of her trademarks. George Steiner in *After Babel* underscores the interrelationship of naming, language, and identity.[7] Geoffrey Hartman observes that "naming and the problem of identity cannot be dissociated."[8] Accordingly, I would first like to bring attention to the problems posed by the act of naming, and then integrate this into my attempt to synthesize elements of thought from those writers who have contributed greatly to our understanding of the paradox of identity and its uneasy relationship with language and creative communication.

As Jacques Derrida has pointed out, names appear to be pure signifiers in that they have a referent—person or place—but no meaning or signified (other than the associations we have with them). Much of Derrida's work explores the idea of the proper name and its relationship to language. In *Of Grammatology* he writes:

> There was in fact a first violence to be named. To name, to give names that it will be on occasion forbidden to pronounce, such is the originary violence of language which consists in inscribing within a difference, in classifying, in suspending the vocative absolute. To think the unique *within* the system, to inscribe it there, such is the gesture of the arche-writing.[9]

There is a kind of simultaneity being invoked here: inscribing within a difference, the unique within the system. This simultaneity or, perhaps, ambiguity, regarding naming that Derrida often plays with is also evidenced by Gayatri Spivak's attempt to summarize Derrida's project, which has to do with the movement of desire around the proper name: "The narcissistic desire to make one's own 'proper' name 'common,' to make it enter and be at one with the body of the mother tongue; and, at the same time, the oedipal desire to preserve one's proper name, to see it as the analog of the *name* of the father."[10] Naming is here related to an attempted merger of the mother principle (narcissism, fusion) and the father principle (Oedipus, uniqueness). Perhaps the key phrase is "at the same time."

For Jacques Lacan, naming is allied with the father principle. The name of the Father is the Law; and the name of the Father operates explicitly in the register of language. Moreover, the subject is always already inscribed in language "if only by virtue of his proper name."[11] This inscription of the subject is most readily apparent when the mirror phase ends and the child takes the father's *nom* in an act of identification, which is also his *non,* that is, the prohibition of incestual union with the mother. At this moment society and the symbolic order claim the child and enmesh her. The *nom* thus comes to signify "mother's desire," which in turn signifies the phallus. This is a result of Lacanian insight through puns: the child's *désir de la mère* means both "desire for the mother" and "mother's desire" which is, symbolically, the phallus. So although the proper name, the name of the father, signifies separation from the mother, separation from the imaginary order (after the mirror phase) and induction into the symbolic order, there is still a trace of desire for the mother (union with the mother) which is also revealed by the punning and the act of induction. In other words, the *non* relates to the desire for the mother and the *nom,* the official separation, is always a reminder of what one was separated from.

Thus it would appear that there is always an alternative or specular name to the proper name or name of the father: a pet name, a baby name, a common name (as Derrida would have it), which signifies a desire for, or a continued attachment to, the original narcissistic union. This secret, private, repressed, common name may be the kind of thing Hartman is referring to when he speculates that

> there may be such a thing as a specular name or "imago du nom propre" in the fantasy development of the individual, a name more genuinely one's own than a signature or proper

name. Signature can always be faked, is there something that cannot be faked? . . . Is it possible to discern a specular word, logos phase, or image of the proper name in the life of the individual?[12]

Hartman leaves this question open. I contend that this logos phase bears a strong relation to what I (following the lead of Heinz Lichtenstein and Norman N. Holland) call an "identity theme." Le Guin, largely because of her preoccupation with naming, especially with private names, intuits that there is a persistent name or identity that cannot be faked and is therefore more genuine than the public designation. And while a proper name confers a kind of public identity, a label of one's distinction or differentiation from others, the private name may represent something that binds rather than divides. Luce Irigaray is working around this idea in her endeavor to establish through language the sort of communication that she desires among "nous: toute(s)"—"our naming system has always hindered this communion. Names appropriate identity and cloister us within the networks of family relations."[13] For Irigaray, it appears, identity is acquired before the proper name is enforced by the family network. Hence, if there is a name that predates the official naming system, it would be allied with identity.

Julia Kristeva maintains that *true* naming and the ability to name arises out of that space (which she calls the "semiotic disposition") that exists prior to the sign (and precedes Lacan's mirror stage) before any language begins to encode the child's "idealities." Kristeva cites clinical evidence to show that the child's ability to name, especially spatial naming, "retains the memory of the maternal impact already evoked within the constitution of semiotic rudiments. . . . The *entry into syntax constitutes a first victory over the mother,* a still uncertain distancing of the mother, by the simple fact of naming."[14] The proper name, however, arises from an "uncertain position of the speaking subject's identity and refers back to the preobjectival state of naming."[15] Furthermore, Kristeva contends that the potential meanings of infantile language and the problem of naming are always at work within our "adult" discourse. She concludes that "naming, always originating in a place (the *chora,* space, 'topic,' subject-predicate), is a *replacement* for what the speaker perceives as an archaic mother—a more or less victorious confrontation, never finished with her."[16] The ability to name, and therefore the entry into syntax, constitute a victory over the mother; however, this victory is not final—it is still uncertain distancing of the mother. The proper name relates to an uncertainty about identity and *refers back* to another naming state, the preobjectival one. Naming in general is a replacement for the archaic mother; but though this is more or less successful, it is never complete. Once again we find this duplicity concerning naming: it is a separation that is not quite a separation, verging on a form of union. Margaret Mahler notes that the "ability to name objects seems to have provided the toddler with a greater sense of ability to control his environment. Use of the personal pronoun 'I' also often appeared at this time, as well as the ability to name and recognize familiar people." Mahler has also witnessed that, although naming, the acquisition of language, aids in separation from the maternal unit, the child is always hesitant about being a person with a name because this designates a loss of symbiosis.[17]

As these accounts indicate, a name represents a kind of duality, perhaps a combination of a victory and a defeat. It can mean a victory over the mother and thus a giving in to the law of the father; that is, it may represent a separation from the maternal order and an inscription into the paternal order of language and society. Or it can mean a continued union with the mother and thus an implicit defiance of, or refusal to recognize the validity and "importance" of the father and the society that he ostensibly represents through language. This double paradigm is implicit in the act of naming; naming is never either/or, it is both/and. Le Guin, consciously or unconsciously, recognizes this duality or duplicity. Although one of her main characteristics is a desire to balance, or perhaps mediate, scrutiny of her work reveals a valorization of the private part of the name, which is a victory over the father—a questioning of paternal or phallic discourse—and a leaning toward the original unity. The private name is a signifier of that preverbal space, prior to the sign; it is, as Kristeva would put it, that archaic disposition that some writers bring to light in order to challenge the closure of meaning.

Thus naming, like language and identity, is marked by duplicity. Identity means both sameness and distinctiveness; yet when speaking of a person's "sense of identity" or "ego-identity" we generally mean, or think we mean, distinctiveness as opposed to sameness. However, as Le Guin's work suggests, and as contemporary psychoanalytic theory bears out, self is always other, to varying degrees. Identity, then, will be regarded throughout this study as one's ability to maintain inner sameness and continuity combined with the awareness of one's self as an entity separate and distinct from one's environment, specifically, one's earliest environment. (Context will dictate which of the two elements needs to be dominant at certain times.) Mine is a concise way of stating Roy Schafer's more elaborate definition:

> Identity implies object representations as well as self representations, specific content themes as well as abstract organizing principles, aspects of the id and superego systems as well as the ego system, and aspects of the surrounding external world viewed historically as well as in cross section and subjectivity as well as objectivity.[18]

Very helpful to this discussion, largely because it seems to apply more directly to literature, is Heinz Lichtenstein's identity maintenance theory. What we describe as the personality of another person, Lichtenstein argues, is an invariant that we remove from the countless sequence of bodily and behavioral transformations during the entire life of the individual. In other words, the individual lives out variations on an identity theme much as a musician might play variations on a musical theme, or as a single mathematical variant might give rise to an infinity of functions. Significantly, one critic shows that Le Guin's works "resemble musical recurrence, that persistence with which a pervasive theme expresses itself in variations."[19] Developmentally, out of the great range of potentialities within a child, its mother-person actuates a specific way of being:

> The mother does not convey a *sense* of identity to the infant but an *identity:* the child is the organ, the instrument for the fulfillment of the mother's unconscious needs. *Out of the infinite potentialities within the human infant, the specific stimulus combination emanating from the mother "releases" one, and only one, concrete way of being this organ, this instrument.* This "released" identity will be irreversible, and thus it will compel the child to find ways and means to realize this specific identity which the mother has imprinted upon it.

The child, then, "obeys" the maternal stimulations; yet this obedience is also a fulfillment of the child's own needs: "In being the instrument, the organ for the satisfaction of the maternal Otherness, the full symbiotic interaction of the two partners is realized for both of them." Although this imprinted identity theme is irreversible, it is capable of infinite variations. Thus man is the protean animal, capable of innumerable identities—he must constantly *create* himself in accordance to an image pressed upon him. Strictly speaking, one can never know another's "primary identity" because it is deeply and unconsciously buried. Formed before speech, it can hardly be put into words; since the mother's specific expectations of the child are "all nonverbally communicated, the child will 'create itself' as he understands those expectations." As the child gradually separates from the mother, it becomes another one in relation to her:

> Thus, its beginning individuality is experienced in terms of a changed relationship with someone else. Its individuality emerges from a state of primary oneness, then into a primitive way of relatedness—at first confined to an I-you relatedness—which is the primary *social* unit. One aspect of this dilemma of human identity is the fact that outside a relatedness to another one it collapses. Only by contrasting themselves one to another can human beings become separate, can they acquire or create an identity. The integral role of the other in the creation of an identity constitutes a grave danger, a profound threat to one's identity through loss, abandonment, or enforced separation. The dangers are real, and they make the alternative—regression to the symbiotic state with loss of identity—an always threatening possibility.[20]

What we have, therefore, is a "special 'existential' imbalance" which is at the root of the precariousness of human existence. The separation-symbiosis polarity or counterbalance is the key to working variations on an identity theme. Lichtenstein's identity theme, it must be noted, is an object-relational concept. Recently, arguments have been made for the use of the object-relations body of theory for historical and sociological studies as well as for insight into the origins of creation and aesthetic experience.[21] By putting the child's relationship to the mother at the heart of psychoanalytic thought, object-relations psychoanalysis focuses attention on the self-other relationships of infancy that shape identity, establish forms of interaction with the environment, and lead to the acquisition of individual autonomy. Winnicott, perhaps the strongest and most progressive voice of the object-relations school, invites us to regard art not as a separate product, but as a process of communication. Winnicott locates play, art, and cultural experience as emanating from the "potential space" between infant and mother, which precedes the clear definition of subject-object boundaries. This intermediate area between the infant's psychological fusion with the mother-environment and the attainment of self-other differentiation constitutes the greater part of the infant's experience. Winnicott uses the terms "transitional object" and "transitional phenomenon" to describe and symbolize "the union of two now separate beings, baby and mother, *at the point in time and space of the initiation of their state of separateness.*" This intermediate area "both joins and separates the baby and the mother." Both inner reality and external life contribute to this middle ground, which exists as a kind of "resting place for the individual engaged in the perpetual human task of keeping inner and outer reality separate yet interrelated." Of course, no human being is free from the strain of relating inner and outer reality and thus the "task of reality-acceptance is never completed."[22] The intermediate area, moreover, simultaneously provides a relief from the strain of this interrelation and symbolizes the problem of coming to terms with the reality principle. As the initial form of intersubjective mediation, this space serves as the prototype for all later communication activity, which must retain its boundary-blurring and boundary-forming aspects.

At this early stage, the mother (or "facilitating environment," according to Winnicott) is giving the infant "the *experience of omnipotence;* by this I mean more than magical control, I mean the term to include the creative aspect of experience." Because this aspect of experience includes communication, Winnicott describes the conflict the infant encounters in communicating, in relation to its transitional object, as a private self that is not communicating but yet at the same time wants to communicate and to be found. The question becomes, then, "how to be isolated without having to be insulated." This conflict is most readily observed in the artist:

> In the artist of all kinds I think one can detect an inherent dilemma, which belongs to the co-existence of two trends, the urgent need to communicate and the still more urgent need not to be found. This might account for the fact that we cannot conceive of an artist's coming to the end of the task that occupies his whole nature.

The two extremes, explicit communication that is "indirect" and silent or personal communication that feels "real"—each of these has its place in the intermediate area where "there exists for many, but not for all, a mode of communication which is a most valuable compromise."[23]

The separation-symbiosis dilemma that Lichtenstein described—and that Winnicott works through in his own terms, particularly by locating a potential space between the two polarities—is closely related to Margaret Mahler's observations. Mahler says that children who encounter symbiotic problems—a fusion, melting, and lack of differentiation between the self and nonself: a complete blurring of *boundaries*—will use the extreme form of separation, "autism," as a "desperate means of warding off the fear of losing whatever minimal individual entity they may have succeeded in achieving." They use autism to "ward off the threatened regression into the symbiotic fusion to preserve individual entity, separate from mother or father." Mahler also adds that when autism conflicts with symbiotic fusion, it is often "accompanied by bisexual conflict." When cases of child psychosis are met at a later stage, pure cases of autistic child psychosis as well as pure cases of symbiotic psychosis are quite rare; mixed cases are frequent because by this time symbiotic mechanisms have been superimposed on autistic structures and vice versa.[24] For Mahler, the main cause for alienation of ego from reality and for fragmentation is the above-described disturbance—autistic and symbiotic infantile psychoses are seen as the "two extreme disturbances of the sense of 'identity.'" If the separation-individuation process is to be successful, two levels must be attained: "(1) the awareness of being a separate and individual entity, and (2) a beginning awareness of a gender-defined self-identity."[25]

Bruno Bettelheim writes of the autistic child's need to separate himself from a reality he no longer trusts or feels to be potentially destructive. The child often strives for a lost image of a satisfying world through fantasy (a world in which he believes he is in control of his fate). He loses interest in a world he feels he cannot change. Accordingly, the child gives up public language: "The autistic child may still try to talk to himself or some imaginary person, or else to some real people but in a private language they cannot understand." Nevertheless, Bettelheim feels, "it is only when communication reaches the symbolic level of language that a self can become fully established with the 'I' clearly separated from the 'you.'"[26]

This crucial idea of entry into the symbolic world of language has been thoroughly investigated by Lacan, who has promulgated the notion of the symbolic order—the language by which society structures our thought and communication.[27] For Lacan, the child's first discovery of sexual difference comes around the same time that it is discovering language. This is because it begins to realize that its relations of difference and similarity to the other speaking subjects around it constitute its own identity as a subject of a certain gender. However, since language is deceptive—"speech was given to man to hide his thoughts"[28]—and "empty" (it is an endless process of difference and absence; nothing can be possessed in its fullness—the child must now move along an infinite chain of signifiers), the subject will never be fully present to himself in language. He will be divided from himself, undergoing a split "by virtue of being a subject only in so far as he speaks."[29] His speech, given to him or imposed on him in that the signifier always appears in the field of the language of his society, will always refer to that autonomous world of language without which the subject cannot be constructed. No person, however, can ever be fully present in the metonymic chain of signifiers and meaning because its effect is to differentiate all identities. Thus the subject is "split." This splitting of the subject had already been intimated in primitive form in the Imaginary order by the mirror phase, where the child discovers a likeness of itself in another (the reflection). Although its relation to this reflection or image is of an imaginary kind—the reflection in the mirror is both itself and not itself, so a blurring of subject and object still remains—it is still a feeling or "illusion" of self-identity, which will never again be felt in the realm of the symbolic. Moreover, there is a sense of alienation produced by this reflected "I" (which is usually represented by the mother, with whom the child identifies) because the child "misrecognizes" itself: the child *is* his own double more than he is himself. Nonetheless, this is an experience, a world, of *"plenitude,* with no lacks or exclusions of any kind: standing before the mirror, the 'signifier' (the child) finds a 'fullness,' a whole and unblemished identity, in the signified of its reflection. No gap has yet opened up between signifier and signified, subject and world."[30] When language enters, it divides this experience of fullness accorded by the Imaginary—we will never again be able to find rest in that single object (the final meaning), the mother's body. We travel along replacements for replacements, metaphors for metaphors, unable to recapture the pure (although "fictive") self-identity and self-completion that we enjoyed in the Imaginary. But the symbolic function must be retained at all costs, because loss of the symbolic function, Lacan warns, is a slide into madness or schizophrenia.

The seeming inaccessibility of this lost realm of the Imaginary is enhanced by our recognition that language is something that is never entirely under our control. The structuralists have been telling us this about language for some time, as have the poets. Christopher Dewdney is a poet who has made an investigation into how and why language has become autonomous, and how one may resist it. In a documented, illustrated, and tightly argued monograph, Dewdney demonstrates that language has diverged from its parallel status with the human species and has become "animated" and taken on a life of its own. This animated language acts on the individual, restricting the limits of conceptualization. The poet, however, by the specialized use of linguistic conventions, is able to transcend the animated language through the use of a special neural system which is unique to the "ontogeny" of the writer. In this system—a special condition of intelligence outside the realm of animated language—" 'I' is an illusion." Since the writer, especially the poet, places such an unusual demand on the speech centers, the demand for "novel configurations," a kind of "schizophrenic fission" takes place (similar to Rimbaud's *"dérèglement de tous les sens"* or Keats' "Negative Capability"), which allows the poet to function beyond his capability. Dewdney calls this renewed ability to function the "Parasite;" the old animated language is called the "Governor" or "Host." Hence, the "artificial energy derived from controlled neurochemical 'schizophrenia' drives the Parasite far beyond the perceptions of its host."[31]

Allying the insights of the poet with those of the linguist and the neurologist or neurochemist, Dewdney's Governor-Parasite opposition is akin to Lacan's Symbolic-Imaginary antinomy. But whereas Lacan tends to value the Symbolic over the Imaginary—without the symbolic function one is doomed to madness, lost in the preoedipal realm of the maternal Imaginary—Dewdney values the "psychotic" state, at least for the poet, because it is a state that undermines and then transcends the standardizing effects of language. Furthermore, the poet has control of this state, of his schizophrenia. This way of thinking is similar to that of Julia Kristeva, whose "semiotic disposition" is a pattern of forces that we can detect inside language. This play of forces has been retrieved by artists (such as Mallarmé, Joyce, Artaud, and Céline) whose language "musicates through letters" and is able to "resume within discourse the rhythms, intonations, and echolalias of the mother-infant symbiosis—intense, pre-oedipal, predating the father."[32] This archaic dimension of language, prediscursive, preverbal, is an immediate expression of the bodily contact with the mother before the "paternal order" of language (related to Lacan's Symbolic and Dewdney's Governor) comes to separate the subject from the mother. In a sense, the Semiotic, much like Dewdney's Parasite, represents a poetic dimension of language that is nonetheless intertwined with language. Although Kristeva's Semiotic corresponds to Lacan's Imaginary in that both are associated with the preoedipal, prelinguistic maternal, and are therefore in contradistinction to the Symbolic, Lacan's Imaginary is more conservative than Kristeva's Semiotic. As Jane Gallop notes, the Imaginary is "comforting, tends toward closure, and is disrupted by the symbolic; the semiotic is revolutionary, breaks closure, and disrupts the symbolic."[33] Although the Semiotic is closely allied with the feminine and the maternal, it is not, Kristeva is at pains to point out (partly by means of her examples from the symbolist poets and avant-garde writers), a language exclusive to women, largely because it comes from that preoedipal period that recognizes no distinctions of gender. The Semiotic thus blurs all distinctions between masculine and feminine and tends toward a "bisexual" discourse. Because the literature of Semiotic discourse is opposed to all fixed, absolute significations, and "since the ideologies of modern male-dominated class-society rely on such fixed signs for their power (God, father, state, order, property and so on)," Terry Eagleton writes, "such literature becomes a kind of equivalent in the realm of language to revolution in the sphere of politics."[34]

Although the writers above are not uniform in method, parlance, or even ideology necessarily, they do complement each other as guides through a certain segment of contemporary thinking.[35] I regard Le Guin's works, at their very basic level, as a major contribution to this segment. What we are dealing with is a kind of zeitgeist, a direction of thought. I will concentrate in this study on the things that unite these theorists with each other and with Le Guin, rather than on the things that divide them. This unitive endeavor is, I hope, one of which Le Guin would approve. Many of the things these thinkers have in common—such as the investigation of preverbal states, which are relationships beyond language; the recognition of the relative bisexuality of the preoedipal stage; the problems posed by splitting or doubling and the occasional concomitant feeling of alienation—will become more evident as this study progresses. For now, I shall underscore the most important and pronounced similarities.

The most evident affinity of these writers is their emphasis on the need for balance and counterpoise. Inextricably intertwined with this is the notion of creativity. For Lichtenstein, variations on a basic identity theme, which is formed in the preverbal mother-child relation, are dependent upon the successful counterbalancing of separation and symbiosis, though at times one will be obliged to dominate the other. Variations, Lichtenstein maintains, "spell the difference between human creativity and a 'destiny neurosis.'"[36] Mahler sees autism, the extreme form of separation, as a last-ditch way of counterbalancing a loss of entity through "over-symbiosis." We all pass through the "normal" autistic phase, which serves to support the need for a feeling of omnipotence; this phase frequently exhibits periods of "hallucination." Some of us experience this feeling of omnipotence and the accompanying hallucinations (which are usually negative or frightening) more than others. This experience is one that the artist is more accustomed to than most and is related to the "psychotic" side of infantile autism. Although Bettelheim focuses entirely on the autistic child and her striving to create a "fantasy" world in opposition to a destructive reality she does not trust, he also stresses the love, communication, and connection that is needed to help the child differentiate and come to terms with the "I" and the "Thou." Winnicott uses the transitional phenomena idea as a way of designating the ceaseless creative compromise—a compromise only some individuals, such as the artist, are able to perpetuate. The compromise is between inner reality and outer reality, private communication and public communication, boundary blurring and boundary forming. Perhaps the most valuable contribution by the ever-slippery Lacan to the present discussion is his insistence, in theories of interhuman relations, on the permanence of the mirror stage (the heart of the Imaginary) which inaugurates our being for another and our being for ourselves. Although Lacan instructs us to be wary of "Imaginary slidings," his discourse is quite consistently a structural analysis of the position of the subject, who always moves at the intersection of the Imaginary representation and Symbolic speech. Dewdney and Kristeva, the first a poet and the latter a Marxian, psychoanalytic, and semiotic thinker, serve to underline Lacan's ideas while focusing his insights more toward the creative aspect of this "intersection." The so-called schizoid mentality, the one that can arise out of the Imaginary realm (which is akin in one aspect to the autistic world and to the "not to be found" world that Winnicott elucidates), tends to counterbalance the orderly world of the Symbolic. It is seen by Dewdney as undermining and transcending and by Kristeva as interpenetrating and calling into question the Symbolic, the Governor, and paternal discourse. Le Guin's canon intuits the need for this precarious and perpetual balance that all these writers are working around. Her tendency is to value the private realm, however. The other levels of meaning in Le Guin's work—mythological, social, environmental, political—also seek to initiate an equilibrium but, I submit, these other balancing feats are rooted in and nourished by the original one. Her leaning toward the archaic, private, preverbal world, the Semiotic side of the counterpoise, effects and informs her political anarchism, for example.

For all of the above, language is that by which our society structures our thought and communication. Because of its standardizing effect, public language is inherently inimical to one who wants to work variations on a model or pattern. Since the artist is the one most concerned with working variations on a theme, creating "novel configurations" (as Dewdney says), she is the one likely to manifest the greatest distrust of language. Periodically, artists are inclined to question the tools of their trade, but the questioning of language has never been such an overriding and widespread concern as it is these days. Beckett, Handke, Pinter, Barth, and Cortazar are some of the most prominent among those searching for a new language, even a nonlanguage. Allied with the movement towards silence are attractive and enchanting but rather peculiar forms of characterization that are inclined to emphasize the schizoid (almost all of Beckett's "characters") and the autistic (Handke's Kaspar Hauser is the most outstanding example).

This relationship between mistrust of language and schizophrenia comes as no surprise, given the preceding discussion. The artist, as far as Dewdney is concerned, can only subvert and overcome the limiting nature of language by instituting a schizoid state in which "I" is an illusion. This state, and the "neologisms" that frequently accompany it, are akin to Bettelheim's analysis of the autistic child who in fact will not use the first person pronoun and who communicates privately, usually in a language of neologism. Only when, and if, the child submits to communicating at the symbolic level of language does the "I" appear, quite clearly separated from the "you." This is related to Lacan's argument: in the Oedipus, the child moves from an immediate nondistanced relationship with its mother to a mediate relationship, due to its insertion into the symbolic order of language, the family, society. Any serious fault in the transition (the Oedipus) rivets the child to the earlier, imaginary relationship, depriving it of subjectivity or the "I," and rendering it schizoid, incapable of making the symbolic substitution inherent in language. Mahler had also noted how the acquisition of language is the cleanest way of making the break from the early states of the normal or psychotic autistically or symbiotically oriented child. Kristeva asserts that the so-called psychotic infantile language is the kind of language that the poet brings to light—it is a revolutionary language. Winnicott also works with the schizophrenic aspect regarding language and communication. He says that "if we look at our descriptions of schizoid persons we find we are using words to describe little children and babies." And it is in children and babies that he finds the double need to communicate and the (at least) equally strong need to remain "incommunicado." To find what the child or schizoid feels or sees, we must "draw on our experience with psychoanalytic patients who reach back to very early phenomena and yet who can verbalize (when they feel they can do so) without insulting the delicacy of what is preverbal, unverbalized, and unverbalizable except perhaps in poetry."[37]

Perhaps the homologue of all this is that these writers are presenting us with a picture of the individual, particularly the schizoid or the artist, as ambivalent (to say the absolute minimum) in her relation to her society: molded by but at odds with the demands of culture, which is instituted through and represented by language. The ambivalence is likely the main reason why maintaining an identity, not to mention working radically creative variations on the basic identity theme, is such a hard-won achievement, if it is ever achieved at all. Hostility to the reality principle can arise simultaneously from a fear of being overwhelmed or subsumed by a social structure that one does not trust and from a desire to find a kind of communion—to be sought for either in or outside of society—which that social system does not provide. This is only one way of stating Le Guin's, and her contemporaries', admirable conflict and project.

The core of this project or "theme" does not really change. Instead, it may elaborate itself and become more sophisticated, more penetrating, depending on the social context and the creative persistence of the individual. This way of looking at a person as containing or embodying an invariant theme, capable of ultraistic variation, is similar to the way any good literary critic *initially* regards a text. As Northrop Frye put it:

> The process of academic criticism begins with reading a work through to the end, suspending value judgements while doing so. Once the end is reached, we can see the whole design of the work as a unity. It is now a simultaneous pattern radiating out from a centre, not a narrative moving in time. The structure is what we call the theme, and the identifying of the theme is the next step. By "identifying a theme" I don't mean spotting it: the theme is not something in the poem, much less a moral precept suggested by it, but the structural principle of the poem.[38]

I shall now attempt to illustrate that in Le Guin's work one *can* spot the primary theme of the novel—or, rather, spot the place or space in the work where the central theme is most firmly inscribed. This spot is related to the identity theme of the protagonist, which in turn is a variation on Le Guin's primary identity theme. The normal structure of her novels is radial, circling about, repeating and elaborating the central theme, which begins with a phrase or image and is elaborated on in a chapter which contains that image, around which the rest of the novel revolves. Le Guin's novels operate in a fashion very similar to the way that Le Guin has described other works as operating: each "goes rolling and bowling about what it is all about."[39]

3

A Wizard of Earthsea:
The Artist as Magician

But we have never, never spoken to each other. And such an abyss now
separates us that I never leave you whole, for I am always held back in
your womb. Shrouded in shadow. Captives of our confinement.
*   And the one doesn't stir without the other. But we do not move*
together. When the one of us comes into the world, the other goes
underground. When the one carries life, the other dies. And what I
wanted from you, Mother, was this: that in giving me life, you still
remain alive.

Luce Irigaray
"And the One Doesn't Stir without the Other"

In his introductory note to *Science-Fiction Studies*'s special issue on Le Guin in
1975, Darko Suvin comments on the lack of articles on her trilogy, lamenting that
they couldn't find anybody to integrate the *Earthsea* trilogy with Le Guin's SF.
Since that time, a number of articles on the trilogy have appeared, but none has
been particularly convincing in its attempt to elucidate the kind of integration that
Suvin is seeking. This attempt is, I think, complicated by Le Guin's well-known
statement that "the 'Earthsea Trilogy' is profoundly Jungian. There's absolutely
no getting around it; it's Jungian through and through. It's the only psychology I
know that comes anywhere near coinciding with it or explaining it. The fact is I
had never read any Jung until long after I'd finished the third book of the
'Trilogy.'"[1] The statements by Le Guin and Suvin are challenging ones. By
offering a psychoanalytic reading of *A Wizard of Earthsea* that will attempt to
coincide with it, or explain it, this chapter attempts to show that there is at least one
other psychology that can come to terms with her trilogy. Once the different
processes of *Wizard* are explained, we will have a theory and practice for
interpreting the whole trilogy. The Jungian readings, while useful, are largely an
illustration of how Jung's Shadow coincides with Le Guin's shadow and hardly do
justice to the detailed insight and artistic complexity afforded us by the trilogy.

This chapter also argues that *Wizard* (1968, the first and, artistically, the finest of the trilogy) establishes Le Guin's primary concern, the basis of every one of her major works—the identity of the creative person. A statement by Le Guin is useful here:

> I said that to know the true name is to know the thing, for me, and for the wizards. This implies a good deal about the "meaning" of the trilogy, and about me. The trilogy is, in one aspect, about the artist. The artist as magician. . . . Wizardry is artistry. The trilogy is, then, in this sense, about art, about the creative experience, the creative process.[2]

As we shall see in the ensuing chapters, it is typical of Le Guin to align herself with her characters. She quite frankly can see herself as a wizard of the trilogy. And she implies that the meaning of the trilogy can reveal a great deal about her, and therefore, necessarily, about her *oeuvre*.

The opening chapter of *Wizard* is where Le Guin's concern with the identity of the artist is established. This chapter, "Warriors in the Mist," introduces the themes, images, and devices that then spiral throughout the remainder of the novel. "The Island of Gont, a single mountain that lifts its peak a mile above the storm-racked Northeast Sea, is a land famous for Wizards."[3] This opening sentence does at least two things at once. First, it embodies the land-sea conflict, which is one of the dominant conflicts in the novel. Second, it symbolizes Ged's plight, and therefore the plight of the artist, which is to differentiate herself—lift her peak—from an environment of which she is a part but which nonetheless has the potential to absorb or overwhelm her. The second paragraph of the novel underscores this by telling us that "the greatest voyager, was the man called Sparrowhawk, who in his day became both dragonlord and Archmage." Names and titles confer identity and help to distinguish one from one's human, and nonhuman, environment. Ged, which is his true, private name, is publicly known as Sparrowhawk, a name that also connects him with his nonhuman environment. He is also called Goatherd and Kelub. This multiple naming betrays an uncertainty about who he is. The "name he bore as a child, Duny, was given him by his mother, and that and his life were all she could give him, for she died before he was a year old" (12). After this primary separation, "there was no one to bring the child up in tenderness" (12). His mother's sister looked after his basic needs as a child but otherwise paid no heed to him, as he, not one for work, roamed the forests and swam in the rivers of Gont. One day, however, he distinguishes himself and wins the attention of his aunt. He overhears her crying out a "certain rhyme" to a goat, which then obeys her. The next day he shouts the words of this strange language to a herd of goats. More and more goats come, "closer, crowding and pushing round him . . . keeping in a knot around him" (13); he begins weeping and bellowing. His aunt breaks the spell and, recognizing that he is in some way special, takes him into her hut, where she usually "let no child enter."

It is by repeating the rhymes of his mother-surrogate, and thereby awakening the potential creative power he has within him, that Duny gains her attention. She then inducts him into the world of artistry and magic, which consists of rhyming, singing, naming, and making use of a private language. It is essentially an oral world and it is a private one; she tells him, "Your tongue will be stilled until I choose to unbind it. . . . We must keep the secrets of our craft" (14). They spend time in her hut around the firepit. At one point,

> She began to sing. Her voice changed sometimes to low or high as if another voice sang through her, and the singing went on and on until the boy did not know if he waked or slept. . . .
> Then the witch spoke to Duny in a tongue he did not understand, and made him say with her certain rhymes and words until the enchantment came on him and held him still.
> "Speak!" she said to test the spell.
> The boy could not speak, but he laughed. Then his aunt was a little afraid of his strength, for this was as strong a spell as she knew how to weave; she had tried not only to gain control of his speech and silence, but to bind him at the same time to her service in the craft of sorcery. Yet even as the spell bound him, he had laughed: (15)

There is a curious kind of simultaneity going on here. His aunt sings through her voice, which is also the voice of another. Duny is both asleep and awake. He is both bound to the aunt and her magic and language and free of it—he cannot speak, but he can still laugh, and this allows him a certain degree of freedom from her. When she does allow him to speak again, she teaches him the true name of the falcon, to which the falcon must respond. The ability to name, conferred on him by his aunt in that paradoxical state of simultaneous symbiosis and separation, is a kind of identity theme. Just after he learns the true name of the falcon, we are told: "This was Duny's first step on the way he was to follow all his life, the way of magery, the way that led him at last to hunt a shadow over land and sea to the lightless coasts of death's kingdom" (15). This "art-magic was child-like" and that "pleasure stayed with him all his life" (16).

The ability to name, this "honest craft" that she teaches him, invests him with a feeling of uniqueness—he stands out from the other children, "liking to know and do what they knew not and could not" (14). Seeing him often in the high pastures with a bird of prey around him, the other children call him Sparrowhawk. "The witch praised him and the children of the village began to fear him, and he himself was sure that very soon he would become great among men" (16). It is important to recognize that, while he has a sense of identity and the self-esteem that should accompany it early in life, he owes this distinction to the witch. His movement among his peers stems from that trance-like state with the witch in which he is both bound to her and distinct from her, in that intermediate area between symbiosis and separation, private language and public language.

Immediately following these episodes, in which Duny acquires his skill, Gont is invaded by Kargs, a people who speak a tongue that is not like any spoken in the Archipelago or the other Reaches. As they work their way up to his village, destroying everything in their path, Duny reflects: "It rankled at his heart that he should die, spitted on a Kargish lance, while still a boy: that he should go into the dark land without ever having known his own name, his true name as a man" (18). Subsequently, he enacts a "fogweaving," a binding-spell that gathers the mists together for a while in one place. He blurs distinctions with this fog to the extent that it forms a wall or boundary between Duny and the villagers, and the potential destroyers. This "blind mist," which is intent on "blurring the world," also introduces the predominant color grey: "A wall of wavering, writhing grey lay blank across the path, hiding all that lay behind it" (22). Because of this grey fog, the Kargs are eventually driven back to the sea; every one of them is killed. Then the grey fog "melted away."

What has happened is that Duny, happily and proudly standing out among his peers, is suddenly threatened with a total loss of identity. It is significant that this loss is associated with naming, with death and, to some extent, with being eaten: he will die "spitted" on a Kargish lance (as if to be roasted) without ever knowing his true name as a man. If, for some reason, these Kargs do not take his life, he would no doubt lose his language: they speak a foreign tongue, which would then become Duny's official language whether he stays in his captured country or goes to their land. He weaves a wall between his potential appropriators and himself. They are absorbed or eaten by the sea, appropriately, at Armouth. When the danger is past, the wall can come down, so the grey fog dissipates. The color grey is here associated with artistic creation and with building a boundary; however, it is not a firm boundary: it blurs more than it separates, but it is effective nonetheless. The color grey, which is omnipresent in the novel, serves two purposes: it continually recalls Duny's deed, a deed which prevented him from losing identity and gave him great renown; and it suggests that in this world of Earthsea, as we see it through the protagonist's eyes, the line between inside and outside, self and other, is often blurred. Grey, the blandest of all colors, combines extremes, especially of black and white.

It must be noted that Duny is not really a part of the battle (his father even knocks him down because he is "blathering" instead of fighting). After uttering the first words that weave the spell, he is silent, in a trance-like state, keeping the illusion intact. The villagers do the fighting, the killing, and the cleaning up. They eventually find him near the great yew, speechless and stunned. Despite their efforts, "he would not speak nor eat nor sleep; he seemed not to hear what was said to him, not to see those who came to see him" (23). This autistic state cannot be cured, and Duny is left to lie "dark and dumb" until the wizard Ogion the Silent (his rune is a closed mouth), carrying a "great staff" of oak as tall as himself, comes down out of the forests and lays his hand on the boy's forehead and touches his lips once. Duny's father says to Ogion, "you are no common man," to which Ogion responds, "nor will this boy be a common man. . . . I have come here to give him his name, if as they say he has not yet made passage into manhood" (24). Ogion leaves and returns on the feast of Sun-return: "The witch took from the boy his name Duny, the name his mother had given him as a baby. Nameless and naked he walked into the cold springs of Ar." As he comes to the bank, Ogion, waiting, "reached out his hand and clasping the boy's arm whispered to him his true name: Ged" (25). Ogion instructs Ged to bid his people farewell, and the two of them leave the village.

Ogion is a wizard and an artist, but he is also someone who can confer a name and therefore an identity. With his "great staff," he also represents the male order, which is able to rescue Duny from the speechless state he brought on himself through the power awakened and invested in him by the witch. The naming scene is one of rebirth and one of simultaneous separation and symbiosis. He is separated from the maternal order when the witch takes back the name given him by his mother. He is then in the "living water" nameless. He receives his true name, Ged, at the same time he leaves the living water. Naming thus signifies separation; it also signifies symbiosis, for as he receives his name while rising out of the water, the nonhuman environment, he is bound to and by Ogion, unified with him by virtue of a name that nobody else knows. However, the naming scene is really only a *repetition* of the naming of the infant when he leaves the water of the womb. The naming scene is meant to be an induction into the realm of the male-artist, into a world with a more advanced language; with his skill, his training, and his staff, he will be recognized by the world at large as someone special, the artist-wizard. But all this is a matter of degree. With the power to name, his acquaintance with the "True Speech," his identity as Sparrowhawk, and the tale of his deed with the fog circulating around the countryside, he has already had as a child, thanks to the witch, the same kind of identity and claim to fame that he will later have as a "man." Yet it seems that he needs the staff, the phallus, the symbol of his ability to separate himself from the trance-like states that, in both conferring and depriving of identity, are necessary to artistic creation. So there is a dialectic set up between the realm of the witch-mother and the realm of the wizard-father: they partake of each other and interpenetrate each other as do the waves of the sea and the shore of the land. The father-phallus-staff symbolizes separation and individuation largely through language, but it is rooted in and parallels the separation-individuation that the child Duny was able to achieve with and through the witch. However, there is never total separation—Ged is bound to Ogion in much the same way Duny was bound to the witch.

Everything that happens later in the novel is a variation on and extrapolation of what we have just witnessed (just as, one might argue, the person Le Guin is now is a complex variation on the person she was as a child). The first chapter of *Wizard*, then, is a microcosm of the novel. If the "psychology" I am using is to explain or coincide with this most important work of the trilogy, there are several things that must be examined: the nonhuman environment, naming, the wizard's staff, and magic and the shadow that arises as a result of it. An ordered elucidation of these four tightly intertwined elements will also explain the other issues raised in the first chapter of *Wizard*—separation and symbiosis, private language and public language, sea and land, boundaries, the function of art—with which the four large motifs are interconnected and which can all be subsumed under the rubric of identity.

A great deal of literature, particularly that in the Romantic tradition and especially Romantic poetry, chronicles a quest for a lost wholeness, an attempt to discover in nature a kind of mirror that will reflect an image of the poet at one with himself and his environment in a unity that precedes differences. This type of quest is an element of all of Le Guin's work, but it is particularly prominent in the trilogy. Ged is a creature of and for nature; his relationship to the nonhuman world seems more important to him than interpersonal relationships. His communion with nature as a child—romping in the forests and swimming in the rivers, rather than working at his father's forge—is paralleled by his relationship with nature as an adolescent and young adult. As Sparrowhawk he can be found in the fields speaking to animals (and later, on occasion, transforming himself into one), and his closest companion is an Otak. His travels and adventures are almost entirely in the nonhuman realm, away from the trade and commerce—or forges—of the human realm.

Harold Searles's large study attests that the nonhuman environment constitutes one of the most important ingredients of human psychological existence, mainly because the infant's differentiation from his nonhuman environment is closely related to his differentiation from the human environment. The richest source of evidence for this hypothesis comes from LSD experiments and from work with schizophrenics, who are unable to distinguish clear boundaries between the self and the nonhuman environment. Children's fairytales also illustrate the interchangeability or the lack of qualitative distinction between the human being and his nonhuman environment. The early phase of oneness with the total environment, which is, for the infant, difficult to distinguish from the mother, is called the animistic period, in which all objects are personified (in the trilogy, for example, all objects have a name and can be spoken to). This period precedes the infant's recognition of his own aliveness, and Searles illustrates how this and subsequent experiences of oneness with "the totality of our environment may also form a vital phase of creativity."[4]

Schizophrenia, at least in the context that Searles regards it, is essentially and potentially a creative state of mind. There is a lack of differentiation between inside and outside, and quite often the schizophrenic (the earliest manifestation of whom is the autistic child) turns "to various elements in his nonhuman environment—to books, to animal pets, to trees, and so on—in search of companionship, the relatedness, the reassurance of there being a meaning in life, which he was not finding to an adequate degree in his relations with other human beings."[5] This can lead to a desire to *become* nonhuman as a means of dealing with or escaping from the superego injunction that he be omnipotent, capable of doing anything. In this state of relationship to the nonhuman environment, there is a relative freedom from words, as contrasted to the human environment. According to Searles, the establishment of firm ego boundaries is necessary to "symbolic thinking," which is "one of the factors which helps to free the child (or the adult who is recovering from schizophrenia) from his erstwhile identification with the non-human world."[6] Nonetheless, an inner conflict persists in the "normal" child and adult—the yearning to become wholly at one with this nonhuman environment and his contrasting anxiety lest he become so and thus lose his own human uniqueness.

The conflict that Searles evinces is that of separation versus symbiosis. It is also related to Lacanian thought in that the symbiotic or preverbal state correlates with Lacan's mirror phase, while the state of uniqueness, or separation, and symbolic thinking correlates with his Symbolic. Indeed Lacan sees the Symbolic as the order that gives man his grandeur and his supremacy over the animal. For Lacan, the dual relationship of the child and his mother-environment covers the human being's initial way of life before he becomes involved in the dimension proper to his humanity, namely the symbolic organization. A child who remains fixed in this pre-Symbolic state would be reduced to the level of animal life—he would not have at his disposal the common symbolic ground for any human relationship. This is what happens with the "psychotic." So whereas Searles tends to valorize this pre-symbolic relationship—man is "ethical" only when the life of plants and animals is as sacred to him as the life of his fellow man—Lacan tends to describe it as downgrading because it can be somewhat subhuman. Le Guin seems to desire a mediation for these types of attitudes, although there is a tendency, particularly in *Wizard* and *Always Coming Home,* to prefer the earlier unity with Mother Nature, problematic as this can be.

When Ged leaves his village as "prentice" to Ogion, he believes that he is going to enter even deeper into the realm of the nonhuman. He thinks that he will learn to "understand the language of the beasts and the speech of the leaves of the forest . . . and sway the winds with his words, and learn to change himself into any shape he wished" (27). This freedom he is feeling, freedom from the binding spells of the witch and her limitations is, again, only a matter of degree. With the possible exception of changing his shape, what he expects to do with Ogion he has been doing all along at home as a child. Although Ogion embodies distinction from the world of woman's magic, he is also equated with the nonhuman, preverbal stages of existence. He is "dark copper-brown; grey haired, lean and tough as a hound" (103). Ogion's home is Re Albi—its name means Falcon's nest. He seldom speaks and is known as Ogion the Silent. As the years go by he becomes "more silent, more solitary than ever . . . Ogion, who spoke to the spiders on their webs and had been seen to greet trees courteously, never said a word to the Lord of the Isle" (139). When he and Ged are first together, his "long, listening silence would fill the room, and fill Ged's mind, until sometimes it seemed he had forgotten what words sounded like: and when Ogion spoke at last it was as if he had, just then and for the first time, invented speech" (31). The isolated, autistic Ogion is the prototype for the kind of person Ged will become—indeed, near the end of the novel, Ged admits that Ogion is his only true master. Ogion's oneness with nature and his silence (and his home as nest) harken back to that period of nondifferentiation. However, Ogion is never in danger of being overwhelmed by this unity to the point of "psychosis." He differentiates himself by means of speech—he speaks to nature but only in the "Old Speech, that language in which things are named with their true names" (30). By means of this language, Ogion remains poised between the world of human and the world of nonhuman, although it is clear that he favors the latter.

Ged's relationship with the nonhuman continues when he leaves Ogion for the wizard school on Roke. In the open court within the walls of the school, he encounters the Archmage of the school:

> As their eyes met, a bird sang aloud in the branches of the tree. In that moment Ged understood the singing of the bird, and the language of the water falling in the basin of the fountain, and the shape of the clouds, and the beginning and end of the wind that stirred the leaves: it seemed to him that he himself was a word spoken by sunlight. (47)

The Archmage is "white and worn as driftwood," and when he spoke his "voice quavered like the bird's voice" (48). Then he begins to speak in a tongue that Ged does not understand, "mumbling as will an old man whose wits go wandering among the years and islands. Yet in among his mumbling there were words of what the bird had sung and what the water had said falling" (48).

Ged's only friend on Roke is Vetch, who "thought no more of performing the lesser arts of magic than a bird thinks of flying" (54). However, Ged does not see a great deal of Vetch, partly because Vetch is older and thus learns at a different level, and partly because he leaves the island after receiving his staff, not long after Ged arrives. Ged's only companion is an Otak, a bright-eyed, furry little creature that has "no call or cry or any voice" (61). He is told that a man "favored by a wild beast is a man to whom the old Powers of stone and spring will speak in human voice" (62). This kind of thing feeds Ged's pride and leads him to feel he has a privileged position with regard to the nonhuman, that he can control it. This feeling of omnipotence is one reason why, just after he changes himself into a falcon, he summons up a spirit from the bottom of the sea. Along with the woman he summons appears a headless, faceless "black beast"; it has "four taloned paws with which it gripped and tore" (75) at Ged. What has happened is that Ged has allowed the boundary between self and nonhuman to disappear; he did not know the words that had power over the beast. The earth is "split apart" and "the fabric of the world" is ripped open. The beast here is the embodiment of this boundary loss. Had it not been for the Archmage closing the rent by "speaking as softly as a tree whispers or a fountain plays" (77), Ged would have been destroyed. Nonetheless, for "four weeks of that hot summer he lay blind, and deaf, and mute, though at times he moaned and cried out like an animal" (77). This is his punishment, by the superego, for failing to be omnipotent. It is a while before Ged is totally human again. Even after his recovery, the new Archmage says to him: "I know what you did . . . but not what you are" (78).

In *Wizard,* then, there is this overriding desire to be at one with, even to become, the nonhuman. However, if one does not know the words, the private language, that keep some semblance of separation between the human and nonhuman, one risks becoming nonhuman, losing one's uniqueness and identity as a human being. The only ones able to maintain this communion with the nonhuman in balance with the human are the wizards, the creative artists, with whom Le Guin allies herself. It is important to remember, though, that the wizard-artist in *Wizard* is not finding an exact midpoint between the nonhuman and the human environment, the Imaginary and the Symbolic; he has little use for the world of trade and commerce, the public language, of Earthsea: Ged "was set apart from them, cut off from them. . . . He was like a cold wind blowing through the firelit room, like a black bird carried by on a storm from foreign lands" (172). He comes to believe that the wise man is one who "never sets himself apart from other living things, whether they have speech or not, and in later years he strove long to learn what can be learned, in silence, from the eyes of animals, the flight of birds, the great slow gestures of trees" (97). Ged favors the presymbolic world, but as the novel progresses he recognizes the dangers involved in remaining in it entirely, and he often longs for human contact. One must be vigilant regarding the potential loss of self. To do this one must learn the Old Speech and the names of all things because, in this sense, knowing a thing's name presupposes that one can distinguish that thing as not being oneself and that one therefore has at one's disposal a signifier of subjectivity and separation. At the same time, knowing that thing's name establishes a bond between the knower and the known.

The previous chapter of this study indicated that whenever someone takes on the problem of naming, there is a certain duplicity noticeable: naming is a type of separation that confers identity, but it is also a separation that is a form of union. This seeming dichotomy is a kind of paradox, which is given clarity by a sentence in *Wizard:* "No one knows a man's true name but himself and his namer" (82). In *Wizard,* as in all of Le Guin's work, naming and language are almost inextricable. Just as there is a true or private language, Old Speech or True Speech, in addition to the public language, so too there is a true or private name in addition to the public one. The power of language exists only when one knows the true or private name of the thing or person over which one wants power; and the incantation or magical phrase must be uttered, almost always "whispered," in the Old Speech: "that language in which things are named with their true names" (30). Although power comes from knowledge of the true name through the Old Speech, communion and unity are also achieved. It is only in extreme circumstances that one should use one's power. Ogion's whispering to the trees and animals signifies his close relationship with them and not his power over them; and to give another person one's true name is to establish a bond of trust, even though the knowledge of that true name gives one power over the other. Ged eventually learns how to make equitable use of private names and speech. At the beginning of his apprenticeship with Ogion, Ged "hungered to learn, to gain power," and he was curious about the function of seemingly useless things such as a weed or a fourfoil flower. Ogion reprimands him for this: "When you know the fourfoil in all its seasons root and leaf and flower, by sight and secret and seed, then you may learn its true name, knowing its being: which is more than its use. What, after all, is the use of you? or of myself?" (29).

There is another important qualification to be made about the ability of words to change things. One can turn a pebble into a diamond with an operative word, but that change is merely an illusion, and diamond will return to pebble unless one accomplished the change by means of the true name: "Illusion fools the beholder's senses; it makes him see and hear and feel that the thing is changed. But it does not change the thing. To change this rock into a jewel, you must change its true name. And to do that, my son, even to do so small a scrap of the world, is to change the world. It can be done" (56). This is explained to Ged by the Master Hand, and it is an echo of an earlier caution by Ogion: "every word, every act of our Art is said and is done either for good, or for evil. Before you speak or do you must know the price that is to pay!" (35). This prudence about change and concern for sameness, which is characteristic of the autistic child, is one of the main characteristics of the novel. Ged's growth and his acquisition of artistic skills parallel his need to be able to distinguish illusion from reality. He can create illusions all he likes, but when it comes to changing the world he must back off. Much of what Ged accomplishes in the novel—his outwitting of the old Dragon, for example—is done through illusion and trickery. His highest achievement comes when he finally acts on his own, with very little use of his skills, to physically make the shadow himself, and therefore keep himself and Earthsea from being harmed. So it appears that the Le Guin text questions, or registers some lack of confidence in, the artist's ability to change the world with her art; there is some change involved in the illusion, and a great deal of beauty, but in the large scheme of things, they are specious and temporary.

Nevertheless, the *potential* of naming, of language, of art, to change the world is always present and we are predisposed to take some comfort in that possibility. Although any change means some degree of disruption to the self, some loss of continuity, it can also mean the kind of rebirth that strengthens identity. Learning the Old Speech, the language in which things are named with their true names, means having the option to change things or to let them remain the same. The Old Speech is aligned with one of the most powerful symbols of the novel—the sea (as mother, as the unconscious): "the way to the understanding of this speech starts with the Runes that were written when the islands of the world first were raised up from the sea" (30). This Old Speech arose during the time of birth—of the land from the sea. It could indeed be a chronicling of this birth. But although birth usually involves separation, this description shows the islands rising from the sea: they never really leave it.

Language, naming, identity, and change are concepts that are skillfully woven into the crucial land-sea (Earth-sea) symbolism. The Master Namer tells Ged:

> Thus, that which gives us power to work magic, sets the limits of that power. A mage can control only what is near him, what he can name exactly and wholly. And this is well. If it were not so, the wickedness of the powerful or the folly of the wise would long ago have sought to change what cannot be changed, and Equilibrium would fail. The unbalanced sea would overwhelm the islands where we perilously dwell, and in the old silence all voices and all names would be lost. (60)

To lose one's name is to lose one's identity, and losing one's identity is equated with being overwhelmed, absorbed, by the sea. When Ged changes himself into a falcon in order to flee his shadow and the beaks of ancient birds, he flies to Ogion, who changes him back to his human form. Ged lies speechless while Ogion ruminates on how, as a boy, he too loved the game of "art-magic," by which he could change into whatever shape he wished. However, "as a wizard he had learned the price of the game, which is the peril of losing one's self. . . . And no one knows how many of the dolphins that leap in the waters of the Inmost Sea were men once, wise men, who forgot their wisdom and their name in the joy of the restless sea" (141). The kind of art that involves radical change can be costly: one can lose language, name, and identity as a human being; and, again, this is represented by absorption into the sea.

The name of this world Le Guin has created—Earthsea—connotes a kind of dialogic junction of the earth and sea. Yet, throughout the novel, as Ged travels from land to sea and from sea to land, there is a definite disjunction between the two. The land can symbolize the male world, the Symbolic, whereas the sea can symbolize the female world, the maternal, prelinguistic Imaginary. Although by the end of the novel there is an attempted union of the two opposites, throughout the novel the sea appears to be the more powerful of the two. The Gontish landsman, for example, looks at the ocean as at "a salt unsteady realm" and "Gontish fishermen fear nothing, not even wizards, only the sea" (37 and 38). Once a year every island of the Archipelago celebrates the Moon's Night and the Long Dance: "One dance, one music binding together the sea-divided lands" (68).

This fear of the sea and its power over the land forms the bedrock of most of the myths and legends of Earthsea, which are essentially matrilineal. The Princess Elfarran was "only a woman," but for her sake "all Enlad was laid waste, and the Hero-Mage of Havnor died, and the island of Solea sank beneath the sea" (63). The famous jewel of Terrenon, which has the potential to wield great power over all "was made before Segoy raised the islands of the world from the Open Sea" (130). On Roke, the "Immanent Grove," where the Master Patterner learns his supreme magery, contains trees that are wise—but "if ever the trees should die so shall his wisdom die, and in those days the waters will rise and drown the islands of Earthsea which Segoy raised from the deep in the time before myth, all the lands where men and dragons dwell" (85–86).

There is a tension set up between the power of the wizard (on land) and the power of the sea. As Ged travels on the "vast sameness of the sea" (170), we are told how "the land sank out of sight as night came over the eastern edge of the world" (161); or, "The haven now was sunk from sight" (184). And Ged must be strong and vigilant to keep his boat afloat amidst the "spitting, hissing seas" (83) and the waves that "hissed and smacked" (185). Ogion's advice to Ged on how to overcome the loss of self that the shadow threatens involves an identity gained through union with the sea: "If he would not be a stick whirled and whelmed in the stream, he must be the stream itself, all of it, from its spring to its sinking in the sea. You returned to Gont, you returned to me, Ged. Now turn clear round, and seek the very source, and that which lies before the source. There lies your hope of strength" (144). In order to overcome the threat of the shadow—which as we see here is practically synonymous with the sea and its source—Ged must name and become one with his origins which, we find at the end of the novel, are the shadow and the sea-land.

Before Ged begins this quest for the source, Ogion equips him with a new staff. The staff here is a symbol of the phallus, the attribute of the powerful—the presumedly omnipotent and omniscient phallic-mother, the father, the king, and so on. Although Ged is a "man," he is still only a fictional character, words on a page: written by a woman. Because of the author-character gender difference and the confusion often produced by this symbol, I would like to look briefly at a portion of psychoanalytic theory that addresses the relationship of the woman to the phallus. Janine Chassequet-Smirgel takes up the controversial "penis-envy" idea that is said by many psychoanalysts to play a prominent role in the life of the young girl. According to her, a girl has

> nothing with which to oppose the mother, no narcissistic virtue which the mother does not also possess. She will not be able to "show her" her independence. So she will envy the boy his penis and say that he can "do everything." I see penis envy *not as a "virility claim" to something one wants for its own sake, but as a revolt against the person who caused the narcissistic wound: the omnipotent mother*. . . . The narcissistic wound aroused by the child's helplessness and penis envy are closely related.[7]

Nancy Chodorow concurs with this view because it places the narcissistic desire for the penis on the correct metaphorical level: "The penis, or phallus, is a symbol of power or omnipotence, whether you have one as a sexual organ (as a male) or as a sexual object (as her mother 'possesses' her father's). A girl wants it for the powers which it symbolizes and the freedom it promises from her previous sense of dependence, and not because it is inherently and obviously better to be masculine."[8] Women, then, do not wish to become men, but want to separate themselves, show their difference from the mother and become complete, autonomous women. To become or become like the father or phallic-mother is a way of enforcing separateness and gives the girl a sense of freedom and independence; thus the phallus symbolizes independence from the powerful (internalized) mother. However, the separation from the mother, for the male or the female, is never entirely complete. The female, in particular, "alternates between total rejection of a mother who represents infantile dependence and attachment to her, between identification with anyone other than her mother and feeling herself her mother's double and extension. Her mother often mirrors her preoccupations."[9] Accordingly, a "girl does not turn from mother to father, but comes to include her father along with her mother in her primary object world."[10] The turn to the father and the taking up of the phallus, then, whatever sexual (and linguistic) meaning it may have, essentially concerns the emotional issues of self and other.

The entry of the female subject into the Symbolic, or her so-called passage through the Oedipus, is dealt with in the Lacanian mode by Julia Kristeva. Kristeva's "semiotic disposition" or "semiotic discourse" corresponds to Lacan's Imaginary. However, as Jane Gallop points out, although Kristeva's Semiotic and Lacan's Imaginary are in contradistinction to the Symbolic in that both are associated with the preoedipal, prelinguistic maternal, Lacan's Imaginary is more conservative than Kristeva's Semiotic. The Imaginary is "comforting, tends toward closure, and is disrupted by the symbolic; the semiotic is revolutionary, breaks closure and disrupts the symbolic."[11] Kristeva sees the Semiotic as a persistent challenge to the Symbolic order—it asserts the return to the pleasures of the preverbal identity with the mother and the refusal to identify with the father and the logic of paternal discourse. Kristeva recognizes, however, as does Chodorow in her own way, that the rejection of phallic power can never be complete because, by refusing the Symbolic, woman (and I would add artist, especially the female artist) risks making herself even more marginal than she already is. Kristeva's solution—which is, as we shall see, very close to Le Guin's—is to balance these two tendencies. The Semiotic and Symbolic can never be mutually exclusive. The Semiotic constantly asserts itself within the Symbolic, thus allowing its openness and renewal; loss of the Symbolic function means absorption into the preoedipal environment and a slide into schizophrenia and madness. Therefore, the "potency" of the Semiotic, Kristeva contends, can never be denied, but can become a social force:

This identification with the potency of the imaginary is not only an identification, an imaginary potency (a fetish, a belief in the maternal penis maintained at all costs), as a far too normative view of the social and symbolic relationship would have it. This identification also bears witness to women's desire to lift the weight of what is sacrificial in the social contract from their shoulders, to nourish our societies with a more flexible and free discourse, one able to name what has thus far never been an object of circulation in the community: the enigmas of the body, the dreams, secret joys, hatreds of the second sex.[12]

The wizard's staff, sometimes potent and sometimes not, is still a (empty?) symbol of power and independence. All along it has helped to keep Ged from absorption into the preoedipal environment and the slide into schizophrenia and madness. When the staff is not available, however, there is usually a protective wall of some sort, like the wall of mist at the opening of the novel. When Ged is first threatened by the beginnings of the shadow, Ogion breaks into the dark room and dispels the creature by means of the "oaken staff in his hand," which burned with a white radiance (34). On Roke, Ged is protected by the "mighty spell-walls that surround and protect Roke Island," and he would have remained protected if it had not been for the "doorway he had opened" (76) by summoning the spirit. He is saved by Nemmerle, who touches his staff to Ged's lips and heart. Eventually Ged earns his own staff, which gives him the freedom to leave the protective wall of Roke.

At Low Torning, where Ged is the official wizard, he has the opportunity to save the dying child of his friend, Pechvarry. He follows the child into death's realm, only to realize that he must turn back. He turns and comes to a low wall of stones. "But across the wall, facing him, there was a shadow." The shadow was on the side of the living and he was on the side of the dead. He decides that he must step across the wall into life, even though it waits there for him. "His spirit-staff was in his hand, and he raised it high. With that motion, strength came into him. As he made to leap the low wall of stones straight at the shadow, the staff burned suddenly white, a blinding light in that dim place. He leaped, felt himself fall, and saw no more" (95). With its licking, the Otak brings him out of his stricken state. Ged then decides that he must confront the horde of dragons because his "barriers of sorcery" and the "spell-walls" that he sets around his house will not protect him against two enemies. And since the "shadow dared not follow him into a dragon's jaws" (101), Ged goes to meet the dragons at sea. They come at him with fiery mouths and open jaws, but he binds their limbs with spells and watches them drown in the "grey sea." He then confronts the huge Dragon Pendor, making sure not to look into its eyes. "He glanced away from the oily green gaze that watched him, and held up before him his staff, that looked now like a splinter, like a twig" (103). However, as they banter in the Old Speech, through a "maze of mirror-words," Ged becomes less intimidated by the huge devouring eyes, the "great grey talons," the large jaws, and the nostrils that were "two round pits of fire," when he realizes that he can threaten the dragon with the dragon's own name. As we hear the sound of his name, we are told that the dragon "had grown old. It was hard now to stir, to face this mage-lad, this frail enemy, at the sight of whose staff, Yevaud, the old dragon, winced" (106).

When he next meets his shadow, his staff—and the magical words and names he can strengthen it with—no longer serves him well. The shadow comes in the shape of a man called Skiorh; it had "devoured Skiorh's mind and possessed his flesh," and it came at Ged wishing to "cast aside the husk of Skiorh and enter into Ged, devouring him out from within, owning him" (121). Ged strikes at him with his "smoking staff," but to no avail. He is forced to drop his staff, which is burning his hand, and runs through the gate of the Court of Terrenon, where he is safe behind the "mighty walls" (126) which are later called "magic walls" (137). When he leaves the castle walls, he makes himself another staff, and with this he fights off the great birds and then changes into a falcon to fly out of the reach of their "iron beaks" to Ogion's home.

As he watches Ogion making him a new staff, he grows sleepy and thinks "himself a child in the witch's hut in Ten Alders village, on a snowy night in the firelit dark, the air heavy with herb-scent and smoke, and his mind all adrift on dreams as he listened to the long soft singing of spells and deeds of heroes who fought against dark powers and won, or lost, on distant islands long ago" (145). This association that accompanies the making of the staff is ended when Ogion hands him the completed staff, which exactly matches Ged's height. Later, while chasing the shadow, using his staff as the boat's mast, he is tricked into running the boat aground. "Salt-blinded and choked, he tried to keep his head up and to fight the enormous pull of the sea," which he is able to do thanks to his staff, which "did not break, and bouyant as a dry log . . . rode the water." Then a tumult of water surges "around him, under him, over him, blinding him, strangling him, drowning him" and he is flung up on shore where he lies clutching the "yew-wood staff with both hands" (154). He then makes his way to a "wall of rain-wet wood" that is a hut into which he goes to recover. It occurs to him that the shadow had tricked him with his own trick, "bringing that mist about him on the sea as if bringing it out of his own past" (161). Shortly after, in a small cove, he finds the shadow behind him in the boat. Realizing that no "wizardry would serve him now, but only his own flesh," he lunges at the shadow, only to grab at air. He "stumbled forward, catching the mast" (his staff) to keep from falling into the sea.

He meets up with Vetch and the two of them head out to confront the shadow on the open sea. When they are past the Lastland, where there is nothing left but sea, they reach a powerful "enchantment of illusion," which makes the "Open Sea seem land." Ged takes his staff and marches out onto this sea-land. His staff shines with a clear white glow; he lifts it high and the shadow is reduced from a figure of a man to a short beast. They meet and "Ged reached out his hands, dropping his staff, and took hold of his shadow, of the black self that reached out to him. Light and darkness met, and joined, and were one" (198). Ged returned to the boat with his staff "grasped in his right hand, and he would not let go of it. He said no word" (198). Later, he stands up "erect, holding his staff in his two hands as a warrior holds his long sword." And he says to Vetch, "I am whole, I am free." Then he bends over and hides his "face in his arms, weeping like a boy." We are told that Ged "had neither lost nor won" (199).

It should be apparent that the staff is something that helps prevent Ged from being drowned, devoured, overwhelmed, absorbed into the environment. There are at least four parallel ways of stating this predominant conflict: phallic assertiveness against oral engulfment (Freud); the Symbolic versus the Imaginary (Lacan); paternal discourse versus the semiotic disposition (Kristeva); and separation versus total symbiosis (Mahler). For the most part, this is a relatively even balance; after all, Ged does come out of all this alive, even though he neither wins nor loses. Whenever the shadow is present, though, the staff itself is of minimal use—walls or boundaries seem to be more functional. In this sense the staff, the power of the wizard, is of little more use to Ged than was the magic he learned from the witch before he earned his staff. This is suggested (in the staff-shaping scene with Ogion) by the feeling that he is back in the witch's hut, dreaming about heroic deeds and about to embark on his most heroic deed to date. Whatever phase or realm the shadow belongs to, it is, at the very least, as powerful as the phallus or the Symbolic order.

Magical thinking is generally recognized to be an early and basic element of the infantile makeup. Geza Roheim's study on magic and schizophrenia illustrates how they both spring from the same roots, these being the child-mother situation, especially when the environment simply means mother, and it is this mother-environment that gratifies all the wishes of the child. There are, in effect, two kinds of magic. The child has magical qualities: a gesture or a word-cry brings him anything he desires. And the environment-mother is magical in that the gratification comes from and through her. Thus the child experiences magic as his own or as the empathic communication or bond with the mother, or as a combination of the two. Since, as Margaret Mahler's studies show, the two forms of childhood schizophrenia are autistic and symbiotic, we can expect that magical thinking arises from either or both of two reactions. The autistic child struggles against any human or social contact that might interfere with his need to command a segment of his inanimate environment; in this he behaves like an insulative "omnipotent magician." The symbiotic child aims to restore and perpetuate "the delusional omnipotent phase of the mother-infant fusion of earliest times—a period at which the mother was an ever-ready extension of the self, at the service and command of 'His Majesty, the Baby' "[13]; here he behaves like a restorative, omnipotent magician. There is a fine line between autistic magic and symbiotic magic, just as there is a fine line between these two phases of "normal" and "psychotic" infantile behavior. Perhaps the easiest distinction is that whereas the symbiotic child is gratified magically and wants to become fused with that power source (which is sometimes good and sometimes bad), the autistic child tries to invest the power in himself as a way of defending himself against this powerful world, of which, though he comes to think of it as a part of himself, he is afraid. The ability to speak or not to speak becomes important. As Bruno Bettelheim says of autistic children: "Words carry magic power for these children—things may or may not happen, depending on whether they say certain things. Most of all, through their use of language, they show that words are very much their private property and are not used for the purposes of communicating and relating."[14]

Magic or omnipotent feelings, therefore, serve two functions, which are described by Roheim in two different ways: "The ultimate denial of dependency comes from the all-powerful sorcerer who acts out the role which he once attributed to the projected images" (of the parents); and "magic originates in the dual-unity situation, and since our basic anxiety is separation anxiety, it follows that all our strivings (magic) aim at a reunion with the object."[15] Although Roheim makes no attempt to resolve this apparent contradiction, it can be seen that one makes use of magic either for union or for independence; quite often, as in Ged's case, one wants both simultaneously. Roheim deduces, in addition, that without belief in magic "we cannot hold our own against the environment and the superego." Elsewhere he says, *the omnipotence which is achieved in magic is a rejoinder to the aggression of the superego"*; and the "archaic superego or mother image is then introjected as the 'bad mother' and begins to kill the subject."[16] The superego's role can be compared to that of a judge or censor. And the self-attacking tendency of the superego supposedly provides an outlet for the subject's own aggressive impulses. Most contemporary accounts postulate precursors of the superego occurring in the preoedipal phases of development. In Charles Rycroft's words, "it is a container of the past."[17] René Spitz lists the three rudiments of a superego as imposed physical actions, the attempt at mastery of gestures by means of identification, and, most importantly, identification of the aggressor.[18] This account of the superego, and Roheim's correlation of the superego with magic and its purpose (which Mahler had helped to clarify), is a necessary prolegomenon to considering the meaning and function of the shadow in *Wizard*.

The shadow is the key to understanding *Wizard*. The plot of the novel turns on whether or not, and how, Ged will be able to come to terms with the beast that he has "unleashed"; at times, other things in the novel seem incidental to the conflict with the shadow, but they are in fact subsumed by this central theme. Ged's first encounter with the shadow is caused by the daughter of an enchantress, whom he meets while roaming the fields around Ogion's house. She is almost a part of the field: "He looked down at the white flowers that brushed against her white skirt" (31). She taunts him in a way that foreshadows Jasper's taunts by asking him if he has the power to call the spirits of the dead, or if he can change his own shape.

When he confesses that he can't, she says, "Are you afraid to do it? . . . Maybe you are too young" (33). Later, in Ogion's house, he searches through Lore Books for a spell of "self transformation." While puzzling over the names and symbols, a horror grows in him that holds him bound in his chair. Beside the "closed door, a shapeless clot of shadow . . . seemed to reach out towards him, and to whisper, and to call to him in a whisper: but he could not understand the words" (34). The door is then "flung wide" and Ogion appears to dispel the thing.

At Roke Ged forms an antagonistic relationship with an older student, Jasper; like the witch-girl, Jasper taunts and teases Ged, injuring his self-esteem. Jasper is an alter ego to Ged. Ged seeks "always to put himself on equal footing with Jasper" and "Ged swore to himself to outdo his rival" (57). However, in this rivalry "which he clung to and fostered," he did not see any of the danger or darkness. One evening the Lord of O visits the school, accompanied by his wife. All the lads are enchanted by her and her beauty is compared to that of Princess Elfarran, for whose sake "all Enlad was laid waste . . . and the island of Solea sank beneath the sea" (63). Jasper performs an illusion for the Lady of O, who cries out in pleasure, "Come with us, live with us in O-tokne." All are pleased with this interaction except Ged: " 'I could have done better,' he said to himself, in bitter envy; and all the joy of the evening was darkened for him, after that" (64).

Months later, while celebrating the night of the Long Dance, Ged transforms himself into a falcon in an attempt to prove that he is superior to Jasper, who goads, "I like the trap you're building for yourself. The more you try to prove yourself my equal, the more you show yourself for what you are" (71). Ged's "black temper" breaks and on Jasper's sarcastic suggestion he decides to summon up a spirit from the dead. They go to Roke Knoll, the hillside whose roots were "deeper than the sea," and Ged decides to call "a woman's spirit . . . Elfarran . . . her bones lie afar under the Sea of Ea" (73). Recalling the spell from Ogion's book, he speaks aloud the words that are unknown to the rest of the group. He cries the name Elfarran until the "shapeless mass of darkness" he had lifted up between his arms "split apart." In the oval of light a human shape appears: "a tall woman looking over her shoulder. Her face was beautiful, and sorrowful, and full of fear." Then the oval widens, "a ripping open of the fabric of the world," and through the "misshapen breach clambered something like a clot of black shadow, quick and hideous, and it leaped straight out at Ged's face" (74). Ged falls, struggling, "while the bright rip in the world's darkness above him widened and stretched" (75). The black beast tears at his flesh. Soon the torn edges of the world are closed together by the Archmage and Ged is left blind, dumb, and mute. When he recovers he is still slow to find words. He is told that if he left Roke now, the thing would "enter into you, and possess you. You would be no man but a *gebbeth*, a puppet" (79). Ged carries on with his studies and learns what he can about the shadow-beast: he reads about another who had summoned up such a thing *"which did devour him out from within and in his shape walked, destroying men"* (85).

The shadow is a signifier of great thematic and semantic importance, as well as a unifying device: it makes connections between many disparate elements in the novel. Jasper, the sorcerer who never does receive his staff, is Ged's double or alter ego. He is also equated with the witch-girl in that they perform the same function: they inflict damage on Ged's self-esteem and break down his belief in his own omnipotence. In their role of judge or censor they represent the superego. Their taunting is directly related to his attempt to prove his omnipotence by self-transformation and by summoning a spirit from the dead. Both appearances of the shadow have to do with the breaking of a boundary—Ogion dispels it by the open door, and Nemmerle must close the gap or re-create the wall of fabric. The first appearance of the shadow leads to the separation of Ged from Ogion, and the second appearance leaves Ged separated from his human, speaking self as well as from the rest of the school. It is also significant that the appearance of the shadow on Roke is equated with the power of woman and the power of the sea—Princess Elfarran was the cause of Enlad being laid waste and the island of Solea being sunk into the sea. She (or her simulacrum) is also, therefore, the cause of Ged's being laid waste and sunk into speechlessness. First of all, she is associated with the Lady of O, and it is this association that made Ged envious of what Jasper had (the adoration of Lady O) and led to his summoning Elfarran as a way of showing that he, Ged, had control over her and could make her his own. Secondly, when she does appear, it is not clear whether the beast uses her as a means of access to Ged or whether she is indeed the beast. Either way, her association with the nonhuman is established, as is her connection with the sea—he summons her from beneath it. Also, it is through his art—a private language and magical naming—that Ged attempts to unite with Elfarran: the connection or union he attains is much more overwhelming than he had anticipated. As a *gebbeth,* it is an omnipotent and archaic power from the past, which exerts its influence by attempting to devour its victim and thus make it nonhuman, or at least a puppet or instrument of its own desires. It is noteworthy that Jasper sees the entire episode as a "trap" that Ged sets for himself. Later, the shadow sets several traps for Ged. Finally, although Ged has always been aloof and cut-off from others, this incident, which also scars his face and results in feelings of humiliation, alienates him from his fellow man even more.

When Ged takes up his position as wizard of Low Torning, he establishes a friendship with a fisherman named Pechvarry. Because of his desire to please Pechvarry, Ged, while attempting to heal his friend's son, disregards the words of the Master Healer—"Heal the wound and cure the illness, but let the dying spirit go" (94)—and sends his spirit out after the child's spirit. There he meets the shadow:

> It was darkness itself that had awaited him, the unnamed thing, the being that did not belong in the world, the shadow he had loosed or made. In spirit, at the boundary wall between death and

> life, it had waited for him these long years. It had found him there at last. It would be on his track now, seeking to draw near to him, to take his strength into itself, and suck up his life, and clothe itself in his flesh. (97)

This encounter renders Ged deaf and dumb, and the child dies. Largely because it causes Pechvarry to turn away from him, this incident is a blow to Ged's newly regained sense of self-esteem. Soon after, he dreams of the thing that looks like a bear with no head or face—"He thought it went fumbling about the walls of the house, searching for the door" (97). He sets up spell-walls and barriers but still dreams of it being inside the house beside the door. "Yet he could not simply flee the trap"; he must first see to it that the islanders are protected from the dragons.

Ged finds it "hard to turn from the bright danger of the dragon," over whom he had triumphed, "to that formless, hopeless horror" (108). Once the shadow catches up with him, he knows it can draw his power out of him; for now, it is watching him and "feeding" on his weakness (113). On next meeting with the shadow, it is in the form of the man named Skiorh. Skiorh taunts Ged for not carrying a knife, accusing him of being afraid to fight. He jeers at Ged and turns away with a scowl:

> Just as he turned Ged saw a change in his face, a slurring and shifting of the features, as if for a moment something had changed him, used him, looking out through his eyes sidelong at Ged. Yet the next minute Ged saw him full-face, and he looked as usual, so that Ged told himself that what he had seen was his own fear, his own dread reflected in the other's eyes. (118)

This mirroring frightens Ged, and he finds Skiorh that night in his dreams. When he and Skiorh are walking together to the Court of Terrenon, the *gebbeth* takes over Skiorh, and there is no face under the peaked hood; it comes at Ged, wishing to enter into him, "devouring him out from within" (121). Ged and his staff have no power against this thing, which calls him by name in a "hoarse whistling voice": "It had begun to whisper and mumble at him, calling to him, and he knew that all his life that whispering had been in his ears" (122).

When he is safe inside the castle, he sleeps and then wakes to find Serret, the former witch-girl who had teased him into invoking the shadow initially: "He had never seen a beautiful woman dressed to match her beauty but once in his life: that Lady of O . . . but this woman was like the white new moon" (126). In a scene that recalls his encounter with the dragon, he finds it "hard to look away from her," and he is almost tricked into trusting her, "moved by the promise of her voice alone" (126). Later, "he felt her eyes on him, and tried to decide what look had come into those eyes when he refused to touch the Stone." That night "he awakened in the dark thinking of the Stone and of Serret's eyes" (132). She tries to convince him of his power and omnipotence: "You are born with the power to control that which is in the sealed room. . . . Before ever you were born it waited for you, for the one who could master it." "She lifted her strange bright eyes to him, and her gaze pierced him so that he trembled with cold" (132–33). As it turns out, Serret, whom Ged associates with the Lady of O (who in turn is connected with Elfarran), has lured Ged into this keep hoping to make him a slave of the Stone. "Once his will had been captured by the power of the Stone, then they would let the shadow into the walls, for a gebbeth was a better slave than a man" (135). Ged refuses to give in and the scene ends with Serret changing into a grey gull and being eaten by the ancient birds, while Ged escapes as a falcon.

The above scenes deal both with Ged's feeling of omnipotence and with the lack of it. It seems that whenever he overrates his power, he is lured into a trap and then his confidence declines. On his trail the entire time is this devouring creature; somehow it is allied with Serret, since it is Skiorh who suggests that Ged go to the court where she resides. However, her connection with the beast is still ambiguous, just as was Elfarran's connection with the beast that arrived with her—both women disappear. It is not clear whether they are in command of the beast, the beast is in command of them, or they are one and the same as the beast. Serret's association with Elfarran, and therefore the sea, and the description of her as being like the new white moon, suggest that she is a maternal figure, though one is not sure whether she is "good" or "bad" or both; she does appear to be on Ged's side as they run from the castle together, but that could be yet another trap—she is, after all, the one who got him into this whole mess in the first place, several years ago. The eye imagery is pronounced and allies Serret with Skiorh and the dragon. Finally, the fact that the shadow cannot speak but can only mumble or whisper suggests that it is from a preverbal past and from Ged's personal past—all his life that whispering had been in his ears. The shadow is able, however, to whisper Ged's name.

Ged finally goes in search of the shadow. He wants to meet it on the sea where he can grip it and "drag it down with the weight of his body and the weight of his death down into the darkness of the deep sea" (150). At last he sees it coming towards him: "So it came over the seas out of the Jaws of Enlad towards Gont, a dim ill-made thing pacing uneasy on the waves" (151). Ged charges straight towards it and it flees, tricking him onto a sandbar. Later, he follows it into a "dark cleft" which is "cavern pocked":

> Now he was coming to the end of the inlet, a high blank wrinkled mass of rock against which, narrowed to the width of a little creek, the last sea-waves lapped freely. . . . A trap: a dark trap under the roots of the silent mountain, and he was in the trap. (164)

The shadow appears behind him in the boat; he lurches for it but it recoils and escapes. At this point he "wished he might be down there in that dark place where sea and mountain met and sleep, sleep on the restless rocking water" (165). As he continues his chase, he discovers that this creature is his double: he is told that some mysterious person who bears his likeness has come and gone without a boat.

With this knowledge, Ged strongly senses his own alienation: "He was set apart from them, cut off from them" (170), and he watches women at looms or with their husbands and children—"Ged saw all these things from outside and apart, alone" (172). When he meets Vetch, Vetch tells him, "I saw a presentment of you or an imitation of you" (173). Ged acknowledges that all his acts have their "echo" in this creature: "Almost with my own tongue it speaks" (177).

At Vetch's house, Ged is relatively content for the first time in a long while. Much of this has to do with Vetch's sister Yarrow, who is "quick and silent as a little fish" (175). She constantly hides "her eyes with her hands" and "her eyes when not hidden were clear, shy and curious" (174). Ged experiences a "dream-peace" in the house and he thinks that by "leaving this house he would leave the last haven he was to know." In "her own house and mistress of it," Yarrow kept busy for the two days of Ged's sojourn making dry wheatcakes for the voyagers to carry. When Vetch goes to finish some matters before the voyage, Ged has a lengthy conversation with Yarrow, which revolves entirely around the subject of food. Meat pie, for example, is only a word, so creating a meat pie with a word would not fill one's stomach. But Ged would not summon up a real meat pie because that would disturb the Equilibrium. Ged then steals a cake from the hot bricks, a cake that would have accompanied him on the voyage. Yarrow takes a cake as well, which would have been Vetch's cake, in order to maintain Equilibrium. At sea, Vetch and Ged drink to Yarrow, who had thought to put a keg of ale aboard.

The last confrontation with the shadow takes place on the open sea, where the sea temporarily turns to land. Ged leaves the boat, holding his shining staff, and walks across the sand-water to meet the shadow:

> At first it was shapeless, but as it drew nearer it took on the look of a man. An old man it seemed, grey and grim, coming towards Ged; but even as Ged saw his father the smith in that figure, he saw that it was not an old man but a young one. It was Jasper: Jasper's insolent handsome young face, and silver-clasped grey cloak, and stiff stride. Hateful was the look he fixed on Ged across the dark intervening air. Ged did not stop, but slowed his pace, and as he went forward he raised his staff up a little higher. It brightened, and in its light the look of Jasper fell from the figure that approached and it became Pechvarry. But Pechvarry's face was all bloated and pallid like the face of a drowned man, and he reached out his hand strangely as if beckoning. . . . Then the thing that faced him changed utterly, spreading out to either side as if it opened enormous thin wings, and it writhed, and swelled, and shrank again. Ged saw in it for an instant Skiorh's white face, and then a pair of clouded, staring eyes, and then suddenly a fearful face he did not know, man or monster, with writhing lips and eyes that were like pits going back into black emptiness. (197)

Ged then lifts his staff and all form of man "sloughed off" the thing as it draws together and shrinks into a small beast that comes forward "lifting up to him a blind unformed snout without lips or ears or eyes." They come together and Ged, "breaking that old silence," spoke the shadow's name and it "spoke without lips or tongue, saying the same word: 'Ged.' And the two voices were one voice" (198). Ged laughs and is jubilant as they leave the scene of the encounter. Feeling "whole" and "free" he comes into the harbor with Vetch; "and Yarrow ran to meet them, crying with joy" (201).

The novel ends with Ged returning to a woman on shore. Yarrow's eyes link her with Serret and the dragon; however, due to the dream-peace Ged experiences in her house, the last haven, and because of the positive oral imagery—the giving of food and the taking of food maintain an Equilibrium—she acts as a "good" maternal figure opposed to the devouring tempting figures of the dragon and Serret. Roheim's study gives evidence that the "evil eye" signifies oral aggression or a desire to eat the child.[19] The prolonged stares of the dragon and Serret, and even the fearful look of Elfarran (which is included in the last view of the shadow), reflect this desire, especially when we consider their associations with the shadow—and how it mirrors Ged's fear in the eyes of Skiorh—whose sole purpose is to devour Ged. Yarrow, on the other hand, hides her eyes, and then gives food, so as to totally remove the threat. Also, to be united with Yarrow has implications of harmony with the nonhuman environment—her name means minnow (and Yarrow "rhymes" with Sparrow). The "women," then, are representatives of Ged's conflicting desire to reestablish the primary narcissistic unity of identity with the environment-mother, as against his fear of the environment-mother (frequently associated with the vulva)—fear of being drowned, sucked in, overpowered. This conflict can be seen in his fear of the dark cleft, the cavern pocked inlet in which he almost drowns and, minutes later, his wish to be down there sleeping on the restless rocking water.

This basic conflict is evoked by the shadow: Ged is fleeing from it for fear that it will devour him, and then he is chasing after it to become one with it. The double paradigm of childhood schizophrenia—autistic and symbiotic—seems to be involved in this conflict. Ged, the solitary artist, is cut-off from the rest of man: he spends most of his time roaming the seas. Even on land, although we receive glimpses of his desires for communion with human beings, he remains apart. With the exception of his desire for oneness with the shadow, he remains apart until the end when, after he and the shadow unite, he is free to join Vetch and Yarrow. The following description of the autistic child describes Ged, or at least one half of Ged, quite adequately:

> But this phantasy (of omnipotence) can be, and often is, shattered. This usually happens when the external object (or event) behaves *suddenly,* so to speak, in such an unpuppetlike way that the child's omnipotent belief breaks down. When his defensive mechanism fails, he feels confronted by, and at the mercy of, a persecutory object that can be said to embody all the content of his destructive impulses. When this takes place he fears his own annihilation, for I think the intensity of the autistic child's anxiety is similar to that to which imminent death gives rise. The experience of annihilation comes about when he feels that the persecutory object is bursting its way into his body and destroying it. This forceful re-entry of the persecutors seems to be the main anxiety-situation in infantile autism.[20]

The symbiotically oriented child, on the other hand, experiences "hallucinations of reunion with the narcissistically loved and hated, omnipotent mother image, or sometimes by hallucinated fusion with a condensation of father-mother images."[21]

It is the nature of symbols to represent and embody many things, and hence we have the protean nature of the shadow. Ged's relationship with his shadow portrays the plight of the two types of childhood schizophrenia. The shadow is omnipotent and it wishes to burst its way into Ged's body; it also embodies his persecutors. These persecutors are the loved and hated father-mother images. All of the people from Ged's past who appear in the last vision of the shadow were those who at one time persecuted Ged or, rather, questioned his omnipotence or did damage to his self-esteem. The condensation effect of the shadow is such that there are no "Mothers" in that vision—but the mother, especially the devouring mother, is represented by the "staring eyes," the "writhing lips and eyes that were like pits."

This shadow, which assimilates the conflicts and devices of the entire novel, represents more than the above, or at least another version of it. That final view of the shadow contains Ged's past; the shadow as superego is described, to recall Rycroft's phrase, as a container of the past. All of these figures judged or censored Ged's actions at one time or another. Roheim stated that the omnipotence achieved in magic is a rejoinder to the aggression of the superego. And throughout *Wizard,* Ged's use of art-magic is a way of offsetting this aggression and thereby maintaining a sense of entity. The superego, however, is also the introject of primary, oral, object frustration, and is often represented with a strong emphasis on oral frustration and inward-turning aggression. This is the archaic superego or mother image that is introjected as the "bad" mother and which begins to kill the subject. Nonetheless, if one can identify with the aggressor, with this image of absolute omnipotence, there follows a reparation after the phase of self (and object) destruction. Ostensibly, this identification leads to the reparation that followed Ged's final meeting with the shadow (the persecutors, the archaic mother, the condensation of father-mother images, the nonhuman environment).

Significantly, Ged's union with his shadow is not told of in the Deed of Ged, which is sung all over the Archipelago. That particular event of his life, the epilogue seems to suggest, could be a lie or, more likely, an illusion, a fiction. This leads us to Lacan's Imaginary stage, a stage that he describes as a "fiction," because all imaginary relationships are "irremediably deceptive." In the mirror phase, which introduces the order of the Imaginary, "all that the subject can be certain of is the anticipated image coming to meet him."[22] Indeed, as *Wizard* progresses, the only thing that Ged is completely sure of is his shadow, his specular other, coming to meet him. In the other, in the mirror's image, the child sees a person with whom he identifies. The mirror relationship is essentially a relationship of the merging of self and other. Nevertheless, there is a strong sense of alienation produced by this identification (just as Ged's sense of alienation is produced by the appearance of the shadow), largely because the subject is his own double more than he is himself. And like the Narcissus-Echo situation, desire for love often becomes a desire for death. Such identification is also a "capture"—Narcissus captured by his image in the water; and the image is a lure, decoying the subject into a trap. This dual relationship is a relationship that is a "'capture' in that the subject and counterpart tend to merge into an undifferentiated whole."[23] This mirror stage, which is the psychological underpinning of *Wizard,* also directs the constitutional aggressivity of the human being, who must continually win his place at the expense of the other, and either impose himself on the other or be annihilated himself. But once the child gains his first positive perception of self, as an other, as an image in the mirror, he is jubilant in anticipation of the functional unity and mobility he may come to possess: it is "an ideal unity, a salutary *imago."*[24] Hence Ged's jubilation when the eyes in which he sees himself reflected transform and become one with his—as one, yet as an other—and allow him mobility and freedom; with this feeling of gestalt he can proceed to another unity with Yarrow.

Prior to the accession to the Symbolic, then, the subject is trapped in this dual relationship with the other, which may be the mirror image of the mother herself. The child identifies with the mother and with the object of her desire. One object of her desire is the father or phallus, and thus the shadow, with which Ged identifies, contains, for example, Jasper (the object of the desire of Lady O) and Ged's father (the object of the desire of Ged's mother). Of course, should the Symbolic authority, represented by the phallus or staff, that ostensibly separates child from mother fail to be recognized, the subject is in danger of "psychosis." On a basic level, this danger is what *Wizard* is all about: Ged–Le Guin, the artist-wizard, flirts with the threat of psychosis—complete loss of identity in oversymbiosis. It is this flirtation that allies Le Guin's discourse with the preverbal or Semiotic discourse. Both offer a challenge to the Symbolic order, asserting the artist's return to the preverbal identification with the mother, and her refusal to completely identify with the logic of phallic or paternal discourse. Ged does not defeat the speechless, whispering shadow—the representative of the preoedipal state; he unites with it and so he "neither lost nor won but, naming the shadow of his death with his own name, had made himself whole" (199). By naming his shadow, he attains that balance of being both a part of it and yet apart from its, at times, negative influence. Therefore, by the act of naming and then clinging onto his staff—which did not have much power over the beast anyway—while still at the mercy of the powerful sea, he maintains the balance, with the scale slightly tipped toward the maternal side. There is no loss of Symbolic function nor the loss of self and descent into madness that it entails; yet there is a recognition that self is always other—out of which identity is created. This is what the artist elucidates, as well as that the preverbal reemerges constantly in the Symbolic, thus guaranteeing its permanent openness and renewal. Therefore, another tale needs to be told, another novel must be written.

4

The Left Hand of Darkness:
The Artist and Human Sexuality

if I come into a room out of the sharp misty light
and hear them talking a dead language
and if they ask me my identity
what can I say but
I am the androgyne
I am the living mind you fail to describe
in your dead language
the lost noun, the verb surviving
only in the infinitive
the letters of my name are written under the lids
of a new born child

Adrienne Rich
"The Stranger"

The Left Hand of Darkness (1969) is the most thoroughly investigated of Le Guin's novels to date. The themes in it that consistently occupy critics are language and communication; sexuality; Le Guin's treatment of characters by means of contrast; detachment, isolation; union and fusion, especially as it opposes or balances isolation; the need for balance; the artistic quest or the role of the creative writer; and death and rebirth. The list is extensive but by no means complete, and it is a tribute to Le Guin's artistry that *LHD* can withstand, indeed it demands, the critical scrutiny it has received. The question still, as Fredric Jameson might put it, is "whether we can isolate some essential structural homology between these themes."[1]

Since inspiration for an artist often comes by means of an aural or visual image accompanied by a very powerful feeling, I suggest that this image is closely linked with the primary identity that was communicated to her in her preverbal days. Le Guin says that a "book does not come to me as an idea, or a plot, or an event, or a society, or a message; it comes to me as a person. A person seen, seen at a certain distance, usually in a landscape. The place is there. The person is there. I didn't invent him, I didn't make her up: he or she is there and my business is to get there too."[2] The goals and concerns of Le Guin's characters are closely related to her own. Le Guin reveals that her protagonist is a component of herself when she speaks of her writing:

> If I could have said it nonmetaphorically, I would not have written all these words, this novel; and Genly Ai would never have sat down at my desk and used up my ink and typewriter ribbon in informing me, and you, rather solemnly, that truth is a matter of the imagination.

Speaking again of how a book comes to her as a person, she says that once she saw

> two of them . . . . They were small figures, remote, in a tremendous waste landscape of ice and snow. They were pulling a sledge or something over the ice, hauling together. That is all I saw. I didn't know who they were. I didn't even know what sex they were (I must say I was surprised when I found out). But that is how my novel *The Left Hand of Darkness* began, and when I think of the book, it is still that vision I see. All the rest of it, with all its strange rearrangements of human gender and its imagery of betrayal, loneliness and cold, is my effort to catch up, to get nearer, to get there, where I had seen those two figures on the snow, isolated and together.[3]

Isolated and together: this paradoxical phrase and image is a succinct state-ment of the novel's overriding theme; it also describes the movement of the novel—from isolation to togetherness and back again, and from boundary to boundary and back again. Hearth tales, myths, scriptures, and reports are regular-ly inserted between each narrative chapter. They act as borders which separate the regular narrative chapters because they are a totally different way of relaying information: in the form of an official report; by an unknown narrator whose hearth tale is from a sound tape collection; a tale which is a version of another tale; a selection from the sayings of a High Priest; or a very primitive version from a pre-Yomesh written text. They are all seemingly crude and fragmented yet complete unto themselves. Although the style of telling forms a kind of hiatus between the narrative chapters, the substance of them is very much a part of the preceding and following chapters—so much so that they seem to blur thematic distinctions and tend to blend in to form one continuous story. For instance, one often finds oneself feeling that an event or image or idea recalled is from one of the narrative chapters when it is actually from one of the myths or tales. In one sense the tales and myths act as signposts to the regular narrative, if we learn how to read them. They can also function, in Geoffrey Hartman's terms, as the narrative within the narrative. Another related instance of separating only to blur or blend is, from chapter 6 on, Genly Ai and Estraven alternative narratives: two different narrators, with two ostensibly different points of view, but it is difficult at times to tell who is who and who said what.

A boundary is something that divides two entities (people, neighborhoods, countries) but it is something that they have in common as well. The novel is barely begun before we encounter boundaries: "The Palace of Erhenrang is an inner city, a walled wilderness. . . . Over it all rise the grim, red, elaborate walls of the Royal House."[4] Within these walls are walls that form another "palace or fort or keep." Inside the walls of Estraven's dwelling Ai encounters the garden which is "small and walled." Inside Estraven's house Ai and Estraven speak of the dispute concerning "a stretch of border in the high North Fall near Sassinoth" (15). This dispute has compromised Estraven and gotten him in trouble. Consequently he has to sever the connection he has formed with Ai regarding bringing the Ekumen (a league composed of eighty or so worlds) to Karhide. Ai's response is that there is "more at stake than a few miles of national boundary" (16). Estraven agrees but hopes that the Ekumen which is "a hundred light years from border to border" will be patient awhile.

The novel is underway: an Envoy or Mobile, representing the Ekumen that wishes to extend its borders to include the planet Gethen, is visiting one of the two countries on that planet. But, because of a border dispute between the two countries, Karhide and Orgoreyn, the potential union is thrown into jeopardy, and the Envoy goes outside the protective walls of the Prime Minister's dwelling, feeling "cold, unconfident, obsessed by perfidy, and solitude, and fear" (21). So ends the first chapter. The main narrative is underway but we are prevented from immediately following it up by the second chapter which is a hearth tale. The tale begins: "About two hundred years ago in the Hearth of Shath in the Pering Storm-border there were two brothers who vowed kemmering to each other" (22). Their kemmering or mating produces a child so, by law, they are forced to separate; this separation causes one brother to kill himself. Since suicide is illegal, the one is blamed for the death of the other and is exiled. On the Pering Ice Sheet, which is contiguous with the Gorbrin Ice that forms the border between Karhide and Orgoreyn, in "the place inside the blizzard," the living brother meets his dead brother, flees from him and goes inside "a white wall of falling snow" (25), after which he is found and taken care of by a community.

Although the first chapter's concern with boundaries appears largely political, the end result is that two people are separated and one is left alone and out in the cold. Borders or boundaries do ultimately separate people from people. The second chapter's concern is with two people who are united and separated and united and then separated again in an area known as the Pering Storm-border. This border is connected with the border in the first chapter, the dispute over which causes the Envoy Ai to separate from the Prime Minister Estraven.

It becomes quite apparent that Genly Ai's experience on the planet has to do with boundaries and barriers. He travels to the city of Rer; between it and Erhenrang "lie eleven hundred miles, and a wall several miles high" (53). Close to Rer is Otherhord, where Ai goes to meet the Foretellers. He encounters them inside a big building, which is walled off by a forest. During the Foretelling, Ai is forced to "set up a barrier" (65) against the group of minds collected in a circle there. On his way to Orgoreyn he encounters another barrier: "Here the border was the Ey, a narrow river but fierce, glacier-fed" (108). ("Ey" and "Ai" are no doubt pronounced the same; the pun implies that Ai is linked with borders or boundaries.) In Orgoreyn, Ai is taken to Pulefen Voluntary Farm, which is "bounded by the Sembensyen Mountains, the Esagel River, and the coast" (175). The working area of the farm itself is surrounded by electric fences. Later, when Estraven rescues Ai from the farm, he clambers up over the dead fence (dead because Estravcn had cut the current) and they head for "the border at Guthen Bay" (201). First they must reach the Gobrin Glacier which stands across the valleys like "a great wall . . . a wall of ice" (219). While attempting to mindspeak with Estraven on the journey, he finds that Estraven "quickly learned to set up the barriers" (254). When they do reach their goal and are resting in Karhide, Estraven informs Ai that they must embark on another stage of their journey, "and this one not towards haven but back to that damned border when Estraven might go back into exile, leaving me alone" (275). Eventually Estraven does just that; he dashes towards the fence of the border hoping to cross into Orgoreyn; Ai sees it this way: "He ran from me, and straight into the guns of the border guards. . . . Then they made me get up, and took me off one way and him another, I going to prison and he into the dark" (284). The novel closes as it opens, with borders (the same border) dictating and symbolizing a separation of two "brothers." Ai's mission is successful, however, and the Ekumen extends its borders to include Gethen, an act which will eliminate the border between Orgoreyn and Karhide. An earlier statement by Estraven about Ai is significant: "this is certain: in his presence, lines drawn on the earth make no boundaries, and no defense" (87). Whatever levels of meaning *LHD* contains, we find that the basic level that connects with and informs all the other levels is about barriers which separate one person from another and the consequences of removing them.

Inextricably intertwined with the boundaries in *LHD* are the device of doubling, the theme of separation, and its counterpart symbiosis. The separation theme, like the novel itself, revolves almost entirely around the Ai-Estraven relationship, and is mirrored in the hearth tales and the myths. The second chapter, "The Place Inside the Blizzard," a hearth tale, is a microcosm of the novel in that two brothers unite and separate and unite and separate; when the tale is done the isolated living brother manages to bring peace to the domain in much the same way that Ai brings the Ekumen and peace to Gethen. "The Nineteenth Day," a Karhidish story, involves a more brutal separation in that one kemmering kills the other but was "mad thereafter and . . . he would always go looking for Herbor, who he thought was somewhere about the Domain" (46). In the tale "Estraven The Traitor," there is a variation on the relation between Estraven and brother-kemmering Arek, which is at one with the Estraven-Ai relationship. In the tale, a young man, Estraven, or Arek of Estre, is out hunting and cannot make his way home after falling through the ice into the lake. He finds a small house, in the rival domain of Stok, and is warmed "back to life" by the owner, Therem of Stok. They touch their hands together, "like the two hands of one man laid palm to palm" (126), and vow kemmering (mating for life). A couple of days later, a party of men from Stok break in and slay Estraven. About nine months later, Therem of Stok visits the people of Estre and gives them an infant child, saying "This is Therem, the son's son of Estre" (127). They keep the name Therem, even though it is a name never used by the Estre clan. As a lad, Therem, like his father before him, goes hunting, but he is attacked by a group from his own clan. He slays all of them and then, wounded, makes his way to the same small house in the forest. Therem of Stok greets Estraven, Therem of Estre, and heals his wounds, and they place their palms together; "their two hands matched, like the two hands of one man" (129). Estraven is then taken home to Estre. Upon the death of his grandfather, Sorve, Lord of Estre, he becomes Lord of the Domain and ends the old border feud between Estre and Stok.

It is a confusing story, mainly due to the duplication and blending of names. But it foreshadows, or retells, or keeps telling, the story of Ai and Estraven. In *LHD,* there is an Estraven-Arek relationship, which is an earlier, sexual one (it actually takes place before the time covered by the novel), and then there is the Estraven-Ai relationship, which is "platonic." These relationships are paralleled in chapter 18, when Ai enters Estraven's mind in Arek's voice. In the tale, there is the Estraven-Stok relationship, which is a sexual one and the Stok-Estraven relationship, which is "platonic." If Ai is the second Estraven of the tale, as the parallel implies, particularly since the second Estraven of the tale brings peace to the Domain just as Ai does, then we are left to ponder a curious sort of inversion, which intimates that Estraven is Ai's mother. Just as the Therem of Stok in the tale (Therem is Estraven's private name, which Ai discovers in chapter 18) gives life to both Estravens, Estraven in the narrative is responsible for the life, the birth, of Ai because of the way he rescues him from Pulefen Farm. He visits the farm and finds Ai sleeping with a group of prisoners "like babies in wombs" (189). He gives Ai a shot to the head with a stunner gun so that he can tell the guards "He's dead" (189) and carries him off. Later, in the tent, Ai "came to life. . . . He set up crying out. . . . That night he talked much, in no tongue I knew" (193). While death is separation, birth is a union, the beginning of a symbiotic relationship; yet it is a separation as well—from the warmth of the womb. Although in the tales death always separates the brothers, in the narrative Ai and Estraven have several separations before the final one when Estraven dies. After each separation Ai suffers a kind of death of his sense of self—he feels afraid, cold, unable to cope alone. When Estraven visits him in Mishnory and then leaves abruptly, Ai tells us, "All at once I was utterly downcast and homesick . . . on my own, alien and isolate, without a soul I could trust" (133). After Estraven leaves the tent to search for food before they begin their journey, Ai wonders "what I would do in this forsaken place if Estraven did not come back" (205). Losing Estraven in the snow, Ai "panicked and began to blunder forward" (256). Away from Estraven in Sassinoth, he confesses that everything "seemed like a play, unreal, bewildering . . . I was uneasy among strangers and constantly missed Estraven's presence beside me" (280). After the final separation, Ai admits, "I had been all in pieces, disintegrated" (289).

The "Estraven The Traitor" tale also insinuates (partly by means of the repetition of "like the two hands of one man") that we are to regard Ai and Estraven as the latest in the line of an endless series of doubles. Indeed, the novel ends with Estraven reborn in his son, to whom Ai is about to tell the story of the ice trip. Although Estraven is a maternal figure, the gradual fusion of the two characters is enough to allow us to flip-flop them as doubles the same way it is done in the tale. Ai and Estraven serve almost identical functions in the plot of the novel; each is an instrument of the other: Estraven is the instrument of Ai, who needs him to achieve his mission on Gethen, while Ai is the instrument of Estraven, who needs him to bring Gethen into the Ekumen in order to avoid the potentially catastrophic border dispute. (Ai is the direct and Estraven the indirect instrument of a larger other, the Ekumen.) As the narrative progresses, it becomes increasingly obvious that the two are one. At the beginning they have one common goal. Difficulties arise, however, and Estraven goes to Orgoreyn, soon to be followed by Ai. In Mishnory, "Estraven's anxious almost frantic manner" infects Ai (166). Outside Pulefen Farm, Estraven, thinking of Ai, begins to feel that "my luck and his life had gone to waste after all" (192). On the journey they speak of themselves as exiles, "You for my sake—I for yours" (222). And later, "We strike a medium, and he shivers outside his bag while I swelter in mine" (223). In the key chapter 18 they are one to the extent that Ai is inside Estraven's head, speaking with the latter's dead brother's voice. Just off the ice, Estraven and Ai are speaking to a group in a "hot shop": " 'Will you look to my friend?' I thought I had said it, but Estraven had" (272). They are separated shortly after this because Ai's fusing with Estraven is such that his sense of entity is in jeopardy; there is little or no distinction between the self and the nonself—a complete blurring of boundaries.

That one can become totally overwhelmed, devoured, by the other, is indicated in the novel by another doubling relation, that of Faxe the Weaver and Estraven. The connections between Estraven and Faxe begin when Ai journeys to speak with the Foretellers. Ai asks Faxe, their speaker and leader, why they practice prophecy. Faxe replies: "To exhibit the perfect uselessness of knowing the answer to the wrong question" (70). In his journal, Estraven writes, "To learn which questions are unanswerable, and *not to answer them:* this skill is the most needful" (153). In Faxe's closing remarks to Ai, he says, "The only thing that makes life possible is permanent, intolerable uncertainty: not knowing what comes next" (71). Later, when Ai is surprised to see Estraven in Mishnory,

Estraven says, "The unexpected is what makes life possible" (122). When Ai returns to Erhenrang after Estraven's death, he encounters Faxe, who is becoming Prime Minister, Estraven's former position; Ai says of Faxe, "He was perhaps on his way up to the eminence from which Estraven, less than a year ago, had fallen" (290). And when the Ekumen ship finally lands "in a roar and glory," Faxe, standing beside Ai, says, "I'm glad I have lived to see this," and Ai thinks, "So Estraven had said when he looked at the Ice, at death; so he should have said this night" (295).

What the doubling of Faxe and Estraven can reveal about the relationship between Ai and Estraven, and how this relationship is linked with the potential for identity loss and the sources of creativity, may be found in one of the most memorable scenes in the novel—the scene where Ai visits the place of the Foretellers, which is "secretive, peaceful, rural," cut off from the rest of humanity by a "forest or a thick wood" (54). Ai is "pursuing this curiously tangible cult into its secret places" (55) so that he can ask, "Will this world Gethen be a member of the Ekumen of known worlds, five years from now?" (62) That this retreat is a creative place is implied (in the Romantic tradition) by its seclusion and isolation and by "the faint whistling sweetness of a Karhidish flute" that greets Ai as he enters the area. It is a place where people dance and practice the Handdarata discipline of Presence, which is a kind of trance: "the Handdarata, given to negatives, call it an untrance—involving self-loss (self-augmentation?) through extreme sensual receptiveness and awareness" (57). When Ai meets Faxe, he instinctively tries to bespeak him, "to try to reach him with the mindspeech" (58). Though Faxe is the only person other than Estraven that he tries this with, Faxe refuses to learn that "art." Nonetheless, Ai concludes that Faxe the Weaver, "whose extraordinary character, as limpid and unfathomable as a well of clear water, was a quintessence of the character of the place" (59).

When it comes time for the foretelling, Faxe has the tellers form a circle. Among them were two Zanies—"They were insane. Goss called them 'time-dividers,' which may mean schizophrenics." When Ai asks if they can be cured, the reply is, "Would you cure a singer of his voice?" (63). There are also five Indwellers, who must remain celibate as long as they are Foretellers (and one of whom must be in kemmer during the foretelling), and a Pervert, someone with a permanent (hormonal) imbalance toward the male or female. "They were all connected, all of them . . . I felt, whether I wished or not, the connection, the communication that ran, wordless, inarticulate, through Faxe, and which Faxe was trying to pattern and control, for he was the center, the Weaver" (65). Notably, in seeking an answer, they are all connected, in union, but separated from the rest of the world; schizophrenia and sexuality, particularly bisexuality, are involved; the communication, the inspiration, if you will, is silent, wordless; and it is woven into a pattern by a centering figure. As they come together the force of "silence" grows, and Ai says:

> I tried to keep out of contact with the minds of the Foretellers. I was made very uneasy by the silent electric tension, by the sense of being drawn in, of becoming a point or figure in the pattern, in the web. But when I set up a barrier, it was worse: I felt cut-off and cowered inside my own mind obsessed by hallucinations of sight and touch, a stew of wild images and notions, abrupt visions and sensations all sexually charged and grotesquely violent, a red-and-black seething of erotic rage. I was surrounded by great gaping pits with ragged lips, vaginas, wounds, hellmouths, I lost my balance, I was falling. . . . If I could not shut out this chaos I would fall indeed, I would go mad. . . . The emphatic and paraverbal forces at work . . . rising out of the perversion and frustration of sex, out of an insanity that distorts time, and out of an appalling discipline of total concentration and apprehension of immediate reality, were far beyond my restraint or control. And yet they were controlled: the centre was still Faxe. . . . In the centre of all darkness Faxe: the Weaver: a woman, a woman dressed in light. The light was silver, the silver was armor, an armored woman with a sword. The light burned sudden and intolerable, the light along her limbs, the fire, and she screamed aloud in terror and pain, "Yes, yes, yes!" . . . "Some light." It was the physician from Spreve. He had entered the circle. It was all broken. (65–66)

This remarkable passage—a more concise, more intense version of what happens in the tent and on the ice in chapter 18—is a condensation of the main concerns of the novel, which revolve around the separation-symbiosis dilemma. Ai is afraid of being drawn in, but when he sets up a barrier he feels even worse, cut-off, on the brink of madness. As he cuts himself off he is overcome by a stew of images that are erotic as well as destructive—devouring mouths and vaginas. Even though it appears that he is able to prevent himself from being drawn in, his mind, while separated, hallucinates and overwhelms him with images of destructive fusion. As he is losing his sense of time and reality, about to go mad, he is reassured by the omnipotent Faxe, who, somewhat paradoxically, is in the center of all darkness yet dressed in light, "burning in a fire" (67). Faxe is controlling, weaving these images into a unity by means of paraverbal forces, similar to the way an artist works. The passage ends with overtones of an actual birth—the screaming, the relief, the light, and a physician to break the bond. Speaking of the weaving imagery in the novel, David Ketterer remarks that "the act of putting together a novel and creating an aesthetic unity can be imaged as a weaving process."[5] Faxe the Weaver is the fire, the creative center; he says, "I serve as the filament" (67). Since Faxe is the double of Estraven, who is also associated with fire and creativity, largely by way of a private name, Harth,[6] and by his relationship with Ai and the Ekumen, we have an emphasis on the idea of creativity, creative communication, as directly aligned with a centering figure. More significant is that creativity comes from a balance of being cut-off and drawn in. This is emphasized, neatly compressed, in the birth-image—birth being both a separation (from the womb) and a union (with the mother). The product, then, arises from a total union of minds and bodies; but once the product is completed, the answer arrived at, the union must be severed or else complete psychosis (as Lacan would define it) will set in. Also important is the feeling that this act is affecting reality in some way, however oblique. The "Yes, yes, yes!" (the product, the only language in the scene), which is an affirmation of life, indicates that Gethen will be united with the Ekumen (which means Household or "Hearth" [136], another creative center); barriers will come down, and Ai and Estraven's purpose will have been served—they can affect reality.

The passage has added psychological insight if one is curious about the melding of sexual images, devouring vaginas, loss of sense of reality, and a woman with a sword. Hans Loewald writes about the "dread of the vulva," which is expressed in such terms as

> being drowned, sucked in, overpowered, and this in regard to intercourse as well as in regard to the relationship to mother. . . . If we assume that one component of the "castration" threat is maternal in origin . . . this component could not be described as interfering with the primary narcissistic position. On the contrary, it would be the threat to perpetuate or re-establish this position, to engulf the emerging ego into the original unity. . . . The original unity and identity, undifferentiated and unstructured, of psychic apparatus and environment, is as much a danger for the ego as the demand . . . to give it up altogether.[7]

Therefore the trance is directly concerned with the origins and problems of ego and identity. We are told earlier in the foretelling scene that the trance involves "self-loss (self-augmentation?) through extreme sensual receptiveness and awareness" (57). One must lose the self in order to gain it. The needed sensual awareness is in line with Lichtenstein's findings that the child's "sensory responses are simultaneously 'outlining' a first '*Umwelt*-otherness' and a first *Umwelt*-defined identity. . . . In the primitive sensory exchanges taking place between mother and infant one could see the precursor of adult sexuality."[8] The trance reveals our original longings and fears, which are connected with that original identity that is imprinted "paraverbally." The trance, then, accurately pictures the problem of ego and reality:

> Dread of the womb and castration fear . . . threatens loss of reality. Reality is lost if the ego is cut off from objects (castration threat); reality is lost as well if the boundaries of ego and reality are lost (threat of the womb). Loss of reality always means loss of ego.[9]

The network of oral imagery in the novel, which can also express itself in literature as losing the boundaries of the self, of being engulfed, overwhelmed, drowned, or devoured, indicates that one of *LHD*'s major interests is the problem of the subject, especially as it constantly has to deal with and integrate the early period in infancy when life revolves around what goes into and what comes out of the mouth. In Gethen, we are told, it is "always the Year One" (2). Karhide is a land where they eat "four solid meals a day . . . along with a lot of adventitious nibbling and gobbling in between. . . . I had got used to eating, as it seemed, every few minutes" (10). Ai concludes that Gethenians have perfected the technique "not only of perpetual stuffing, but also of indefinitely starving" (11). Throughout the first chapter, Ai is obsessed with the Tibe's teeth: "long, clean, yellow teeth . . . more teeth" (8); "every tooth seemed to have a meaning" (9); "long yellow teeth" (9); "teeth bared across his shoulder at me" (9)—all of which appears nonsensical except as it relates to orality and the central theme of separation and union. It makes sense of Ai's recalling that Estraven had been implying that he "should get away from the city and the court. For some reason I thought of Tibe's teeth" (42), because to leave, to separate, means to avoid being devoured. Ai speaks of Gethen as an inimical world where punishment is prompt: "death from cold or death from hunger" (99). In Orgoreyn, the usage of the word "commensal" includes all national and governmental institutions and it means "to eat together" (109). And the Orgota language "drips off one's teeth like sugar-syrup" (132). In "Estraven the Traitor," Estraven's body is thrown out "for the wild beasts to eat" (127). And in the chapter on the creation myth, the ice-shapes crawl out of a deep crevasse and are melted by the sun: "As milk they melted, and the milk ran into the mouths of the sleepers, and the sleepers woke. The milk is drunk by the children of men alone and without it they will not wake to life" (238). This makes again a connection between birth, orality, creativity, and identity (the boundaries of "self" are melted). In addition to unifying the novel, the oral imagery informs and expands upon the central themes.

The imagery is most abundant and intense in the scenes which describe the journey across the ice cap, where Ai and Estraven become one. The journey is marked by pitfalls: "creeks and ravines" (204); "a deep, cold porridge of rain-sodden snow" (219); "sleet on one's lips [that] tastes of smoke and sulphur" and "crevasses—some wide enough to sink villages in" (230). "A hissing mutter fills the air . . . it fills all the interstices of one's being" (226). Eventually, particularly as they appear to be near the end of their journey, one realizes that what is being described is a vast *body,* probably maternal, that Ai and Estraven are travelling either inside of, outside of, or both. Ketterer is close to this idea when he remarks that the "crevasses become cracks in an eggshell with Genly and Estraven both inside and outside."[10] Estraven writes of how they go back and forth, "seeking the end of a slit in the ice that would swallow a sledge whole. . . . I shall be glad to get off this slit and wrinkled ice-arm between two growling monsters" (226). And the "arm between Drumner and Dremegole is only one finger, and now we are on the back of the hand" (227). Volcanic projectiles "hiss loudly" as Estraven proclaims "Praise then Creation unfinished!" (227). This anthropomorphizing (or gynomorphizing) is continued with this description: "The world around us, ice and rock, ash and snow, fire and dark, trembles and twitches and mutters. Looking out a minute ago I saw the glow of our volcano as a dull red bloom on the belly of vast clouds overhanging the darkness" (229). The ice tries to "choke the fire-mouths with silence," yet it speaks: "There is nothing, the Ice says, but Ice.—But the young volcano there to northward has another word it thinks of saying" (231). The idea that the ice is a live maternal body is reinforced in the chapter on the creation myth, previously quoted, which interrupts the journey part of the narrative. Ice equals milk and birth/creation: "The ice shapes . . . let the sun melt them. As milk they melted. . . . That milk is drunk by the children of men alone and without it they will not wake to life" (238). The chapter "Homecoming" opens with a description of the region, which is covered with "sunken pits" and false floors of snow "that might subside with a huge gasp all around you . . . areas all slit and pocked with little holes and crevasses" (263). During a blizzard they "lay in the tent for three days while the blizzard yelled at us, a three-day long, wordless, hateful yell from the unbreathing lungs. . . . The three-day shriek died down into a gabbling, then a sobbing, then a silence" (268). As they ski on past "protruding tongues of glacier . . . up abreast a valley-mouth . . . out of that gorge howled a gale that knocked us both off our feet." To which Ai comments, "The Gobrin Ice has spewed us out of its mouth" (270).

The journey charts the precarious course the infant takes in its early months, when it is still dependent on the symbiotic unit yet is just barely beginning to realize some need for differentiation. Fear of reengulfment, fear of the vulva, is great for one who is attempting to individuate—and this is what Ai is attempting, although his total at-one-ness with Estraven and the overwhelming environment suggest that he is close to total regression to the symbiotic state with loss of identity. The images of the inside and the outside of the body relate to an occurrence during the symbiotic phase: "There is a shift of cathexis from inside the body, from the predominantly visceral position of the autistic phase to the periphery, the sensory perceptive organs."[11] This is mingled with the attempt to differentiate or individuate. On the subphase, Mahler writes: "Characteristic behaviours that make possible the demarcation of self from nonself are visual and tactile exploration of the mother's face and body."[12] And finally, when Ai comments that they have been spewed out of the mouth (that is, born or reborn), he is speaking metaphorically, but it is appropriate at this point, especially if we continue to regard the ice and snow as representing mother, because the "process of emerging from the symbiotic state of oneness with mother in the intrapsychic sense . . . is the 'second,' the psychological, birth experience."[13] This under-scores Lichtenstein's statement that the "process of self-creation is a permanent rebirth."[14]

The novel continues in a tightening spiral, delineating ever more accurately the same phenomenon. The center of the spiral is the image of two men pulling a sledge. This image is most completely explicated in chapter 18, "On the Ice." It is the center of the novel: the place, the space, where Ai's (and the basic component of Le Guin's) identity theme is most firmly inscribed. The themes, images, and devices which permeate the novel are digested in this chapter—and they all stem from the question of simultaneous separateness and sameness. The chapter opens with as complete a description of fusion as is possible:

> Sometimes as I am falling asleep in a dark, quiet room I have for a moment a great and treasurable illusion of the past. The wall of a tent leans up over my face, not visible but audible, a slanting plane of faint sound: the susurrus of blown snow. Nothing can be seen. The light-emission of the Chabe stove is cut off, and it exists only as a sphere of heat, a heart of warmth. The faint dampness and confining cling of my sleeping-bag; the sound of the snow; barely audible, Estraven's breathing as he sleeps; darkness. Nothing else. We are inside, the two of us, in shelter, at rest, at the center of all things. Outside, as always, lies the great darkness, the cold, death's solitude.
>
> In such fortunate moments as I fall asleep I know beyond doubt what the real center of my own life is, that time which is past and lost and yet permanent, the enduring moment, the heart of warmth. (240)

The most prominent thing about this passage is that there is no clear recognition of inside and outside. (Even past and present are fused.) The wall of the tent is the ostensible boundary between inside and outside yet the wall itself becomes outside, but only the audible outside: it is the whispering of blown snow, the whispering, perhaps, of the mother. And, as indicated partly by the use of semicolons, Estraven is equated with the sound of the snow, with darkness, and with the confining cling of the sleeping bag, which was earlier referred to as a womb (189). So Estraven is simultaneously inside and outside; he is one half of the dual-unity inside, which is separated from the hostile world at large, and he is also the whispering, breathing other that seems to be outside but isn't quite. There is, then, just a faint recognition that the other is both me and not-me. The sensation communicated by the other—a sensation which makes Ai believe that he is experiencing that time which is past and lost yet permanent, "the real center of my own life"—is communicated aurally: nothing can be seen. This con-fusion nonetheless corresponds well with Mahler's findings regarding autism and symbiosis: "Whereas in primary autism there is a deanimated, frozen wall between the subject and the human object, in symbiotic psychosis there is a fusion, melting, and lack of differentiation between the self and the nonself—a complete blurring of boundaries."[15] In this instance the frozen wall is the tent and the human object is the outside environment which we earlier saw as a human body. The fusion and melting is that which takes place between Ai and Estraven, and Ai and the sound of the environment, which is also equated with Estraven. So Estraven is equated with the comforting (and threatening) maternal womb and also with the maternal ice-wilderness body. This is not quite as contradictory as it seems because symbiotic and autistic structures frequently superimpose themselves on each other. This superimposition, which Le Guin has so beautifully depicted, is in line with her search for a balance of separation and symbiosis, "together and separate at once," as Douglas Barbour has aptly phrased it.[16] Also important in this context is the Chabe stove. In this passage it cannot be seen—it exists as a sphere of heat, a heart of warmth, and it is always *between* Ai and Estraven. The Chabe stove is the main symbol of creative communication in the novel; creativity is something which comes out of, and creates, the simultaneous bridge and barrier between self and other. Without the "little heater-stove," Ai admits, they "would never have got fifty miles" (204) together. And it is the sale of the stove that allows Ai to make the vital communication with the Ekumen.

Ai's reverie in the tent is broken by hunger. "I was hungry, constantly hungry, daily hungrier. I woke up because I was hungry" (241). They eat and then they continue their journey over a land replete with crevasses, gorges, and biting storms. But they "seldom talked . . . it was necessary to keep the mouth closed and breathe through the nose,"or else one would "gasp in a lungful of razors" (244). The losing of boundaries of self, which is manifested in the network of oral imagery in the novel, is rooted in this chapter. Ai and Estraven gradually find themselves stepping out of the tent into nothing. They cast no shadow and they leave no track. "No sun, no sky, no horizon, no world. A whitish-gray void, in which we appeared to hang. The illusion was so complete that I had trouble keeping my balance" (260). By the end of the chapter "that bland blind nothing- ness about us began to flow and writhe" (261). The inanimate becomes animate. "I saw a huge black shape come hulking out of the void towards us. Black tentacles writhed upwards, groping out. I stopped dead in my tracks" (261). The chapter then ends with a decision to take a slightly different route.

What has happened is that by the end of the chapter the relationship has developed into such a totally symbiotic one that Ai is in danger of being complete- ly overwhelmed by the other. He frequently desires death and has to be "coaxed" into living by Estraven—"I hated the harsh, intricate, obstinate demands that he made on me in the name of life" (245). More and more he finds himself craving the warmth of the tent, "an enveloping, protecting ambiance" (245). He also notices a change in Estraven: "His face in the reddish light was as soft, as vulnerable, as remote as the face of a woman . . . and I saw then, and for good, what I had always been afraid to see in him: that he was a woman as well as a man" (248). This confrontation and Ai's fear were inevitable. The entire novel moves to put these two into a situation where Ai has to deal with his sexuality, his gender identity. One critic has written that in *LHD* "homosexuality is on the whole covert, though the emotional temperature of the relationship between Genly and Estraven . . . rises (it approaches the boiling point in chapter 18), and through Genly's loss of a clearly defined sex role threatens to make all sex repellent to him."[17] In an ambisexual society, homosexuality is an issue only for Ai, the outsider; nonetheless, the scene does point out Ai's problems with gender identity, which are seen throughout the novel mainly by his distrust of Estraven and Gethenians due to the "sense of effeminate intrigue" (8) and "effeminate deviousness" (14) and "the soft supple femininity that I disliked and distrusted in him" (12). In the caravan en route to Pulefen Farm, Ai tries to hide from a prisoner who is attracted to him. At the Farm he has "a certain feeling of being a man among women, or among eunuchs" (176). It is fitting, however, that all of this comes to the fore in a scene where the identity problem is most evident. For Ai on Gethen, there is enough ambiguity, enough potential strangeness in the sexual act with an ambisextrous person to powerfully test his identity. In the tent Ai does, to a large extent, come to terms with his sexual identity—he learns what his sex role is in relation to the other.

Accordingly, Ai and Estraven do not copulate: "It was from the difference between us, not from the affinities and the likenesses, but from the difference, that love came: and it was itself the bridge, the only bridge, across what divided us. For us to meet sexually would be for us to meet once more as aliens" (249). In other words, difference is what keeps them together as lovers but simultaneously keeps them apart sexually: yet another version of Le Guin's insistence on having symbiosis and separateness at the same time. Insofar as Estraven is also a mother-figure for Ai, then copulation would be inappropriate and would indeed be to meet as aliens; if there is to be love between them, it must therefore arise out of the (sexual) *difference* (separation) between them. The sexual act would thus be a complete giving in, an admission that one is not adequately individuated, and the consequence of the act would be loss of self. Ai of course wants to be both a part and apart. Le Guin's invention of an ambisexual society is a crafty way of finding a compromise: becoming one with an ambisexual person is akin to a child's "hallucinated fusion with a condensation of father-mother images,"[18] and it also avoids, or solves, the problem of having to separate one sex from another, which is tied in with one's gender identity, when one has to say and believe, firmly, "I am male" or "I am female." It is, in effect, another blurring of boundaries. Also, to behave, to yield, in a feminine way, Ai seems to feel, is to dissolve or be transformed; yet to act in an aggressive way is to allow "standards of manliness, of virility" to complicate one's "pride" (218). As an ambisexual, one can blend or balance the two. The figure of the androgyne itself connotes a kind of balance, or at least a kind of ambiguous unity. The ambisexual Gethenian, then, is an extremely rich construct because it designates so many of our sexual preoccupations—which stem from our earliest days—and because it allows a variety of readers to respond in a bewildering variety of ways.

Once the sexual barrier is dealt with (or avoided?), Ai and Estraven are able to move to an even more intimate level of communication by getting rid of the language barrier. They both believe that it is time Estraven learns the "mind-science." Estraven asks Ai if there are special teachers of the skill. Ai replies:

> Yes. Not on Alterra, where there's a high occurrence of natural sensitivity, and—they say—mothers mindspeak to their unborn babies. I don't know what the babies answer. But most of us have to be taught, as if it were a foreign language. Or rather as if it were our native language, but learned very late. (250)

Mindspeech is thus a different kind of language; it is the most private language in that it attempts to go beyond spoken language and its lies, and because it can be learned—or imprinted like one's identity theme—in the preverbal stage. Ai tries to bespeak Estraven, expecting an easy passage because Estraven is an adept of the Handdara. However, Ai tries until he "felt hoarse of brain." Finally they decide to sleep.

> Within a minute or two he was sliding into sleep as a swimmer slides into dark water. I felt his sleep as if it were my own: the empathic bond was there, and once more I bespoke him, sleepily, by his name—"Therem!"
>
> He sat bolt upright, for his voice rang out above me in the blackness, loud. "Arek! is that you?"
>
> *"No: Genly Ai: I am bespeaking you."*
>
> His breath caught. Silence. He fumbled with the Chabe stove, turned up the light, stared at me with his dark eyes full of fear. "I dreamed," he said, "I thought I was at home—"
>
> "You heard me mindspeak."
>
> "You called me—It was my brother. It was his voice I heard. He's dead. . . . This is more terrible than I thought." (252–53)

We discover that Estraven's brother was also his mate or kemmering. Although brothers on Gethen are allowed to couple, to commit incest, they are not allowed to vow for life. "In those days as now, full brothers were permitted to keep kemmer until one of them should bear a child, but after that they must separate" (22)—so we are told in chapter 2, "The Place Inside the Blizzard." When Ai, in chapter 18, speaks of himself and Estraven as "inside the blizzard" (260) it is clear that we are to make the connection between Estraven and brother, and Estraven and Ai; that is, Ai equals Arek. Mindspeech therefore has a sexual connotation—or at least an erotic connection is implied because they have just vowed to avoid sex when they move into mindspeech, only to have Ai speak as Estraven's mate. So it is an even closer union than sexual union, partly because there is no possibility of deceit.

Mindspeech, in addition to its implications of fusion here, is also connected with the idea of naming, which is somehow tied in with the potential danger involved in attempting to supersede the language barrier. When Ai sees how disturbed Estraven is by the mindspeech, he apologizes. Estraven replies: "No. Call me by my name. If you can speak inside my skull with a dead man's voice then you call me by my name! Would *he* have called me 'Harth'? Oh, I see why there's no lying in this mindspeech. It is a terrible thing" (253). Estraven is eventually able to bespeak the name "Genry." However, it does not come easily for him—"he could not take it for granted. He quickly learned to set up the barriers" (254). Ai speculates that as a Gethenian, being "singularly complete," Estraven experiences telepathic speech as a "violation of completeness."

> Every word he said rose out of a deeper silence. He heard my voice bespeaking him as a dead man's, his brother's voice. I did not know what, besides love and death, lay between him and that brother, but I knew that whenever I bespoke him something in him winced away as if I touched a

wound. So that intimacy of mind established between us was a bond, indeed, but an obscure and austere one, not so much admitting further light (as I had expected it to) as showing the extent of the darkness. (255)

The link between private language, naming, and wounding is separation. When Arek is placed once again within Estraven's mind there is, for Estraven, the recollection of the symbiosis, the sexual union, only to be followed by the wounding—separation and exile (the tale "Inside the Blizzard" also suggests that Estraven is responsible for the death of his brother). Naming and wounding are also equated by Estraven's remark that Ai's name is a "cry of pain. . . . I asked his name, and heard for answer a cry of pain from a human throat across the night" (229). And although naming in the novel is given a magical function—to know a person's name is to know the essence of that person; one curses and can bring ill on another by means of a name—it is something that can be both public and private. Estraven has three names: Estraven, his public name; Harth, which is a private name, one that he gives to Ai; and Therem, his most private name—the one that Ai discovers through mindspeech. The Envoy is Ai's public designation (he's also known as the Mobile to the Ekumen); Mr. Ai is also public and formal; Genly Ai is both public and personal; Genry is the private name used by Estraven. The multiple naming fits well with an uncertainty about who one is; it is as if to say "I am a number of parts; I am not a whole."

Mahler writes about language and naming as a critical part of the child's growing ability to function at a greater distance from the mother's presence. "The ability to name objects seems to have provided the toddler with a greater sense of ability to control his environment. Use of the personal pronoun 'I' also often appeared at this time, as well as the ability to recognize and name familiar people."[19] The choice of "Ai" ("I") betrays an unconscious concern with that early process. That Ai-I is a cry of pain further underlines the wounding that accompanies separation. But the naming is, perhaps, more than this. It almost always distinguishes one's sex. And naming is a matter both of conferring a name and of receiving a name; ostensibly, the conferrer whispers it frequently, stirs one to life with it, initiates the potential for individuation. So a name, at its deepest level, is both one and two; one's name is the emblem of one's difference, of what sets one apart, but it is always connected with the namer, which is the most private part of the name. This preoccupation with, this questioning of the source and meaning of names, is carried on by Geoffrey Hartman. He queries: "There may be such a thing as a specular name or 'imago du nom propre' in the fantasy development of the individual, a name more genuinely one's own than a signature or proper name. . . . Is it possible to discern a specular word, logos phase, or imago of the proper name in the development of the individual?"[20] Le Guin intuits that there is a specular name and the Therem-Arek-Ai scenario suggests that the specular name is either the source or the end of identity and doubling.

In the scene where Ai and Estraven are whispering each other's names in their private language, Le Guin's text is registering an insight into the fact that in the process of individuation, in the infant's attempt to establish its own boundaries apart from the (m)other, there is often a fusion and confusion of the two. Sometimes the "I" is the child; sometimes the (m)other; sometimes both. Through mindspeech Le Guin imitates the condition of unity that existed before the differentiation of consciousness and language. In this sense language, public language, is a necessary evil: it keeps us away from the unity we strive for (as individuals in relationship to other, be it mother, father, or community) but it prevents us from being overwhelmed by that state. It is therefore appropriate, after Ai and Estraven have established this deepest bond, that Ai is terrified when he is separated from Estraven. At one point they are trudging along, "then came another blizzard whooping up in our faces":

> Within two minutes of the first strong gusts the snow blew so thick that I could not see Estraven six feet away. I had turned my back on him and the sledge and the plastering, blinding, suffocating snow in order to get my breath, and when a minute later I turned around he was gone. I shouted and could not hear my own voice. I was deaf and alone in a universe filled solid with small stinging gray streaks. I panicked and began to blunder forward, mindcalling frantically, *"Therem!"*
> Right under my hand, kneeling, he said, "Come on, give me a hand with the tent."
> I did so and never mentioned my minute of panic. (256)

The fusion-confusion of "I" and "Thou" and the overlapping of separation and symbiosis are again evident. With no language or other barriers between them, Ai is vulnerable to being suffocated by the maternal unit, represented simultaneously by the environment and Estraven. Separated from Estraven he feels alone and begins to panic. He makes the connection with Estraven by means of the private language and they are, once more, ready to set up their private symbiotic world away from and yet, simultaneously, within the hostile environment. Furthermore, Ai is beginning to shut out the "real world": *"Down there,* for us, had come to mean the south, and the world below the plateau of ice, the region of earth, men, roads, cities, all of which had become hard to imagine as really existing" (257). They have become the essence of each other to the extent that eating together is a stronger bond than speaking together: "Eating was so engrossing a business that we never talked anymore while we ate . . . not a word said till the last crumb was gone" (259). Lichtenstein writes of the connection between orality and identity: "Oral language serves in both cases the thought of being both inseparable and being the 'essence' of the other one. . . . Symbiotic experiences blurring the person's boundary between himself, the 'objects' of the 'real world' are, if they dominate the individual's perception of himself and the world, an important characteristic of insanity."[21] Thus it is no surprise to see the chapter end with Ai hallucinating—believing he is being overcome by the Esherhoth Crags, which he thinks to be almost within arms reach when they are miles away. The oneness established on the ice, instigated by a hostile environment, is largely due to the breaking down of sexual and language barriers. Therefore there is no increase in the recognition that there is an "I" and a "Thou"; there is some recognition as they mindspeak less and less and then complete recognition when Estraven dies at the border. At the end of the novel, however, we see Estraven reborn in his son and it appears that Ai's need for a "Thou" to differentiate the "I" will continue.

The doubling in the novel arises out of this state of undifferentiation, in which the "I" is not yet differentiated from the "not-I" and in which inside and outside are only gradually coming to be sensed as different. Ai is Estraven and Estraven is Faxe, therefore Ai is Faxe. Just as the novel moves around separation and symbiosis so Ai is at times one with Faxe and/or Estraven and at other times he painfully realizes his difference from them. To Le Guin's imagination the double must die in order for the single to live, however precariously and alone. As long as there is a double, there is some recognition of "not-I." Nonetheless, the chance of losing the "I" altogether is always near. Once the double is killed off, the single, shattered momentarily, is free to gain its individuality in contrast to the "not-I." One must lose in order to gain. The suggestion that the doubles are also maternal figures is in accord with the idea of losing in order to gain—in infancy, we give up union with a nurturing other to gain individuality. The idea of the mother-as-double also comes from R. A. Spitz, who calls the mother the "auxiliary ego" of the infant.[22] Mahler speaks of the child's desire to restore and perpetuate the "delusional omnipotent phase of mother-infant fusion—when mother was an extension of the self."[23] Lichtenstein writes that even "as the infant separates slowly from the original symbiotic state, the mother and child respond to each other as if they were extensions of one another, both physically and psychically." Also speaking of mirroring and narcissism, Lichtenstein contends that what

> is dimly emerging in this mirror is not a primary love object, but the outlines of the child's own image as reflected by the mother's unconscious needs with regard to the child. In this first, archaic mirroring experience of the child a primary identity emerges which may be called narcissistic. It is not yet a sense of identity for that presupposes consciousness. I see in it a primary organizational principle without which the process of developmental differentiation could not begin.[24]

In unison with what the infant sees is what she feels in regard to the mother's unconscious needs. There is not yet a sense of differentiation, but this is the start of the child's being able to consolidate her own identity, and it is equated with doubling. Lacan writes about the mirror phase in the early development of what will eventually become the child's ego. "By the complaisance of the mirror the child sees itself for the first time as a coordinated being and, triumphantly, jubilantly, assumes that image. But what is found by means of the play ('je-jeu') with the mirror is really a double rather than a differentiated other."[25] The double, it would appear, is somewhere between union and separation. A variation of this is a childhood companion or alter ego that can remain with one into adulthood: "the little man became established primarily before the mother existed as a separate entity, and identification with her occurred only later, after she had become an object distinct from himself. Many features of the mother were then added to the image of the little man."[26] Robert Stoller writes of a double called Charlie who "was created . . . to help her survive her inability throughout infancy and childhood to reach her mother."[27]

In *LHD* the double is a compromise, a mediator, a balance of two mutually contradictory tendencies, both of which threaten the individual's existence: final separation from the mother versus the total loss of identity and personal death involved in total reunion with her. As long as there is a double somewhere in the novel, the implication is that the precarious balance is being maintained. That is why we find another Estraven at the end of *LHD* in his son Sorve Harth. And the novel ends with the beginning of yet another novel by Ai. Alone and feeling alienated from the rest of Gethen after Estraven's death, he is, at the end of *LHD*, once again in a safe enclosure with a warm fire burning, about to retell the tale of the Gobrin Ice, how Estraven died, and about "the other worlds out among the stars—the other kinds of men, the other lives" (301).

Winnicott believes that it is "only in being creative that the individual discovers the self"; and if the artist "is searching for the self, then it can be said that in all probability there is already some failure for that artist in the field of general creative living. The finished creation never heals the underlying lack of self."[28] Therefore, another creation must come about. The bulk of this discussion has been insinuating that Ai embodies the artist and her basic concerns. This is seen in his doubling relation with two creative centers, Estraven and Faxe. Faxe is the Weaver, as is Ai, who, at one point, is trying to remember "how I had meant to weave the story" (182). There are other signs that Ai's purposes are creative. At the opening of the novel, he conjoins facts, art, imagination, and childhood: "I'll make my report as if I told a story, for I was taught as a child on my homeworld that truth is a matter of the imagination" (1). He is known as a "highly imaginative monster" (13) and his stories about other worlds are regarded as "baseless fiction" (30). His mindspeech is "an art that would change the world entirely" (69); it is "the 'Last Art'" (254). He tells us that "an essential part of my job," known as "Farfetching," is "highflown speculation" and "tends to find expression not in rational symbols, but in metaphor" (147). At Pulefen Farm, when he tells a "story about people who live on another world" (181), his listener is "puzzled by the injection of the teller into the tale" (182). When Ai and Estraven complete their journey, Ai thinks the "saga is over" (277).

Estraven also is a writer; his "writing was both an obligation and a link with his family, the Hearth of Estre" (208). In Karhide after the journey, Estraven tells his hosts "the whole tale of our crossing of the Ice," and he tells the story in such a way that it becomes "a saga, full of traditional locution and even episodes" (276). As one of the Handdarata, Estraven is both writer and foreteller. The connection between a tale teller and a foreteller is made early in the novel, when King Argaven refuses to believe Ai's "tales and messages" because what they give is as "useful an answer as I might get from any Foreteller" (39). The Foretellers have the "power of seeing (if only for a flash) *everything at once:* seeing whole" (204), much like Ai as Farfetcher, who is adept at "the intuitive perception of a moral entirety" (147). Vital to the foretelling are the "time-dividers" or schizophrenics, people, if you will, with the ultimate identity problem.

One purpose of writing is to communicate, and the role of Ai, Estraven, and Faxe, who are all one, is just that. Estraven's initial role is to communicate with the people of Karhide; later, in addition to communicating with Ai, he communicates his private thoughts and details of the ice trip to his Domain. The origins of Faxe's communication are wordless, woven out of a union between a small group of people, and later passed on to one person; later his job is to communicate with the people of Karhide. Both Faxe and Estraven, then, have a private as well as a public form of communication. This is more obvious with Ai, whose private language is the mindspeech, and whose native tongue is also unknown on Gethen. Publicly his job is to find out if this isolated planet is "willing to communicate with the rest of mankind" (138). The communication will be made via Ai's ansible communicator, which will "produce a message at any two points simultaneously" (37). He eventually loses his ansible, the ostensible bridge between two peoples, but, thanks to the Chabe stove, he is able to purchase "ten minutes of private transmission to private reception" (279). This private communication that creates a simultaneity, a oneness, is linked with the identity question in the novel and to the writer who wishes to establish a link with the reader. That Le Guin feels this way is evidenced by her statement concerning writing and storytelling: "But by remembering it he had made the story his; and insofar as I have remembered it, it is mine; and now, if you like it, it's yours. In the tale, in the telling, we are all one blood."[29]

The writer, then (Le Guin at least), ultimately wants to break down barriers between people. Ai "brings the end of kingdoms and commensalities" (86); "in his presence, lines drawn on the earth make no boundaries, and no defense" (87). Also in any writer's dreams is the hope of influencing reality; she would like to "show us the new road" (19); because of Ai, "the alien who lay ill, not acting, not caring, in a room in Sassinoth, two governments fell within ten days" (287). This desire to influence reality is also essential to the makeup of the autistic child:

> The experience that his own actions . . . make no difference is what stops him from becoming a human being, for it discourages him from forming a personality through which to deal with the environment. . . . Unless we can also influence reality, things are just as destructive for our

efforts to develop a personality. . . . I can now be more specific about what essentially the autistic *Anlage* consists of: it is the conviction that one's own efforts have no power to influence the world, because of the earlier conviction that the world is insensitive to one's reactions. . . . But since the autistic child once had some vague image of a satisfying world, he strives for it—not through action, but only in fantasy.[30]

Like the autistic child, the artist moves into his own private reality, largely to create; in his fantasy world he can affect that reality, influence the inner environment, away from the symbiotic unit. This fantasy world is a re-creation of the symbiosis and the problems involved in allaying the possibility of total dissolution. So the writing, the text, *is* the bridge, the balance, between autism and symbiosis, as the double of the protagonist *is* the bridge between isolation and dissolution. Both the work and the double are attempts to remain poised, precariously, between two extremes. Freud's use of the bird's egg as a model of a closed system helps us with the kind of thing Le Guin is getting at by having Ai move into three creative spaces where fire and warmth is the vital element, and from which a line of communication is thrown:

A neat example of a psychical system shut off from the stimuli of the external world and even able to satisfy its nutritional requirements autistically . . . is afforded by a bird's egg with its food supply enclosed in its shell; for it, the care provided by its mother is limited to provision of warmth.[31]

The first bird's egg or place is inside the forest, inside the building, inside the circle, with Faxe as the filament, the fire, discovering that union with the Ekumen will take place. The second is inside the tent, warmed by the Chabe stove, forming a bond with Estraven; the tent in turn is "inside a huge frosted-glass ball" (265) which is the environment of the ice-cap, also a "white, soundless sphere" (265). From that space originates the actual communication with the Ekumen. The final place is inside a building which is cut "from the steep mountainside to which it clung" (298). Inside the building Ai is led to the "Inner Hearth," where he will tell and retell his tale to his listeners, because in the telling, all are one blood.

The drive towards endless productivity, endless creativity, also implies a wish for immortality, which in turn suggests a desire for a timeless world of bliss. Jamèson believes that the appeal and fascination of *LHD* "surely derives from the subterranean drive within towards a utopian 'rest' . . . towards some ultimate 'no place' of a collectivity untormented by sex or history."[32] The wish for a timeless, uninterrupted region of immortality in *LHD* is hinted at early in the novel, when King Argaven snaps, "Are you immortal?" Ai replies,

"No, not at all, sir. But the time-jumps have their uses. If I left Gethen now for the nearest world, Ollul, I'd spend seventeen years of planetary time getting there. Timejumping is a function of travelling nearly as fast as light. If I simply turned around and came back, my few hours spent on the ship would, here, amount to thirty-four years and I could start all over." But the idea of timejumping . . . with its false hint of immortality had fascinated everyone who listened to me. (37)

The hint of immortality is omnipresent in *LHD*, especially if we agree that timelessness and immortality stem from a common source. The myths, tales, and religions in the novel, along with the eternal order promised by the Ekumen (not "political, not pragmatic, but mystical" [250]) are all timeless, which suggests a needed continuity, a way of avoiding separations and interruptions. A quest for timelessness and immortality stems from a deeper wish to avoid discontinuities which marred the earliest relation with the other, the untormented no-place that Jameson speaks of. In later life, Erik Erikson has shown, political ideologies, personal love, or religious faith can all serve the maternal function, gratifying "the simple and fervent wish for a hallucinatory sense of unity with a maternal matrix."[33]

The drive toward unity and oneness characterizes the novel. Lacan has said that the "illusion of unity, in which a human being is always looking forward to self mastery, entails a constant danger of sliding back again into the chaos from which he started."[34] But as we have seen, this drive or illusion in *LHD* is always deconstructed by the separation motif, which is connected with Lacan's symbolic order. The balance or mediator was partly conveyed by and embodied in the idea of the double, which is also aligned with the immortality idea. Endless creativity involves doubling—that is implied by the tales, particularly the "Estraven the Traitor" tale that informs and extends *LHD*, which ends with the beginning of another double relation that is linked with the original one. Otto Rank has shown how "a positive evaluation of the Double as immortal soul leads to the building-up of the prototype of personality from the Self," and that originally the double, "a representative of the individual's past . . . was an identical self (shadow, reflection), promising personal survival in the *future*."[35] This primary level of the novel that we have been exploring engenders the relatively optimistic note on which the novel ends.

The Left Hand of Darkness, to sum up, is incubated by an image of two men pulling a sledge; that image is specifically expanded upon in chapter 18 ("On the Ice"), and is vividly complemented in the dreamlike scene of the Foretelling. Around this the novel spins. The central phrase or image does say it all—isolated and together. Two men joined and separated by a sledge travelling over an ice-cap that joins and separates two countries. Inside their sledge are their tent, their Chabe stove, and their food. Outside the sledge are two people trudging along, braving the cold, avoiding hissing volcanoes and bottomless crevasses. Outside, they seldom talk. Inside they are united by the warmth of the stove, the food, the conversation: they speak about the past, the present, the future; they speak about the important themes of life. In short, they speak about what they are going through—emotionally, sexually, politically—and how they are progressing on their journey to Karhide, which will bring them out of their isolation and bring the planet out of its isolation to unite with the Ekumen, the rest of mankind.

The space inside the tent, in which there is symbiosis and communication with virtually no barriers is totally separated from the rest of the world by the boundary created by the tent. The image—isolated and together—is the attempt to balance autism and symbiosis. The private language of the autistic child (Ai and Estraven are the only ones on the planet using mindspeech) creates a private world, yet it is a world created out of and about a symbiotic state—a symbolic way of trying to attain, again, symbiosis. According to Lichtenstein and Mahler, one gains identity by way of symbiosis, but one must always be wary of complete regression to that state at the expense of that precarious identity. The artist seems willing to take the risk because complete separation leads to loneliness and alienation. The object of the artist, nevertheless, is akin to the object of the autistic child: to absorb herself in her private world of fantasy in order to fulfill the desire to perpetuate the "delusional omnipotent phase of mother-infant fusion—when mother was an extension of the self."[36] Largely because of its concern with creating identity, *LHD* is not only a work of art, it is a model for creative consciousness itself. But there is no product, only an endless productivity, which is a priceless form of creative communication.

5

The Lathe of Heaven:
The Artist as Dreamer

Is the journey my invention: Do the night, the sea, exist at all, I ask myself, apart from my experience of them? Do I myself exist, or is this a dream? Sometimes I wonder. And if I am, who am I? The Heritage I supposedly transport? But how can I be both vessel and contents? Such are the questions that beset my intervals of rest.

John Barth
Lost in the Funhouse

In *The Left Hand of Darkness,* Le Guin uses boundaries or barriers as the structuring principle of the novel. In *The Lathe of Heaven* (1971), she continues her concern with boundaries in a more cryptic fashion: they become doors, walls, and windows which separate inside from outside. This separation of inside from outside is first suggested by the memorable and enigmatic "jellyfish" passage that begins the novel. The polarities from which the novel builds—dream-reality, rebirth-death, silent communication-explicit communication, continuity-change, symbiosis-separation, creativity-destructiveness, female-male—arise out of this passage. It is actually a powerful image, in a synecdochical relation to the whole of *Lathe* and is the place where Le Guin's identity theme is most firmly inscribed.

Current-borne, wave-flung, tugged hugely by the whole might of ocean, the jellyfish drifts in the tidal abyss. The light shines through it, and the dark enters it. Borne, flung, tugged from anywhere to anywhere, for in the deep sea there is no compass but nearer and farther, higher and lower, the jellyfish hangs and sways; pulses move slight and quick within it, as the vast diurnal pulses beat in the moondriven sea. Hanging, swaying, pulsing, the most vulnerable and insubstantial creature, it has for its defense the violence and power of the whole ocean, to which it has entrusted its being, its going, and its will.

But here rise the stubborn continents. The shelves of gravel and the cliffs of rock break from water baldly into air, that dry, terrible outerspace of radiance and instability, where there is no support for life. And now, now the currents mislead and the waves betray, breaking their endless circle, to leap up in loud foam against rock and air, breaking. . . . [ellipses in text]

What will the creature made all of seadrift do on the dry sand of daylight; what will the mind do, each morning, waking?[1]

The first paragraph is both pleasant and unpleasant. The relationship between the jellyfish and the ocean is built on trust. Although it is ostensibly a symbiotic relationship—"pulses move slight and quick within it, as the vast diurnal pulses beat in the moondriven sea"—it is essentially a relationship between one overpowering being and another one which remains dependent on the power of the other. Although the tugging and pulling of the jellyfish has negative intimations, the fact that it "hangs and sways" gives a feeling of carefreeness or, perhaps, suspension of anxiety. Whatever the case, the jellyfish is protected, and the first paragraph seems particularly positive when the stubborn continents and the hard shelves and cliffs rudely disrupt the oceanic unity, the continuity, the feeling of permanence. The "dry, terrible outerspace" sets itself against what we can only assume is its opposite, a moist innerspace. There is then a separation, a break, which is seen as a betrayal by the waves, the moist element. But the "endless circle" and the ellipses after "breaking" suggest that this separation, which is a birth or rebirth, is repeated over and over. The final sentence asks whether the jellyfish, the *mind,* coming from the sea, alone now, will be able to survive in the reality of daylight. Can this vulnerable creature make the *transition* from sea to land? The presentation of daylight and waking as the result of a separation implies that night and sleeping (which necessarily include dreaming) constitute the situation before the break.

The sea image is a recurrent one in *Lathe:* the Aliens are sea-turtles who are in their own element in the world created by George Orr; all of Boswash is imperiled because "the polar ice kept melting and the sea kept rising," whereas Portland "was not threatened by rising water: only by failing water" (29); and while Orr in his sleep "saw the depths of the open sea," his wife Heather hears "the roaring of a creek full of the voices of unborn children singing" (136, 96). The jellyfish passage evokes the child in the womb, and the breaking of water can be the breaking of the waters of the womb at birth. If the moondriven sea is a symbol of the maternal matrix, then this matrix is also equated with night and sleeping. Sleeping means dreaming and dreaming in *Lathe* means the power to create. Identity is created out of symbiosis, and it is something that has to be constantly re-created. George Orr, the mild-mannered, fragmented protagonist of *Lathe,* is constantly being reborn and he is signified by the insubstantial jellyfish of this passage. He has "skin like a fish's belly," (40) and he is always trying to "get off the hook" (67, 77). Dr. Haber calls him a "moral jellyfish" (126).

We have seen how closely Le Guin associates herself with her protagonists. Both her primary relatedness to the world and her sense of herself as an artist derive from a fusion of herself and her sea-mother. From the diurnal pulses of the sea comes the metamorphic (and metaphoric) quality of life—out of this relationship with the sea comes the power to create. It is significant that the word *diurnal* comes from the word *journal* and that *journal* derives from *deity:* the artist as inscriber and as god. The brief jellyfish passage, then, contains the basic structure and movement of the novel, from inside to outside, and is the bedrock for the themes of the novel, all of which are bound up with the central problem of the artist's need to create an identity. Indeed, George Klein attests that "the role which falls to George Orr is in some way a metaphor of the artist in our world"[2]; this critic, however, gives no evidence to back up his claim, nor does he even hint at the dynamics involved.

The narrative opens with a blurring of inside and outside connoted by the absence of eyelids: "His eyelids had been burned away, so that he could not close his eyes, and the light entered into the brain, searing." He is apparently sitting outside—"He was on the cement steps; a dandelion flowered by his hand" (7)—but when he opens the door, he finds he is actually inside, on the balloonbed. He opens the door to move into another space, "the endless linoleum corridor"; he moves out toward it, "trying to hold on to the wall, but there was nothing to hold on to, and the wall turned into the floor." Suddenly he is back on his bed. Mannie, his landlord, appears and asks him what his problem is. "'Couldn't find the fit,' he said, meaning that he had been trying to lock the door through which the dreams came but none of the keys had fit the lock" (8). A medic appears with a hypodermic that offsets the nausea. He leaves and the door is shut. Inside again are he and Mannie on the bed. The first chapter ends: "Out of the darkness of closed eyes, the mist rising all round, Mannie's voice said remotely, 'Ain't it great to be alive?'" (10).

On reading the first chapter, the reader finds it as difficult as George Orr to get his bearings because inside is outside and outside is inside. Inside can mean inside a room but it can also mean inside Orr's mind. When the wall becomes the floor one gets a feeling of being suspended in the void, much like the jellyfish. And somehow this confusion of inside-outside is associated with dreams: he had been trying to lock the door through which the dreams came. But do the dreams come from the inside or the outside, or both? When the chapter ends, the mist rising all round, we are not sure whether the mist is rising inside the closed eyes or outside the closed eyes, inside or outside the room with Mannie. This distinction is difficult to make, partly because it is the nature of mist to blur distinctions. Thus the main structural device of barriers or doors, which ostensibly separates inside from outside, is allied with dreams, mist, and birth. Mannie, as a mothering figure, is there and says, "Ain't it great to be alive."

Chapter 2 begins with Dr. William Haber in his "interior Efficiency Suite" gazing at a big photographic mural of Mount Hood on "one of the windowless walls." He can hear the elevator whine up and stop, "the doors gasp open; then footsteps, hesitation, the outer door opening. He could also, now he was listening, hear doors . . . in offices all up and down the hall and above him and underneath him. . . . The only solid partitions left were inside the head" (11). George Orr enters Haber's office—"Dr. Haber's Palace of Dreams"—and tells him that his most intense dreams change the outside world at large. After much discussion

Haber hooks Orr up to his dream machine, the "Augmentor," and has him dream one of his "effective" dreams. Orr promptly changes the mural of Mt. Hood into a mural of a racehorse. Whether Haber notices this change or not Orr does not know, because Haber gives no indication, and Orr's dreams change reality retrospectively. The chapter ends with Orr leaving and Haber looking at the mural wishing he could afford an office with a view. A few days later Haber is climbing the steps of the Oregon Oneirological Institute and passing through "the high, polarized-glass doors. . . . It was only March 24, and already like a sauna-bath outside: but within all was cool" (48). He passes his "well-enameled receptionist" en route to his "outer office" and then he "strode on into the inner sanctum."

> Dropping briefcase and file folders on the couch, he stretched his arms, and then went over, as he always did when he first entered his office, to the window. It was a large corner window, looking out east and north over a great sweep of the world: the curve of the much-bridged Williamette close in beneath the hills; the city's countless towers high and milky in the spring mist, on either side of the river; and suburbs receding out of sight till from their remote outbacks the foothills rose; and the mountains. Hood, immense yet withdrawn, breeding clouds about her head; going northward, the distant Adams, like a molar tooth; and then the pure cone of St. Helens, from whose long gray sweep of the slope still farther northward a little bald dome stuck out, like a baby looking round its mother's skirt: Mount Rainier. (48)

This view must be kept in mind because approximately half of the novel takes place inside this new office, which Orr, through Haber's suggestion, has created. Much is made of the large window because through it they can judge what effect Orr's dreams are having on outer reality. Also significant is that Orr has made art—a mural of Mt. Hood—become reality: the real Mt. Hood. Inside the office are Orr, Haber, and the Augmentor (and Heather on two occasions, each as a different Heather). Outside is the scene described above, which, with its milky towers in the mist, Mt. Hood breeding clouds about her head, a molar tooth, and a sight of a baby looking round its mother's skirt, is maternal in character, vaguely erotic, and somewhat threatening, but beautiful nonetheless. In this context, reality is maternal.

Orr also meets the other character in the novel, Heather Lelache, in a small windowless space: "Miss Lelache sat behind the screen of bookcases and files that semi-separated her semi-office from Mr. Pearl's semi-office, and thought of herself as a Black Widow" (40). She sits, "hard, shiny, and poisonous," waiting for her victim. Orr enters, explains that Haber is exploiting him by using his dreams to change reality, and they agree to try to get Haber on an invasion of privacy charge. She is to sit in on one of Orr's sessions, ostensibly to check out Haber's new machine, the Augmentor. She enters Haber's office:

> She snapped and clicked. Heavy brass snap catch on handbag, heavy copper and brass jewelry that clattered, clump-heel shoes, a huge silver ring with a horribly ugly African mask design,

frowning eyebrows, hard voice: clack, clash, snap. . . . In the second ten seconds, Haber
suspected that the whole affair was indeed a mask, as the ring said: a lot of sound and fury
signifying timidity. (50)

Heather's vulnerable inner self is protected from the outside world by her hard,
shiny surface and her suit of armor. In addition, she has a "chitinous voice" (47)
and a "squamous personality" (82). She and Orr are attracted to and trust each
other, and she is going to end Haber's exploitation of him.

This exploitation brings the three of them together in Haber's office. In this
particular session Orr will dream a dream, suggested by Haber and prompted by
the Augmentor, which will cure him of feeling "crowded in on . . . squeezed,
pressed together" (54). Orr dreams and suddenly the "shift, the arrival, the change
comes about." Heather stares out the window in shock and terror. Haber realizes
she is aware of the change: "She had stood beside the dreamer; she was there at the
center, like him. And like him had turned to look out the window at the vanishing
towers fade like a dream . . . miles of suburb dissolving like smoke" (57). In Orr's
earlier dream, the one that gave Haber his new office and position, Haber recalls
"the walls change around him, had known the world was being remade" (58). Orr
and Heather leave. The chapter ends with Haber looking out the window, at a
greatly diminished population, "raising his glass to his creation," toasting a better
world. Whatever Orr-Haber may change, however, the mountains and the mist
always remain. Another important observation is that the shift, the change, the
rebirth, had to do with walls changing and the dissolution of a large part of the
outer reality.

The novel progresses from space to space, through windows and walls. Orr moves
to his apartment, then back to another session with Haber, then to his cabin in the
forest. Heather moves to a restaurant to meet Orr, who does not show up, then to
Orr's apartment, then to his cabin. (Haber, as far as we are concerned, never
moves; until the very end of the novel we only see him in his office.) Inside the
cabin Heather assures Orr of his ability to change reality. "I sure have been trying
to run on two tracks with one set of wheels ever since. I walked right into a
wall. . . . The wall was *there* now but it wasn't *there* now. . . . I saw what
happened to the city! I was looking out the window!" (86). They decide that she
should hypnotize him so that he can sleep and dream a positive, relatively
harmless, effective dream: "dream that the Aliens aren't out there on the moon any
longer" (95). While Orr sleeps, Heather goes to the "door and stood half inside,
half outside for a while, listening to the creek shouting and hollering eternal praise!
. . . it had kept up that tremendous noise for hundreds of years before she was
born, and would go on doing it until the mountains moved. . . . It seemed, like the
voices of unborn children singing" (96). No sooner does she shut the door on the
unborn children and lie down on the floor to sleep, than the cold, hard, too bright

sunrise comes through the window. "The hills muttered and dreamed of falling into the sea, and over the hills . . . the sirens of distant towns howled. . . . The wolves howled for the world's end. Sunrise poured in through the single window, hiding all that lay under its dazzling slant" (96). She awakens Orr, who informs her that the Aliens have landed. Even though the only change that Orr brings about is the Aliens' landing on the earth, their arrival is accompanied by changes that connote death and rebirth. Just before they land Heather is sweetly haunted by voices of unborn children; hills dream of dissolution into the sea; there is a howling for the world's end; but the blazing sunrise suggests rebirth, recalling Orr's awakening at the beginning of the novel, and blurs distinctions with its dazzling slant.

The military, knowing there is an Alien landing but not quite sure where, is shelling everything in sight. Meanwhile, Haber waits in his office for Orr, who finally arrives with Heather. "Just as they entered Haber's office the glass burst out of the great double window with a shrill, singing sound and a huge sucking-out of air; both men were impelled toward the window as if toward the mouth of a vacuum cleaner" (103). Heather is sent downstairs to keep her hand on the emergency generator while Haber hooks up Orr so that he can dream them out of the burning, exploding world. While Haber is putting Orr under hypnosis an ovoid object appears in "opaque glare outside the glassless window." Haber screams at Orr to dream that "we're at peace with everybody!" As the object comes closer, Haber tries to protect the Augmentor with his body. The snout of the object, "looking like oily steel, silver with violet streaks and gleams, filled the entire window. . . . Haber sobbed aloud with terror but stayed spread out there between the Alien and the Augmentor" (105). It crunches itself into the window frame and the snout whirls and falls on the floor. "From the hole that gaped behind it, something emerged. . . . a giant turtle. Then he realized that it was encased in a suit of some kind, which gave it a bulky, greenish, armored, inexpressive look like a giant sea turtle standing on its hind legs" (105). The Alien enters and informs Haber that they are attempting to make a peaceful arrival, then disappears "into the dark cavity." Orr awakens and recalls his dream which corresponds exactly to what had just occurred. Haber replies, "But that's not a dream! That happened!" (107). Haber wants Orr to "simply get *rid* of the Aliens" but Orr refuses and Haber is obliged to telephone and call off the military.

There are several things to note about this scene. By filling the space left by the broken window, the Aliens are being allied with a work of art (the mural of Mt. Hood) and with a permanent reality (replacing the mountain scene). Since this reality is implicitly maternal, the Aliens are also connected with the concept of a maternal reality. Because the ship is lodged in the area that separates inside and outside, the implication is that the Aliens function as a transition from inside to outside or, in other words, as symbolic of that transitional space between subjectivity and objectivity. This is underlined and expanded upon by the fact that Orr has dreamed them up (subjective) and then they appear in the flesh, coming from the external (objective) world. This confluence of dream and reality, the basis of the novel, is most vivid in this scene, especially when we find ourselves in Haber's position, not really knowing if the Aliens just happened to come by while Orr was dreaming—and therefore all his dreams are about what is going to happen anyway—or whether Orr dreams simultaneously with changing outward reality, or whether he does in fact change reality. The appearance of the Alien in a threatening armored suit, which encases a kind and passive being, connects the Aliens with Heather, who is so clearly described as a creature with a carapace. This scene also fits Haber into Orr's situation more tightly than we've seen so far in the novel. It is, after all, his space, his office; and he has his hands on the Augmentor, which is connected to the trancap on Orr's brain. He gave Orr the command to dream of peace; but then it is Haber who, in reality, brings about peace with his phone call, thus fulfilling Orr-Haber's dream-wish. In this case he is Orr's instrument, much as Orr has been his. Another matter to note is that the Alien's appearance from a dark cavity has connotations of a birth. Finally, the idea of communication is significant. The communication level that Haber-Orr and the Alien reach, with Haber-Orr inside and the Alien in a transitional space, is responsible for ending the destruction in the outside world.

Toward the end of the novel, Orr happens upon a group of buildings which "had grown up, like swallows' nests in a cliff" (130) under a large piece of the old freeway that ended abruptly in mid-air. The sign above the window of one of the shops says "Antiques," and in the window Orr can see handmade pottery, an old rocker, and other cultural litter from the recent past. And there is

> a stack of old hi-fi 45 rpm records, marked "Gd Cond," but obviously scratched. Just the sort of place, Orr thought, where Heather's mother might have worked for a while. Moved by the impulse, he went in.
>
> It was cool and rather dark inside. A leg of the ramp formed one wall, a high blank dark expanse of concrete, like the wall of an undersea cave. From the receding prospects of shadows . . . from these tenebrous reaches of no-man's-things, a huge form emerged, seeming to float forward slowly, silent and reptilian. The proprietor was an Alien.
>
> It raised its crooked left elbow and said, "Good day. Do you wish an object." (131)

Indeed, Orr's task is to move away from the pool of subjectivity, the inside area, and to distinguish it from what is real, outside, the object world. The object he is seeking is Heather Lelache. The Alien, who is dream-created by Orr, is willing to help. Orr's first question is, "In your language, what is the meaning of the word *iahklu?*" (131). To which the Alien responds, "incommunicable. Language used for communication with individual-persons will not contain other forms of relationship. Jor Jor" (132). Orr then asks if he ever knew anyone named Lelache because, as he says, "I have lost Lelache." To this the Alien observes, foreshadowing the ending, "Crossings in mist." Orr's final question is, "Is there any way to control *iahklu,* to make it go the way it . . . ought to go?" The Alien, not pleased with his own efforts at "bridging the communication gap," goes to the front window and brings Orr a Beatle record, "With a Little Help From My Friends." Orr leaves with the record, feeling more real and at ease than he has in a long while. He feels "a part of" the world, "not separate from it. I walk on the ground and the ground's walked on by me, I breathe the air and change it, I am entirely interconnected with the world" (133). Orr goes home, shares some cannabis with Mannie, puts the record on Mannie's record player, and wakes up to his wife Heather. They had been married seven months.

What we have witnessed is Orr moving to an inside space, a nest, a womb-like undersea cave. It is a quasi-symbiotic state from which he emerges with an object, a record, which corresponds to the word *iahklu*. With this object in hand, he moves from the inside to the outside and begins to feel comfortable in the world. He then moves to another inside space, his home at Mannie's, and by the repeated playing of this object he is able to create the subject/object which he has been seeking. He reaches a state of oneness with Heather—"They hung on to each other, in touch at all available surfaces, absolutely unified" (135)—only to lose her again shortly after. One reason he loses her is that this Heather is too much like him: she is passive like him, she is gray in skin color like him (his very first words to her are, "You should be brown" [135]), and she has no armor—this is not the person we met earlier with a carapace of bangles and clothing. Without the *difference* of color and the firm outer surface, Orr stands once again to lose the differentiation between self and nonself and risks dissolving into the other. This possible dissolution of self or other is dramatically depicted shortly after Orr is labelled normal by Haber, who is dreaming his dreams for him. Orr and Heather are riding in a funicular car, heading back to stop Haber from dreaming. Orr tells her to look out the window. The river had run dry and the buildings of Portland were melting. "They were getting soggy and shaky like jello left out in the sun." The corners ran down the sides leaving "great creamy smears." "It was the presence of absence. . . . It was horrible and it was nothing" (146–47). With Heather gone—"she sank down in a ball curled about the center of her own being, and fell forever through the dry abyss"—Orr is able to make it to "the last door":

> He pushed it open. On the other side of it there was nothing. "Help me," he said aloud, for the void drew him, pulled at him. He had not the strength all by himself to get through nothingness and out the other side.
>
> There was a sort of dull rousing in his mind; he thought of Tiua'k Ennbe Ennbe, and of the bust of Schubert, and of Heather's voice saying furiously, "What the *hell*, George!" This seemed to be all he had to cross nothingness on. He went forward. He knew as he went that he would lose all he had.
>
> He entered the eye of the nightmare.
>
> It was a cold, vaguely moving, rotating darkness made of fear, that pulled him aside, pulled him apart. (147–48)

He turns off the Augmentor and he is reborn: "the world reexisted" (148).

After leaving Haber and the Augmentor, Orr is trying to find his way home when he is stopped by an Alien, who persuades him to come with him to his apartment. In bed, about to sleep, Orr "clearly sensed the pity and protective compassion of the Alien standing across the dark room. It saw him, not with eyes, as short-lived, fleshly, armorless, a strange creature, infinitely vulnerable, adrift in the gulfs of the possible: something that needed help" (152). Sometime later, Orr visits Haber at the Federal Asylum. An orderly takes him up to Haber's room in the North Wing. "The doors leading into this wing and the doors of all the rooms in it were heavy, with a little spyhold grating five feet up, and all of them were locked" (152). Inside, Orr finds Haber staring at the void: "He was looking at the world as misunderstood by the mind: the bad dream" (153). He realizes Haber is "lost" and tries to speak to him but can find no words. When he returns to the "Kitchen Sink," he hears a voice that reminds him of his ex-wife's. It is the Heather of the earlier part of the novel. "His wife had been a gray person, a far gentler person than this one, he thought. This Heather carried a big black handbag with a brass snap, and probably a half pint of brandy inside; she came on hard" (155). Orr asks her out for a cup of coffee and the novel ends: "He went out with Heather into the warm, rainy afternoon of summer. The Alien watched them from within the glass-fronted shop, as a sea creature might watch from the aquarium, seeing them pass and disappear into the mist."

The final chapter continues the movement of the novel, through doors, windows, and walls, from outside to inside and inside to outside. Orr makes a home with a creature that is well-protected from the outside world by its shell. In contrast, Orr is fleshly and armorless, something that needs help—this has not changed since the beginning of the novel. Another thing that has not changed is that Haber is once again inside a series of doors in a small windowless room. Apparently, however, there are no solid partitions left inside his head, and he is doomed to stare into a void; by sitting and staring into the nightmare, Haber has taken over Orr's early role. And Heather is once again the Heather with the hard exterior. The ending implies a new beginning: "To go is to return" (156). The beginning, moreover, like the ending, involves Orr's attempt to establish a relationship that will not create a dissolution of the self. Although Heather's hard shell implies that a relationship between two separate entities is difficult but possible, the setting implies that the blurring of boundaries will continue: they move from an inside that is not clearly distinguishable from the outside. Inside is a creature with a hard exterior, like a creature in an aquarium; outside in the rain is also a creature with a hard exterior; what separates the two is a window, suspiciously transparent; and the ubiquitous mist continues to blur distinctions. The rain symbolizes rebirth and recalls Mannie's statement, "Ain't it great to be alive," at the beginning of the novel. Since *Lathe* ends as it began, with the mist rising all round, and with no *clear* demarcation between inside and outside, we can only assume that another story must be told: to go is to return.

Lathe, then, is constructed so as to draw attention to the need to separate inside from outside by hard surfaces. Once alerted to this, we can make other connections which lead us into the narrative within the narrative. For example, the novel opens with an epigraph, the first line of which is, "Confucius and you are both dreams, and I who say you are dreams am a dream myself." This says that a dream can be, or is, a speaker, a person; it implies that, if we are all dreams, we cannot distinguish one from another; and the question it begs is, if we are all dreams, what is reality? The novel suggests several other things about dreams. Dreams are equated with some life-giving, nurturing force: "You were depriving yourself of dreams. . . . Do you try to deprive yourself of food and water, Mr. Orr? Have you tried doing without air lately?" Without dreams one becomes "irritable, hungry, unable to concentrate" (13). The notion of dream as nurturer is underscored by statements such as "What did you dream, George? Let's have it, hot off the griddle" (35). Dreams are allied with infancy: "the mind's lack of recall of most dreams had puzzled him. Nonconscious thinking, whether in infancy or dream, apparently is not available to conscious recall" (38). The statement, "The dream is the aquarium of the night," looks forward to the Alien in the aquarium and makes the dream, like the novel perhaps, into a container that holds "strange animalities . . . obscure undermakings of miracle, growths and vanishings within a murky depth" (78). Mt. Hood, which is depicted as art becoming reality and vice-versa, as well as an immovable maternal presence, is also allied with a dream: "This building could stand up to anything left on earth, except perhaps Mt. Hood. Or a bad dream" (117). Mannie is obliquely connected with the dream; while he spoke with Orr, "there were long gaps in the conversation, reflections of the large holes in the fabric of Mannie's mind, worn thin by the application of innumerable chemicals over the years" (134). This recalls the statement, "The void was there. This life lacked realness; it was hollow; the dream, creating where there was no necessity to create, had worn thin and sleazy. If this was being, perhaps the void was better" (130).

This statement suggests something else: the initial purpose of the dream is a creative one—to fill a void, close a gap, make present an absence. The idea of the dream as creative act and creative object is worked through the novel: "When you *see* another man's dream as he dreams it recorded in black and white on the electroencephalograph . . . you don't speak of dreams as 'unreal.' They exist; they are events; they leave a mark behind them" (17). This notion of dream as text is expanded upon: "eight pens scored a permanent record of the brain's electrical activity. . . . It was a scene he never tired of, the all-night movie" (23). Although we all dream, going through this "performance every night, four or five times," Orr's dreams exhibit a kind of "brainstorm": the "pattern seems to resemble an effect that's been observed in electroencephalographs of men hard at work of a certain sort: creative or artistic work, painting, writing verse, even reading Shakespeare" (56). Orr as dreamer-artist is further emphasized by statements such as that his "version" of a dream "sounds like a good science-fiction movie" (75); "When you're dreaming effectively your entire brain is involved in a complexly synchronized pattern of emissions . . . a kind of counterpoint effect that is to ordinary d-state graphs what Beethoven's Great Fugue is to Mary Had a Little Lamb" (102). Just as one of the objectives of art is continually to discern the relationship between illusion and reality, so dreaming in *Lathe* investigates that space between dream and reality. At one point Orr says, regarding his dream of the end of the world, "I've told myself ever since that it was a dream. That *it* was a dream! But it wasn't. This is. This isn't real. This world isn't even probable. It was the truth. It was what happened. We are all dead, and we spoiled the world before we died. There is nothing left. Nothing but dreams." To which Heather responds, "So what? Maybe that's all it's ever been. . . . What does it matter whether you call it real or dreams? It's all one—isn't it?" (93–94). Some other things to note about dreams in *Lathe* are that a rebirth occurs each time Orr dreams effectively; that the Aliens are said to be "of the dream time"; that there are two types of dreams, public (effective) and private (those that don't affect reality); and that although dreams, fantasies, are a substitute for action, they are seen to have the potential power to change the world into that perfect, peaceful place we all dream of. All of the above are contained within the metaphor of the dream, which is itself contained within a novel that is structured around the separation of inside and outside. How, then, does one homologize all of this? And how does the homology relate to Le Guin's identity theme? If we see the dream as an ingenious device by which to explore the human mind—one that contains an inner world of object relations by which the writer is compelled—and the territory that exists, or doesn't exist, between self and other, then we are on our way to finding new relationships in the novel and the homologue, which is a variation on Le Guin's identity theme.

J.-B. Pontalis writes that "the dream process is originally linked to the mother: the variation of scripts that are represented in it, and even the range of meanings . . . unfold against the background of this exclusive relationship."[3] The variation of scripts in *Lathe,* which are contained in the dream idea, unfold against the background of this exclusive relationship. Furthermore, "Dreaming is above all an effort to maintain the impossible union with mother, to preserve an undivided totality, *to move in a space prior to time.*"[4] Certainly the jellyfish enclosed in the sea is an image of this undivided totality. One must remember that Orr has two types of dreams: those that are private, his alone, and those that are effective—they are taken from him, projected into the outside world, which they change and dissolve into; they are no longer his. The one private dream that Orr shares with us does connote the exclusive relationship that Pontalis speaks of: "His dreams, like the waves of the deep sea far from any shore, came and went, rose and fell, profound and harmless, breaking nowhere, changing nothing. They danced the dance among all the other waves in the sea of being. Through his sleep the great, green turtles dived, swimming with heavy inexhaustible grace through the depths, in their element" (152). This is very much a symbiotic and subjective condition, in a "space prior to time." It gives a sense of "oceanic unity" which Freud related to that first unity. There is also the sense of the boundlessness of the symbiotic state as Margaret Mahler describes it.

The turtles, or Aliens, are Orr's creation and they are the most prominent representation of the exclusive relationship. Orr puts them on the moon: "It was no longer pleasant to exchange glances with the moon. It symbolized neither the Unattainable, as it had for thousands of years, nor the Attained, as it had for a few decades, but the Lost. . . . The Aliens held the moon" (82). The Lost, however, is found again when Orr dreams the Aliens to earth, and they appear first in that transitional space between inside and outside; later, by means of a word (*iahklu*) and an object (record) and a job (making tools) they try to help him make the transition from subjective objects to objects objectively perceived. It is a long slow process and it is questionable whether Orr (or indeed any of us) makes a completely successful transition. Also, the uncertainty about the relationship between the record and the word *iahklu* designates an uncertainty about the relation between words and things, between language and reality. The Aliens, as Orr first created them, "didn't realize until they landed that humans depend upon *verbal* communication" (107). When they do master human modes of communication, such as speech, they speak with toneless voices which come from the left elbow. At one point an Alien "issued flatly: 'Jor Jor' . . . After a moment Orr recognized his own name in the Barsoomian bisyllable" (121). The Alien then gives Orr a phrase, "Er'perrehnne" which he repeats, trying to understand its meaning, and later mumbles in his sleep as "air per annum." The Alien responds, "Speech is silver, silence is gold. Self is universe" (122). It is an important exchange in the novel. It is the naming scene and it is enacted substantially in a private language that implies there are three languages: the language of speech, the language of silence, and some critical phrases, untranslatable, that are in between speech and silence—and that all three are bound up with a definition of self. Just after this exchange, Orr finds himself with a strengthened sense of identity:

> And, quick as a thief in the night, a sense of well-being came into him, a certainty that things were all right, and that he was in the middle of things. Self is universe. He would not be allowed to be isolated, to be stranded. He was back where he belonged. He felt an equanimity . . . it was the mood of his childhood. . . . These last years he had lost it. . . . Four years ago, four years ago in April, something had happened that had made him lose that balance for a while. . . . Now, all at once he was back where he belonged. He knew that this was nothing he had accomplished himself. (123)

Orr achieves his balance with help from his friends: Mannie, Heather, and especially the Aliens, who help him create an identity out of fusion with a larger entity. Orr says of the Aliens, "there was always a connection between us . . . I am entirely interconnected with the world" (133). It is after muttering *Er'perrehnne* (which is responded to "soundlessly" by the "protective compassion of the Alien") before surrendering to sleep and to dreams that break like waves of the sea, that Orr finds himself quite firmly established in reality; by the end of the novel he seems able to leave his anxiety behind and concentrate on creating "tangibles" that have "Good balance." This is also done under the protective compassion of the Alien. From his inside space Orr is able to move outside with Heather, "the fierce, recalcitrant, and fragile stranger, forever to be won again" (156). According to Winnicott there is a transitional object that assists an infant in achieving the kind of precarious balance that Orr achieves. The object can be "perhaps a bundle of wool or the corner of a blanket . . . or a word or tune, or a mannerism—that become vitally important to the infant for use at the time of going to sleep, and is a defence against anxiety." The object is accompanied by an "organized sound" which "usually has a word used by the adults partly incorporated in it."[5] In Orr's case the "words" *iahklu* and *Er'perrehnne* correspond to dreaming and getting help from friends, both of which refer directly to the Beatles record. Orr falls asleep with these words and he also falls asleep listening to the record. Winnicott is more specific about the function of the transitional object:

> It is true that the piece of blanket (or whatever it is) is symbolic of some part-object, such as the breast. Nevertheless, the point of it is not its symbolic value so much as its actuality. Its not being the breast (or the mother), although real, is as important as the fact that it stands for the breast (or mother).
>
> When symbolism is employed the infant is already clearly distinguishing between fantasy and fact, between inner objects and external objects, between primary creativity and perception. But the term transitional object, according to my suggestion, gives room for the process of becoming able to accept difference and similarity. I think there is use for a term for the root of symbolism in time, a term that describes the infant's journey from the purely subjective to objectivity; and it seems to me that the transitional object (piece of blanket etc.) is what we see of this journey of progress towards experiencing.[6]

Once Orr realizes that he does have a little help from his friends, symbolized by the record, the transitional object, he is confident that his private dreams are not simultaneously public; he awakens, then, with a sense of rightness and realness, knowing he has separated his inside world (private dream) from the outside world (effective dream) by feeling a part of and no longer apart from the "real world."

This shift from one who is able to create new universes to one who takes exquisite pleasure in creating small objects ("Mr. Orr is expert with tangibles") accords with Winnicott's observation: "In relationship to the transitional object the infant passes from (magical) omnipotent control to control by manipulation (involving muscle eroticism and coordination pleasure)."[7] This is not an easy passage and it takes Le Guin an entire novel to dramatize it. Mahler tells us that in the early stages of the symbiotic state in infancy—which would correspond to Orr and his dream-mother early in the novel—"the infant behaves as though he and his mother were an omnipotent system—a dual unity within one common boundary. . . . the sense of boundlessness of the oceanic feeling. . . . It describes the state of undifferentiation, of fusion with the mother, in which the 'I' is not yet differentiated from the 'not-I' and in which inside and outside are only gradually coming to be sensed as different."[8] This of course describes the central problem of *Lathe*, which is structured around this dilemma and into which is implanted the uneasy feeling of omnipotence that Orr has vis-à-vis his dreams. Quite early in the novel, when Orr recounts his first effective dream, he realizes that what he desires, and therefore dreams, does not translate properly; his dreams frequently decide to do something else. He tells Haber, "Dreams are incoherent, selfish, irrational . . . I didn't want to kill poor Ethel. I just wanted her out of my way. Well, in a dream, that's likely to be drastic. Dreams take shortcuts. I killed her" (17). For the rest of Orr's fifteen odd dreams in the novel, he recognizes more and more that he is unique and alone, and he must separate himself from that relationship with his dream which becomes personified by Haber—"I must get away from Haber" (67). Mahler writes that "along with the beginning of awareness of separateness comes the child's realization that mother's wishes seemed to be by no means always identical with his own—or contrariwise, that his own wishes did not always coincide with mother's. This realization greatly challenged the feelings of grandeur and omnipotence . . . what a disturbance to the bliss of dual unity!"[9] Eventually the infant's belief in his own *and* his parent's omnipotence must recede, to be replaced by autonomous functioning.

By the end of the novel, Orr is functioning relatively autonomously; he has moved from omnipotent control to control by manipulation, first by realizing that his wishes do not always coincide with his dream-mother's and then by making use of subjective objects (Mannie, Alien, Heather) and transitional objects (*Er'perrehnne, iahklu,* record). However, it is not the object per se that is transitional. As Winnicott says, "The object represents the infant's transition from a state of being merged with the mother to a state of being in relation to the mother as something outside and separate."[10] Mannie helps Orr make this transition by always being home, by letting Orr say he borrowed his pharm card, and by giving him the cannabis and the record player. Heather assists by just being in the world as something he can love and then by corroborating that what Orr creates or changes does in fact come into being: this is akin to "the mother's special capacity for making adaption to the needs of her infant, thus allowing the infant the illusion that what the infant creates really exists."[11] The Aliens also help by naming him and thus giving him a sense of a private and separate yet unified self: he has two names, George and Orr, George Orr; out of this the Aliens make two identical names, Jor Jor. Also, by their form of communication, somewhere between public language and silence, they help make the differentiation. As Bettelheim says, "It is only when communication reaches the symbolic level of language that a self can become fully established with the 'I' clearly separated from the 'you.' "[12] In this light, the "word" *iahklu* is no longer a complete puzzle: *i*–ahkl–*u*.

In terms of the reading put forward here, the movement of *Lathe* corresponds remarkably well to the transitional object theory. With her hard surface, the equation of her with her handbag, Haber's reference to her as "the Lelache" (54, 55), and her situation as the love object in the novel, Heather is a fine candidate as an object to which Orr can relate. The Aliens, who are originally created out of Orr's mind, are aquatic creatures as he (as jellyfish) is, and because there was "always a connection" between them, they are the primary subjective objects of the novel. Yet, as we have seen, Heather often functions as the subjective object (as opposed to an object objectively perceived), and the Aliens function as objective objects; the connections, then, between Heather as object and the Aliens as subject (with Mannie somewhere in between)—for example, both have hard surfaces and soft centers, both are maternal figures, and the Aliens are sea turtles while Heather is "like Baltic amber, or a cup of strong Ceylon tea" (111)—are strong enough to suggest that subjects and objects are separate yet interrelated and that the inner and outer reality that the infant must distinguish is still basically maternal. Hence the dialectic of private versus public dream in the novel. It still must be emphasized that Heather is the objectively perceived object once the infant has made the transition to that state of awareness with the help of his transitional object. Moreover, Heather, along with the Aliens and Mannie and, to some extent, the effective dream, are inextricably intertwined with the transitional process and, as such, become closely allied with the transitional object (they are, after all, the friends that help). In addition, "sometimes there is no transitional object except the mother herself," and a "true transitional object" is an "almost inseparable part of the infant." And, as *Lathe* depicts, gradually "the transitional phenomena . . . become diffused . . . become spread out over the whole intermediate territory between 'inner psychic reality' and 'the external world as perceived by two persons in common,' that is to say, over the whole cultural field."[13]

The idea of communication and creativity is intimately allied with this difficult transition from relating to subjective objects to relating to objects objectively perceived. Communication and creativity in turn are bound up with the central dilemma of autism-symbiosis. In the early stage, as we have seen, the facilitating environment is giving the infant an experience of omnipotence. By this, Winnicott means more than magical control; he means "the term to include the creative aspect of experience. . . . The infant experiencing omnipotence under the aegis of the facilitating environment *creates and recreates the object*, and the process gradually becomes built in, and gathers a memory backing."[14] In *Lathe* the facilitating environment is mainly the dream, which allows Orr to create and recreate Heather. First she is Heather Lelache, the Black Widow, the hard lawyer; then she is Heather Orr, a gray and somewhat timid person, who is the secretary of a legal partnership; finally she is Heather Andrews, a black legal secretary who "came on hard." Communication with the three Heathers is explicit but superficial because none of them gets to know the true George Orr; there are "so many different memories, so many skeins of life experience, jostling in his head" (109) that he doesn't know how much each of these Heathers remembers about him and his relationship with her. Just as he and the first Heather appear to be on their way to reaching an understanding, she disappears as a consequence of an effective dream. The second Heather knows that Orr is "ill" but seems to have little knowledge of his tendency to change the world with his dreams. For her it is unbelievable that Haber, "a world leader and a great scientist, should have spent all these weeks of personal therapy on George, who wasn't anybody. But, of course, George's case was very important, researchwise" (138). The third Heather can only remember, she says, somewhat facetiously, that "you thought you dreamed things that came true. Didn't you? And the doctor was making you do more and more of it, and you didn't want him to" (155–56).

The other thing that Orr creates and re-creates is reality itself (which, being maternal and objective, is associated with Heather as well). Orr is sent to Haber for help when he is confronted with the fact that he cannot control his dreams. However, on only his second visit to Haber, he realizes he must get away from him because he "felt exposed, used" (31). He tells Heather, "What I object to is his using me as an instrument" (43). Haber refers to him as "the weak tool" (108). Orr's largely ineffectual rebellion against Haber, and his search for help in being cured and retrieving his dreams for himself, constitute the plot of the novel. The narrative within this narrative relates to Orr's fear of being exposed and therefore to Winnicott's discussion of a person's "right not to communicate. This was a protest from the core of me to the frightening fantasy of being infinitely exploited. In another language this would be the fantasy of being eaten or swallowed up. In the language of this paper it is *the fantasy of being found*."[15] Similarly, Pontalis tells us that "the dream cannot be *shared*. Thus dream-space is a *territory*. . . . The dream is an inner object which the dreamer keeps for himself. . . . The dreamer attaches himself to his dreams so as not to be cast adrift." Pontalis adds that "the dream is aiming at a permanence." Speaking about the visual aspects of the dream he writes:

> The dream screen then should not only be understood as a surface for projection, it is also a surface for protection, it forms a screen. . . . The dream screen protects one—against the inside. . . . That which I can see, which I can represent to myself, is already something that I can hold off: the annihilation, the dissolution of the subject is held aside.[16]

Orr's predicament involving his dreaming with Haber's intervention and assistance now becomes clearer. There is a part of Orr that wants and needs the effective dreaming, and there is a part of him that needs to separate himself from it. This dilemma is the autism-symbiosis conflict that the artist feels so acutely. The effective dreams are an almost perfect way of representing the dream screen which protects Orr against the inside. For example, George's first effective dream involves his aunt: "I was seventeen. I was still living at home, and my mother's sister was staying with us. . . . She was kind of in the way. It was a regular three-room flat, and she was always there. Drove my mother up the wall. . . . Well, I had a lot of sort of anxiety dreams and this aunt was always in them" (15–16). She is continually making a play for Orr, coming in to his bedroom in topless pajamas and trying to get him to "handle her" at the movies. So Orr dreams her into a car accident and kills her. The next day, "No Ethel on the couch. There wasn't anybody else in the apartment, just my parents and me" (16). With this wish-fulfillment Orr has done two things: he has removed the thing that was getting in the way of him and his parents, and by killing her he symbolically commits the act of incest that he had been avoiding.[17] His first effective dream, then, is a simultaneous union and separation: the killing is a sexual union with the symbolic mother and a separation from her—her death; but this separation allows him to be, once again, the child alone with the parents. After Orr describes this dream to Haber, it becomes increasingly difficult to distinguish between Orr's wishes and Haber's wishes. Before this melding occurs, however, we are fairly safe in saying that Orr's greatest wish is to be reborn.

Again, the novel opens with the separation of the jellyfish from the sea and with Orr waking on the cement steps, ill from radiation. Later in the novel Orr explains to Heather what happened: "'Do you—' he stuttered several times. 'Do you remember anything about April, four years ago—in '98'? . . . 'That's when the world ended,' Orr said. A muscular spasm disfigured his face, and he gulped as if for air. 'Nobody else remembers,' he said" (92). He tells about people starving, then of the nuclear war and himself trying to get out of the city, into Forest Park. He finds himself in the situation we find him at the beginning, sitting on cement steps:

> "I was dying. . . . Everything else was dying. And, then I had the—I had this dream." His voice had hoarsened; now it choked off. . . . "I dreamed about being home. I woke up and I was all right. I was in bed at home. Only it wasn't any home I'd ever had, the other time, the first time. Oh God, I wish I didn't remember it. I mostly don't. I can't. I've told myself ever since that it was a dream." (93)

This dream-vision depicts Orr as stranded jellyfish (he gulped as if for air) contending with that primary separation, the wound of birth, the prelude to psychic development which is subject to related wounds or traumas. The novel is a series of deaths and rebirths: every time Orr has an effective dream he is born again into a new reality. This compulsion to repeat painful experiences, noted often by Freud, is currently recognized as an identity search. Mahler describes the separation-individuation phase as a kind of "second birth experience," as "a hatching from the symbiotic mother-child common membrane. This hatching is just as inevitable as is biological birth."[18] When Orr falls into his trance-sleep before dreaming, he is "like a man shot dead" (22, 140). When it is time to come out of the dream, his name is repeated: "His name. Who called? No voice he knew. Dry land, dry air, the crash of the strange voice in his ear. Daylight, and no direction. No way back. He woke" (31). This emphasis recalls the crash of the waves as the jellyfish is left on the dry sand of daylight and looks forward to other births, changes, separations: "His mouth had gone dry. He felt it: the shift, the arrival, the change" (57); "But now his dry and silent grieving for his lost wife must end" (156). Bettelheim contends that the greatest emotional need of an autistic child is "to be reborn into a new life. This idea . . . had to be carefully hidden behind a neologism, revealed only in secret languages."[19] In Orr's case the secret language is the dream itself; later it is the language employed between him and the Aliens, which corresponds with the end of his effective dreaming. As Pontalis writes: "the power of speech is an answer to the imaginary power of the dream, and takes its place."[20]

Lichtenstein applies the idea of rebirth directly to identity:

> Keats linked these "negative capabilities" with the poet's "lack of identity": "A Poet is the most unpoetical of anything in existence; because he has no identity—not one word I ever utter can be taken for granted as an opinion growing out of my identical nature—the identity of everyone begins to press upon me.". . . Keats's statement "that which is creative must create itself" describes the very process of the psychological birth of the human infant, and beyond that, implies that this process of self creation is a permanent "rebirth."[21]

It becomes apparent that Orr's constant need to recreate himself by way of the dream is related to his lack of identity. Orr's feelings of being overwhelmed or pressed upon are described before he eliminates them with a dream. Outer reflects inner and present reflects past when Orr as jellyfish and infant finds himself in a crowded train: "He stood out of reach of strap or stanchion, supported solely by the equalizing pressure of bodies on all sides, occasionally lifted right off his feet and floating as the force of crowding (c) exceeded the force of gravity (g)" (28). Later, he "swayed as he stood holding a swaying steel handle on a strap among a thousand other souls. He felt the heaviness upon him, the weight bearing down endlessly. . . . He was afraid that if he lost hold and had to submit entirely to force (c), he might get sick" (37). When asked by Haber what style of daydream he favors, Orr replies, "Oh—escape. . . . Getting away. Getting out from under . . . it's more the city, the crowding, I mean. Too many people everywhere. The headlines. Everything" (33-34). After one of his effective dreams, Orr wakes "feeling broken and abraded, as one might after making an enormous physical effort to resist an overwhelming, battering force" (36). Orr's relationship with the dream, like that of the jellyfish with the sea, is, as Lichtenstein describes the mother-child relationship, "not a relationship between two persons, but a form of coexistence between one overpowering being and another one which long remains in a position of unconditional surrender to the power of the other. . . . In this most intimate interaction, the child is affirmed as being there as the mother's extension, on the basis of the nonverbal responses of mother and child to one another."[22]

When Orr as artist, like Keats, feels "crowded in on . . . squeezed, pressed together" (54) he is goaded by Haber into creating a world in which he has "all the elbow room there is." Consequently, if he sees fewer people in the outside environment, on the dream screen, he feels less threatened, overwhelmed, squeezed, on the inside. Unfortunately, each creation (like each poem by Keats perhaps) does not allow him much further sense of identity. Winnicott helps here—with his idea of the fantasy of being found that relates to being exploited, overwhelmed, swallowed up—when he writes: "In the artist of all kinds I think one can detect an inherent dilemma, which belongs to the co-existence of two trends, the urgent need to communicate and the still more urgent need not to be found. This might account for the fact that we cannot conceive of the artist's coming to the end of the task that occupies his whole nature."[23] Orr needs to dream but his intense dreams reveal him as much as conceal him. So the finished creation never heals the original wound. Whereas in *The Left Hand Of Darkness* Genly Ai begins another creation, another report or novel, at the end of that novel, Orr is constantly obliged to create and re-create until, near the end, he acquires a different language and a more concrete way of creating: kitchen tools, egg whisks with good balance that, like the mural of Mt. Hood, can hang on the wall (155). When he shows Heather some of the things he's designed, she says, "You're a real artist. It's beautiful" (155).

As artist creating identity, Orr is concurrently an "autist." Descriptions of autistic children and their mechanisms fit Orr to a tee. Bettelheim found that a common trait of the autistic child is that he simultaneously feels "helpless to react when he is acted upon . . . and his actions control the universe."[24] Mahler writes:

> It would seem that autism is the basic defense attitude of these infants for whom the beacon of emotional orientation in the outer world—the mother as primary love object—is nonexistent. Early infantile autism develops, I believe, because the infant personality, devoid of emotional ties to the person of the mother, is unable to cope with external stimuli and inner excitation, which threaten from both sides his very existence as an entity. Autism is therefore the mechanism by which such patients try to shut out, to hallucinate away . . . the potential sources of sensory deprivation. . . . They cannot cope with stimulation from the external world. They cannot mediate between two sets of stimuli. In short, it seems as though these patients experience outer reality as an intolerable source of irritation.[25]

Reality is a source of irritation for Orr, and he deals with it by means of his handy gift of hallucinating it away, creating another world more to his liking.

Perhaps the only positive thing Haber does for Orr is to try to coax him into living more in the world—"People can't live alone, after all; to be put in solitary is the worst kind of confinement! We *need* people around us" (55). Orr's response is to try to get away from Haber, yet he keeps coming back to be put to sleep; there he is "out of communication. That's what strikes humans as uncanny about sleep. It's utter privacy. The sleeper turns his back on everyone" (60). Orr had effectively eliminated his aunt, his parents, and Heather (only to bring her back again). There is therefore no consistent emotional tie with a mothering figure. While Winnicott sees the creation and re-creation of the object as necessary to that difficult transition period, Bettelheim, speaking specifically of the autistic child, is more blunt: "This is exactly what these children hallucinate: the person behind the feeding, the person whom they never reached emotionally and whom they both search for, and wish to get rid of."[26] Although, as we shall see later, this "person behind" is also Haber, during the novel Orr finds himself grieving the "loss of a woman who had never existed" (115). Nonetheless, the love object, like the created work or world, is absolutely necessary to the autistic child if he is to develop. "There is no conceivable human environment in which the autistic child could maintain his shell against the demands of the outside world. Indeed, the prerequisite of personality development, and the first requirement for treatment of the autistic child, is to lure him into contact with a human love object."[27] Luring Orr into contact with Heather is one of the main functions of the Aliens. The love object is necessary to break the shell or break down the wall that the child has set up. Elsewhere, Mahler writes that in "autism there is a deanimated, frozen wall between the subject and the human object," whereas in "symbiotic psychosis there is a fusion, melting and lack of differentiation between the self and the non-self—a complete blurring of boundaries."[28] The autistic/artistic dilemma is plain: the love object must be created and re-created to maintain a connection with the world and a sense of self, but this very creation, this tether, has the potential to break down the boundaries, crack the shell, eliminate the sense of entity that the autistic child is striving to maintain. "Thus we often see children whose psychosis had primarily the characteristics of a symbiotic disturbance, but who then used autism in a desperate attempt to ward off the threatened regression into symbiotic fusion to preserve individual entity, separate from the mother or father."[29]

Orr, as jellyfish, is a creature without a shell. Yet Le Guin uses an egg metaphor to describe Orr's relation with women and his potential loss of identity. Freud uses the bird's egg as a "neat example of a psychical system shut off from the stimuli of the external world and able to satisfy even its nutritional requirements autistically."[30] A dictionary definition of an egg is "an animal reproductive body consisting of an ovum together with its nutritive and protective envelopes and having the capacity to develop into a new individual capable of independent existence."[31] At one point Orr looks into his refrigerator after he has created a world without "squeezing": "There was more food in it than he had ever seen in a private refrigerator in his life. In his other life . . . where an egg was the luxury of the month—'Today we ovulate!' his halfwife had used to say when she bought their egg ration" (70). An essential part of Orr's creation, then, is a world in which there are more eggs. Orr then wolfs down a starving man's meal that begins with hard-boiled eggs. He later has a meal with Heather in which they "had to divide everything in half, even the fifth egg" (90). Susan Wood writes, "it is by scrupulously sharing the five eggs which his depopulated dream-world has provided for them that they assert reality—the validity of individual perception and experience."[32] Shortly after, isolated in the cabin, Heather is about to hypnotize Orr in hopes that he will create yet a better world by taking the Aliens off the moon: "She set the oil lamp in the center of the table, amidst eggshells and wreckage. 'Just keep your eyes on it and don't go to sleep' " (94). With a sense of play-acting, and with Orr in her power, she contemplates what amounts to the artist's dilemma: "A person who believes, as she did, that things fit: that there is a whole of which one is part, and that in being a part one is whole: such a person has no desire whatever, at anytime, to play God. Only those who have denied their being yearn to play at it" (94). At the end of the novel, Orr recognizes Heather when he hears her saying "I'd like one of those egg whisks" (154); and it is after examining his handiwork that she calls him an artist.

The artist is thus in an oblique way associated with the egg—the autistic unit which has potential for individual identity. This is enhanced when we discover that Orr is "the goose that laid the golden eggs" (69). The golden eggs are Orr's creations; therefore the work of art is an autistic unit, the self-enclosed product of an autist-artist. However much the "autist" desires to make contact, to participate, to come out of his shell—Haber tells Orr, "Stick your neck out of your shell, then, and live *fully!*" (120)—the result can be dissolution of self. Consequently, after Orr realizes that he is responsible for the new starvation-free world, "He was near cracking" (62). Haber adds, "If he cracks, of course, he'll crack completely; probably in the catatonic schizophrenic line" (64). Later, Orr says to Haber, "I am cracking. . . . Don't you see that I'm going to pieces?" (78).

Orr never does go to pieces. He is able to maintain balance largely by beginning to act on his own and also by way of the Aliens, who help him make the temporary transition to object love. Although the autistic child characteristically strives for a satisfying world not through action but through fantasy, "selfhood begins when they start to come out of their total isolation and begin to act—both in their own behalf, and to some minimal degree in respect to the other."[33] Orr acts and simultaneously recognizes the other when he goes to Heather for help. With her help the Aliens arrive, and he feels a sense of the continuity and sameness that is another characteristic of the autistic child: "It is the endless repetition of sameness that attracts them because it seems to assure them that nothing ever changes."[34] Indeed, everyone in the novel changes except Orr. He even remains living in the same house on Corbett Avenue despite all that happens, and he consistently resists change. "I don't want to change things!" (17); "I have no right to change things" (44).

Like all of Le Guin's protagonists, Orr attempts to stay in the center. Just as Haber-Orr's creations have made Portland "the home of the World Planning

Center . . . the Capital of the Planet," (110) so too Le Guin takes pains to show that Orr is in the center. For purposes of hypnosis, Orr is "3 on the susceptibility scale. . . . Right in the middle of the graph" (20). Heather believes he is "the strongest person she had ever known, because he could not be moved away from the center" (84). The results of a battery of tests reveal the same pattern everywhere: Orr sits "smack in the middle . . . Creative/destructive . . . Both/neither. Either, or. Where there's an opposed pair, a polarity, you're in the middle; where there's a scale, you're at the balance point. You cancel out so strongly that, in a sense, nothing is left" (118). Mr. Either-Orr (as Heather refers to him) really has no identity, and his entire life consists of trying to maintain the balance between autism and symbiosis: he is destined to continually create himself out of that center, transitional space where he hopes to remain. The use of narcotics and pep pills to keep him from being overwhelmed by the force of the dream "left him emotionally off-balance" (32). Haber tells him: "You are afraid of *losing your balance*. But change need not unbalance you" (119); and "The more things go on moving, interrelating, conflicting, changing, the less balance there is—and the more life. . . . Stick your neck out of your shell, then, and *live fully*" (120). Orr reflects that "four years ago in April, something had happened that had made him lose that balance" (123). That was the death of the world and Orr's rebirth: the original wound, birth, is one of the main threats to Orr's unbalance that can only be overcome, so it appears, by the discipline or art of toolmaking—making objects with "Good balance."

This balance also manifests itself in the relationship between Orr and Haber. Whereas Haber is in favor of creating and changing, Orr is in favor of letting things be. As Haber becomes more obsessed with playing God, Orr becomes more reluctant to produce any change whatsoever. As Haber gets larger and more important, Orr continues as a relative nobody; by the end of the novel, however, Orr can say he "Outgrew 'em." Together, as doubles of each other, they portray the artist *engagé* who desires to change the world (or at least hopes that her work will have some effect on outward reality) but yet wants to remain detached, in her own private space, with some semblance of entity that would be lost in the push and squeeze of politics and business. Either way, there is a certain amount of God-playing. Haber tells Orr, "There will be none of this tension between your will to nihilism and my will to progress, your Nirvana wishes and my conscious, careful planning for the good of all" (127).

There are a number of details in the novel to suggest that Orr and Haber are one. Neither Orr nor Haber has the shell to exit self-sufficiently; like Orr, Haber is "soft and exposed," protected only by his "inadequate flesh" (105). They both need a hard protective boundary because the self is felt to be soft and vulnerable; hence the need to fuse with hard objects—Orr with Aliens and with Heather, and Haber with the Augmentor. To yield in a passive way is to melt, dissolve, or be

transformed. The sexual ambiguity manifested by the characters is most pronounced in the Orr-Haber relationship. Orr is described as a slight, fair, almost
feminine creature. He has hair "like a little girl's, brown and fine, a little blond
beard; soft white skin like a fish's belly; meek, mild, stuttering" (40). When he
first met Haber he "fingered his necklace nervously" (21). There "was an
acceptant, passive quality about him that seemed feminine, or even childish.
Haber recognized in himself a protective/bullying reaction toward this physically
slight and compliant man. To dominate, to patronize him was so easy as to be
almost irresistible" (21). Although Haber discovers that Orr is more resilient than
he first thinks, their relationship must be seen as having these homoerotic
overtones. Haber's fear of being overwhelmed by relationships or crowds is, like
Orr's, balanced by his fear of being alone. This is expressed in largely sexual
terms:

> Haber considered himself a lone wolf. He had never wanted marriage nor close friendships, he
> had chosen a strenuous research carried out when others sleep, he had avoided entanglements.
> He kept his sex life almost entirely to one-night stands, semipros, sometimes young women and
> sometimes young men; he knew which bars and cinemas and saunas to go to for what he wanted.
> He got what he wanted and got clear again, before he or the other person could possibly develop
> any kind of need for the other. He prized his independence, his free will.
> But he found it terrible to be alone. . . . (100)

While Haber is a large, soft male with feminine tendencies, and Heather is a small,
hard female with masculine characteristics, the Aliens' sexuality is much more
ambiguous. Though "indestructible" in their armored suits, they are most noted
for their unaggressiveness. "What they actually looked like, inside the turtle suits,
was not clear in Orr's mind" (144); "was there in fact any substantial form within
that green carapace, that mighty armor?" (132) These creatures remain a sexual
puzzle. Ambiguity concerning sexuality is, according to Mahler, symptomatic of
the autistic-symbiotic conflict. Sexual ambiguity is also prominent wherever
doubling occurs, as we saw in *The Left Hand of Darkness*. And wherever there is a
doubling relationship, it seems, one of the products of that relationship is a
creative one.

From the beginning to the end of the novel, Haber insists that he and Orr are in
"this thing" together. Although Haber uses Orr's dreaming power to fulfill his own
wishes for a better world, it is not evident whether these wishes are not also Orr's,
because his "screwball" brain, his primary process thinking, continually produces
results that Haber does not expect. So it is never entirely clear whether Orr's
wishes become Haber's wishes or vice versa. We do know, however, that Orr's
dreams erase everybody's memories but his and Haber's. Also sure is that Haber
hopes to take over Orr's dreams by printing a model of his brain. Orr's main task
throughout the novel is to get Haber out of his head (46) and prevent Haber from

taking over his dreams: "Instead of preventing me from having effective dreams, you're going to start having them yourself. I don't like making the rest of the world live in my dreams, but I certainly don't want to live in yours" (125). Eventually Haber acquires the template of Orr's brain emissions during effective dreaming. And when the Augmentor synchronizes the generalized e-state pattern with Haber's own d-state, "Then this world will be like heaven, and men will be like gods!" (128). Eventually the big load is taken off Orr's shoulders and put onto Haber's: Orr is cured, normal, and Haber has effective dreaming capability. Haber's first and only effective dream is a disaster; it is an effective nightmare which "had undone connections. The continuity which had always held between the worlds or timelines of Orr's dreaming had now been broken. Chaos entered in" (149). By switching off the Augmentor, Orr is able to stop the "unmaking"; he severs the connection between himself and Haber and between dream and reality. Haber sits, alive, but dead: "The eyes looked straight-forward into the dark, into the void, into the unbeing at the center of William Haber" (148). The time period during which the world is almost destroyed and then renewed—the time at which Orr makes the separation from Haber, and from the "gray" Heather—is referred to by everyone as "The Break." Orr later says that it "took the entire will power, the accumulated strength of my entire existence, to press one damned OFF button" (151).

There are at least three ways to view the Haber-Orr doubling relationship. The first one is that it is a depiction of the process of ego-splitting as described by Freud. Splitting is a process in which the ego is altered as it attempts to defend itself. One "current" in mental life disavows another, both existing and acting as if independent of each other, that is, split-off. "On the one hand, with the help of certain mechanisms the person rejects reality and refuses to accept any prohibition; on the other hand, in the same breath he recognizes the danger of reality, takes over the fear of that danger as a pathological symptom and tries subsequently to divest himself of the fear."[35] Haber rejects the limitations put on him by reality: he gladly has his wishes come true, and he is on his way to the ultimate gratification. Orr, early in the novel, recognizes the possible consequences—the end of the world—and conveniently finds/invents Haber, who gladly takes up Orr's burden. So the ego (Le Guin) can have her cake and eat it too. Once sanity is restored, Orr is ostensibly able to progress without the need for his clever solution.

The second way we can look at the Haber-Orr relationship is as a father-son (daughter) relationship. This view is necessary to be consistent with the dream as maternal body, put forth by Pontalis, which the dreamer views as his own territory. Haber, then, is the interfering father of the later phase of psychosexual development. He is breaking up a union that the child wants but, realistically, will have to give up sooner or later. The demands of reality here, which can cause the splitting referred to, also are connected with the loss of ego boundaries. Hans Loewald (who advocates swinging from a paternal concept of reality to a maternal one, a concept that *Lathe* appears to endorse) writes, "It would be justified to look at the defensive function of the ego . . . from an entirely different point of view. What the ego defends itself, or the psychic apparatus, against, is not reality but the loss of reality, that is, the loss of an integration with the world such as it exists in the libidinal relationship with the mother and with which the father seems to interfere."[36] These comments may be collocated with Orr's thoughts as he visits Haber in the Asylum:

> He was looking at the world as misunderstood by the mind: the bad dream.
> There is a bird in a poem by T. S. Eliot who says that mankind cannot bear very much reality; but the bird is mistaken. A man can endure the entire weight of the universe for eighty years. It is unreality that he cannot bear.
> Haber was lost. (153)

Haber's interference as father also recalls the "stubborn continents" interfering with the jellyfish-sea unity. With the supposed resolution of the Oedipus complex, Haber, Orr's double and father, is left with the bad dream, the bad mother. The process of the splitting of the object (into good and bad) in the struggle to cope with unhappy real life experiences leads to a splitting of the ego in the struggle to maintain relations with both the good and bad aspects of the mother and other family figures. As father, one could argue, Haber is killed off—he no longer is capable of competing for the dream-mother or interfering with the child's ego-reality integration. And since it seems that the double must die in order for the single to live, we can say that Haber as double is eliminated as well. But he is still alive, and he is, as double, keeping the bad mother in check. So the theory that, if there is a double somewhere in the novel the balance is being maintained, appears to hold true as well. As double, Haber helped Orr maintain that delicate balance of separation and symbiosis. By his presence and by his giving Orr dream-suppressant drugs, he helped to keep him from being overwhelmed by the dream; yet he also prevented the total separation of Orr from his dreams by having him dream by way of the Augmentor. Once the Aliens were created, as transitional objects, Orr is able to enter, as Winnicott says, that "intermediate area of experience, unchallenged in respect of its belonging to inner or external (shared) reality [which] constitutes the greater part of the infant's experience, and throughout life is retained in the intense experiencing that belongs to the arts."[37]

The creative aspect of the Haber-Orr relationship is critical to the third way of viewing their relationship, that of mother-son (daughter). Haber is maternal largely through his relationship with the Augmentor—his "Baby"—which bears a striking resemblance to the mother-infant imprinting process described by Lichtenstein. Haber is overpowering in the same way that the dream is. Orr's relationship with Haber, like his relation to effective dreaming and like the mother-child relationship, is an unequal one. It is, as Lichtenstein has said, "a form of coexistence between one overpowering being and another one which long remains in a position of unconditional surrender to the power of the other."[38] Haber's power is described in terms of the fish image: "Haber had him hooked, and with more than one hook. . . . Haber had a moral line on him, then, but where he really had him caught was on the legal hook" (67). Haber retains his protective/bullying relation to Orr, and Orr remains in a state of surrender until near the end.

Lichtenstein emphasized that "mother and child respond to each other as if they were extensions of one another, both physically and psychically. . . . the child is defined as being there as the mother's extension, on the basis of the nonverbal responses of mother and child to one another."[39] The doubling relation can be seen in these terms—Orr is present as Haber's extension. This is underscored by Orr's statement, "He keeps calling me by my name; I think it's to remind himself that there's someone else present" (138). The nonverbal responses are represented by the fact that Orr's dreams are recorded in "black and white," thereby further serving Haber's needs in that he will be able to construct a template of Orr's brain in order to dream effective dreams himself. It has already been pointed out that Orr is Haber's instrument. For Lichtenstein, identity is an experience of a potential instrumentality for another one. This begins with an imprinting process:

> The mother does not convey a *sense* of identity but an *identity:* the child is the organ, the instrument for the fulfillment of the mother's unconscious needs. . . . The specific stimulus combination emanating from the mother releases one concrete way of being this organ, this instrument. This identity will be irreversible and thus it will compel the child to find ways to realize this specific identity. . . . The mother imprints not an identity but an identity *theme.*[40]

The creativity theme runs through Haber's interactions with Orr. The creative motif, in Haber's case, is more conscious than unconscious—Haber needs to create a better world in a relatively organized way, but he needs Orr to fulfill this need. The following statements constitute an imprinting process that creates an identity theme to which Orr ultimately responds: "You haven't seen the help your own mind can give you, the ways you can use it, employ it creatively" (32); "Don't be afraid of your unconscious mind! It's not a black pit of nightmares. . . . It is the wellspring of health, imagination, creativity" (78); "What I'm doing is making this new capacity [of the human brain] *replicable*. There's an analogy with the invention of printing" (127). The new capacity of the human brain is—through works of art, in Le Guin's case—to create itself, to know itself. This capacity, exemplified by the dream metaphor, is simultaneously a "gift" (107; 127), a "crazy performance" (146), and "the meaningless writing of the mad" (138). The Augmentor is created by Haber and it is equated with him; whenever we see him, he is beside his Baby, which he then hooks onto Orr. It is a concretization of the mysterious interaction between mother and child (it is both mother and child). As well as being the baby with "exposed entrails" (117), it is "the Dream Machine" (20). It nurtures and imprints: it picks up the d-sleep patterns in order "to feed them back to the sleeping brain, amplifying its own emissions" (24). As symbolic of the interaction between infant and mother, the result of which is a creative act or object, the Augmentor functions to fill a void, close a gap. "Our hypnosis plus the Augmentor will ensure that we get them, get across the neurophysiological and temporal gulf of sleep, right into dreaming" (21). "The gap we have to bridge" is, no doubt for Le Guin, that between inner and outer, female and male, mother and child. The artist's task is to explore that transitional area between self and other. The Augmentor allows Orr to do this and then records it in black and white.

However, the original process is nonverbal; it is a silent communication through the images generated by the dream. The verbal communication made with Haber is ineffectual—Orr is unable to communicate to Haber his need to interact with the world without being overwhelmed by it. The simple "words" *iahklu* and *Er'perrehnne* are communicated to Orr in "Barsoomian bisyllable" during a trance and take the place of the Augmentor. Orr has this communication with the Aliens in a trance which produces an effect that, as far as Haber can understand, only the Augmentor can create: "Queer stuff going on in your cortex there, and I wasn't even feeding your cortex at all with the Augmentor" (122). Eventually, Orr, with a little help from his friends, is able to "override the pattern stimulation from the Augmentor" (141), and then separate from the Augmentor and Haber altogether. It should be clear that two things are happening. First, the language of the Aliens is overriding and replacing the silent muttering of images that the augmentor stimulates. Second, this language allows Orr to transform the abstract dreaming process into a concrete object—a tool with good balance. This is done in the transitional space that the Aliens represent, and it accords with Winnicott's contention that, for the infant, true communication arises out of silence. One must recognize

> the non-communicating central self, forever immune from the reality principle, and forever silent. Here communication is not non-verbal; it is, like the music of the spheres, absolutely personal. . . . Explicit communication is pleasurable and it involves extremely interesting techniques, including that of language. The two extremes, explicit communication that is indirect, and silent or personal communication that feels real, each of these has its place, and in the intermediate cultural area there exists for many, but not for all, a mode of communication which is a more valuable compromise.[41]

The compromise (balance) of silent communicating (dream images) and explicit communication (with Haber, who "seemed not to know the uses of silence" [140], and with the world at large) is the Alien language ("Incommunicable. Language used for communication with individual-persons will not contain other forms of relationship. Jor Jor" [132]). This balance of private and public language corresponds to and stems from the artist's balancing of autism and symbiosis. Orr as artist will continue to attempt to "make distinctions (make compromises) that exist between phenomena in terms of their position in the area between external or shared reality and the true dream."[42] The end of the novel, once again, is still a beginning, "To go is to return." The separation of self from other is not a clean one, and never will be. Only a window—treacherously transparent, breakable, and therefore threatening to let inside become outside entirely—separates Orr from the sea creature inside (outside?). Outside (inside?), the mist blurs the distinction between him and Heather; but Heather has a hard surface. The precarious balance is temporarily maintained.

6

The Dispossessed:
The Artist and Politics

Let me speak the mother tongue
and I will sing so loudly
newlyweds and old women
will dance to my singing
and sheep will cease from cropping and machines
will gather round to listen
in cities fallen silent
as a ring of standing stones:
O let me sing the walls down, Mother!

Ursula K. Le Guin
"Invocation"

The majority of the criticism on *The Dispossessed: An Ambiguous Utopia* (1974) has necessarily focused on the nature and the ramifications of the social, political, and philosophical theories that are concretized and ostensibly endorsed in the novel.[1] In addition to being a novel of ideas, there is evidence to suggest that *TD* is very much a story about the exceptional creative individual. Le Guin describes the origin of *TD*:

> It too began with a person, seen much closer to, this time, and with intense vividness: a man, this time . . . [he] may have come from a childhood memory of Robert Oppenheimer as a young man. But more vivid than any visual detail was the personality, which was most attractive—attractive, I mean as a flame to a moth. There, there he is, I have to get there this time. . . . There he stood, quite untouched. Catch me if you can!
>   All right. All right, what's your name. What is your name, by the way? Shevek, he told me promptly. All right, Shevek. So who are you?

She tells us that in the process of "trying to find out who and what Shevek was, I found out a great deal else, and thought as hard as I was capable of thinking, about society, about my world, and about myself. I would not have found out or been able to communicate any of this if I had not been doggedly pursuing . . . the elusive Mrs. Brown."[2]

As usual, Le Guin's comments on the genesis of her work are intriguing and revealing. The image of a person comes to her, a man: but the "man" is transformed or qualified by the elusive Mrs. Brown, with whom he is allied. Mrs. Brown is the one Virginia Woolf uses in her statement that "all novels begin with an old lady in the corner opposite."[3] In Le Guin's case, the person comes to her as a man, from a childhood memory, and then leaves her again—catch me if you can! She is finally able to catch him and pin him down by means of his name. She wants to become one with him, as the moth does the flame. In getting to him, she finds out a great deal about herself. So Shevek comes to represent Le Guin, but he is also an Other, a memory, an old woman, a place to get to. Although Le Guin admits that *TD* is a didactic and idealistic book, she also believes that it is a novel, "because at the heart of it you will not find an idea, or an inspirational message, or even a stone ax, but something much frailer and obscurer and more complex: a person." This belief is confirmed for her by the fact that almost every reviewer,

> however carried away he gets in supporting or attacking or explaining the book's themes and ideas, somewhere in the discussion has mentioned its protagonist by name. There he is!—there, if only for a moment. If I had to invent two entire worlds to get to him . . . it was worth it. If I could give the readers one glimpse of what I saw: Shevek, Mrs. Brown, the Other, a soul, a human soul, "the spirit we live by. . . ."[4]

On the most fundamental level, then, *TD* is about one person. Le Guin, Mrs. Brown, and the Other either constitute Shevek or are fragments of this split subject. This is implied in a later statement by Le Guin: *"The Dispossessed* was meant, so much, to be a book about two people and it ended up to be a book about one person with satellites."[5] This statement is significant in at least two ways. First, it suggests that all the other characters in the novel are subordinates, dependents, fragments, doubles, of Shevek. Second, it equates a person with a body in space.

To understand how Le Guin's identity theme manifests itself in *TD*, how it germinates and informs theme and structure, it is important to recognize that the two planets, Anarres and Urras are, in Le Guin's creative imagination, physical bodies: Shevek and Other, Le Guin and Mrs. Brown, and variations thereon. There are several fine touches in *TD* that suggest an equation or a correlation between person and planet, inner world and outside environment: "We don't leave Anarres, because we *are* Anarres. Being Tirin, you can't leave Tirin's skin;"[6] Shevek's view outside his window on Urras gave "an impression of complex wholeness such as he had never seen, except, perhaps, foreshadowed on a small scale in certain serene and thoughtful human faces" (52); Anarres is referred to as "child Anarchia" and Abbenay, the chief "city," is "the mind and center of Anarres" (78); in fact, Abbenay means "mind" (77). Vea, on Urras, has breasts "like the snow." Near the end of the novel, Shevek tells Keng, "You don't believe in Anarres. You don't believe in me" (281).

This need to endow the external world with something of the self and vice-versa is a preoccupation both of the artist and of the developing infant. It ultimately symbolizes the ego-infant's "original tendencies towards re-establishment of the primary narcissistic unity or identity with the environment (mother)."[7] Takver, specifically, comes to represent the environment-mother. Her association with the moon, a universal maternal symbol, is one example. Feeling alone and exiled on Urras, Shevek thinks of home: "He had seen the Moon rise . . . over the dry plains of the past; over the roofs of Abbenay, with Takver watching it beside him" (72). When he and Takver initially form the "bond," she is "sitting among the delicate bushes of moonthorn," and they watch each other in the "steadily growing moonlight." In this setting they become fused: "He had a feeling of unlimitedness. . . . Behind Takver's head the sky was brightening with moonrise. . . . 'Yes, that's it,' he said, without self-consciousness, without any sense of talking to someone else" (146). Shevek later queries, "Which is moonlight, which is Takver?" (154). On Urras, it was "as if the beauty and strangeness of the beasts and plants of Urras had been charged with a message for him by Takver" (123). And Takver is one of those whose "umbilicus has never been cut. They never got weaned from the universe. . . . It was strange to see Takver take a leaf into her hand, or even a rock. She became an extension of it, it of her" (150).

Shevek's relationship with Takver as mother-environment, their coming together, their separation, their coming together again, is the bedrock of his relationship with the world(s) at large. This correlation is delicately depicted when they make love in the darkness: they "circled about the center of infinite pleasure, about each other's being, like planets circling blindly, quietly, in the flood of sunlight, about the common center of gravity, swinging, circling endlessly" (258). Shevek's crossing the abyss of space in order to communicate with, and perhaps unite with, Urras, is built upon a much earlier attempt to bridge a gap:

> We came, Takver thought, from a great distance to each other . . . over years, over abysses of chance. It is because he comes from so far away that nothing can separate us. Nothing, no distances, no years, can be greater than the distance that's already between us, the distance of our sex, the difference of our being, our minds; that gap, that abyss which we bridge with a look, with a touch, with a word. (258–59)

The quality of the communication, the mutuality of that first relationship, Le Guin seems to suggest, can dictate the quality of the male-female relationship and, in turn, the quality of the social relationship. Thus, "the real mutuality and reciprocity of society and individual" (267) stem from and parallel Shevek's "mutual commitment with Takver," a relationship that "had remained thoroughly alive during their four years' separation" (268).

Contemporary psychoanalytic writers, including Lacanians, have consistently depicted the interrelationship of individual and society, of inside and outside; the quality of that relationship greatly depends on the early stage in life when mutual trust is established and from which a (potential) identity can develop. Heinz Lichtenstein in turn believes that one's ability to work creatively and independently with society depends on how well the original identity theme is "received." Although psychoanalysis has investigated why one never submits unequivocally to the demands and interdicts of society—Shevek and all Le Guin's protagonists are prime examples of this—there is that need of the person to feel part of a whole and to enact her part as creatively as possible within it. The original feeling of relatedness to a whole is the mother-child unit: "In this unit the mother-*Umwelt* would correspond to the surrounding total organism, and the infant to an organ within this totality."[8] It is after the breaking up of this unit that, according to Edith Jacobson, its reestablishment is sought by processes of identification with the mother. The infant's "playful imitations of what the parents do are first only forerunners of ego identifications. . . . This presupposes a transition from desires for a complete union with the mother to a striving to become only 'like' her."[9]

Since one of my claims is that Le Guin is investigating the separation-individuation process, this desire to be like the mother should be evident in the novel. Shevek's relationship with Takver represents that earlier stage: it is one of complete unity. The person Shevek (and Le Guin) most wants to be like, to become, is Odo. Le Guin's short story, "The Day Before the Revolution," which was written after *TD*, is about the last days of Odo, the "drooling old woman who had started a world revolution," and who is regarded as "if she were some kind of All-Mother, the idol of the Big Sheltering Womb." In a preface to the story, Le Guin describes her state of mind after the completion of *TD*: "When it was done I felt lost, exiled—a displaced person. I was very grateful, therefore, when Odo came out of the shadows and across the gulf of Probability, and wanted a story written, not about the world she made, but about herself."[10] Le Guin's feeling of being lost, exiled, is typical of Shevek's experience throughout the novel (Odo is also referred to as "an exile" [82]). This feeling is temporarily allayed for Le Guin when the gulf is closed between her and Odo; in much the same fashion, Shevek's feelings of isolation are alleviated when, for example, the gap is closed between him and Takver or when he crosses the abyss to arrive "home" in Urras or Anarres.

Odo is the mother of the society of Anarres; she gave birth to the Odonians: "Our society, here, is a true community wherever it truly embodies Odo's ideas. It was a woman who made the Promise!" (266); "she renewed the relationships of men" (71). From her prison cell in Drio on Urras, Odo did the writing that inspired and formed the philosophical and political framework for the Odonians on Anarres. Pictures of Odo in her prison cell are common on Anarres; "a framed amateur painting of Odo in prison" (252) is one of the things that takes Shevek back to his childhood. *TD* is replete with prison imagery, which serves to equate Odo and Shevek. Shevek's decision to unbuild walls leads him to "this little room, this prison" (7) on the freighter *Mindful,* which is taking him to Urras. After several weeks on Urras, Shevek queries: "Having locked himself in jail, how might he act as a free man?" (219). In his room at the university in A-Io on Urras, which he calls his "gracious prison cell" (223), he finally sits down to complete his Temporal Theory, which will, he hopes, have the effect of unifying people as did Odo's writings from a not so gracious prison cell. He eventually escapes from his jail at the university and makes his way to the leaders of the subversive Odonian movement on Urras. He writes pieces for the newspapers for them with the hope that "all prison doors will fly open" (238). There are other ways that Le Guin depicts Shevek's identification with Odo. Prior to his decision to go to Urras, the birthplace of Odo and, as a result, Anarres, he comes upon a statue of Odo in a park in Abbenay. He is able to "comprehend" Odo, "whose face he had known since his infancy, whose ideas were central and abiding in his mind" (82). In effect, Odo has instigated a way of thinking and behaving for him. Like Shevek, "Odo was an alien: an exile," and "the young man sat beside the statue in the twilight, one almost as quiet as the other" (82). Later in the novel, when Takver sees how Shevek is overworking himself at his desk, "she would have cried out as Odo's husband, Asieo, did once, 'For God's sake, girl, can't you serve Truth *a little at a time?*'" (152). Before the uprising in A-Io, one of the leaders tells Shevek, "You are an idea. A dangerous one. The idea of anarchism made flesh." A young girl interjects: "Then you've got your Odo. . . . After all, Odo was only an idea. Dr. Shevek is the proof" (237).

Another dimension of Shevek's identification with Odo is added when we consider his isolation on both Anarres and Urras, which parallels the alienation of Anarres from Urras. For Lichtenstein, alienation is one aspect of a central human problem: "this problem derives from man's lack of an innate 'identity,' thus compelling him to define himself in terms of his instrumentality for someone or something else."[11] Shevek is Odo's instrument; he is the "proof." Without a Shevek—"I am Anarres"—Odo's work can bear no fruit. Through and as Odo, Shevek can work variations on his identity theme. However, it is more complicated than this. Odo is, if we listen to Le Guin, one of several satellites, a fragment or double of Shevek (as are others such as Rulag, Gvarab, and Takver, who all play their parts in his individuation process). As physical bodies, the two planets Urras and Anarres also represent a mother (Urras) which gives birth to a child (Anarres). Both are in a position of instrumentality for each other: Urras needs Anarresti natural resources; Anarres needs Urrasti machine parts. Keng says,

"Perhaps Anarres is the key to Urras" (275). The two planetary bodies are doubles of each other, known as "the Twin Planets" (63). Early in the novel, Tirin says, "I never thought before . . . of the fact that there are people sitting up on a hill, up there, on Urras, looking at Anarres, at us, and saying, 'Look, there's the Moon.' Our earth is their Moon; our Moon is their earth" (33).

The relationship between the two planets parallels the infant's attempt to establish its own boundaries apart from those of the mother, and the occasional fusion of the two; the mirroring of the two planets (and their alienation from each other) recalls Lacan's mirror stage. At some times the "I" is the child; at other times it is the mother; at still other times it is both. As Loewald states, "The less mother and child are one, the more they become separate entities, the more will there be a dynamic interplay of forces between these two 'systems.' As the mother becomes 'outside,' and hand in hand with this, the child an 'inside,' there arises a tension between the two."[12] This relationship is nicely evoked at the opening of the novel:

> There was a wall. It did not look important. It was built of uncut rocks roughly mortared. An adult could look right over it, and even a child could climb it. Where it crossed the roadway, instead of having a gate it degenerated into mere geometry, a line, an idea of boundary. But the idea was real. It was important. For seven generations there had been nothing in the world more important than that wall.
>
> Like all walls it was ambiguous, two-faced. What was inside it and what was outside it depended upon which side of it you were on. . . . The wall shut in . . . the rest of the universe. It enclosed the universe, leaving Anarres outside, free.
>
> Looked at from the other side, the wall enclosed Anarres: the whole planet was inside it, a great prison camp, cut off from other worlds and other men, in quarantine. (1–2)

Le Guin, with her accustomed skill and economy, provides the essence of the novel in a few sentences. The wall is something that separates Anarres from the rest of the universe, particularly from the planet Urras. It is a real boundary but it is really an idea, something concrete made abstract and vice-versa. This idea of separation has existed since the birth of that planet for the Odonians. It is important; it is necessary. But one is not sure whether it is a positive thing or not. It is ambiguous and two-faced. Inside can also be outside. This confusion of inside and outside recalls the opening of *Lathe*. In *Lathe* we were made to experience this confusion; in *TD* we are simply told. We are told that the wall allows Anarres to be outside and free. This seems positive. Then we are informed that the wall makes Anarres a prison camp cut off from other worlds. This identifies Anarres with Shevek, and also makes the connection with Odo, whose ideas from prison gave birth to the Anarresti. Again, much is made of Shevek being a lonely, isolated creature. He tells one woman, Gimar—significantly, after she has declined his offer to copulate—"I haven't really ever known anybody. You see how I didn't understand you. I'm cut off. Can't get in. Never will" (40). On Urras: "It was not that they cut him off; it was that—as always—he cut himself off from them. He was lonely. . . . The trouble was that he was not *in touch*. He felt that he had not touched anything, anyone, on Urras in all these months" (117). Shevek, as Anarres, can be seen as

> the autistic child who clings to a boundary dividing that which is felt to be good and to be his self, from that which is felt as bad and alien. He has made a shell of a boundary out of fear of a persecutory world—a shell which is a defense against confusion and loss of differentiation between an inner "good" and an outer "bad" world.[13]

The novel is structured around the idea of a wall separating a "good" and a "bad." Anarres and anarchism are good while Urras and propertarianism are bad. Shevek's inner, creative self is good, yet irritated by an outside world that makes certain demands. The main action of the novel, however, is Shevek's attempt to come to terms with the good and the bad of the different worlds; *TD* charts his growing dissatisfaction with conditions on Anarres and his attempt to reestablish communication with Urras, followed by his growing dissatisfaction with Urras, which he leaves in hopes of returning home to Takver and Anarres. The first and last chapters of the novel take place in that space that both joins and divides the planets and, accordingly, partakes of the good and the bad. The other chapters alternate between Anarres (the past) and Urras (the present); we see the two planets through Shevek's eyes. As George Slusser put it, the "point of contact between two worlds is the hero's mind."[14] Since it is a fundamental axiom of psychoanalytic thought that the individual inhabits two worlds, the outer world of the present and the inner world of the past, it is clear that these two planets embody Shevek's endeavor to come to terms with inner and outer realities. The boundary between the two realities can be solid, but it can also blur. For as the novel progresses, it becomes less and less clear what is good and what is bad. It is clear, however, that there is an intermittent tension and a constant flow between child and mother, inside and outside, Anarres and Urras, which represent an urge to reestablish the original unity. Shevek, like Le Guin, the artist, personifies and documents this tension and flow.

It is difficult to correlate precisely artistic activity and autistic activity. Each involves a retreat in order to create. Margaret Mahler puts the autistic child's situation succinctly: "After withdrawal from the object world, he recreates in his own internal reality both the subject and the object, the mother and himself."[15] This kind of withdrawal is characteristic of Shevek from the beginning. At the opening of the first Anarres chapter, there is a room with eleven babies settling down to their nap. Shevek, two years old, sits alone in "the square of yellow sunlight from the window, staring up the sunbeam with an earnest and stupid expression" (21). We are told that his mother has just been posted to Abbenay. Soon, another child wanders over and tries to take over Shevek's spot. Shevek screams and cries "Mine sun!" The scene ends with the matron telling Shevek's father, referring to the departed mother, "I hope you get posted together soon" (22), while Shevek sobs in his father's arms. This is juxtaposed with the next scene, where Shevek, a boy of eight, is explaining his theory (Zeno's paradox) to the rest of the classroom: if you throw a rock at a tree it can never hit it—"there's always a place, only it's a time really, that's halfway between the last place it was and the tree. . . . *It can't reach the tree*" (23). To the rest of the class, Shevek is speaking another language. The director tells him, "Speech is sharing—a cooperative act. You're not sharing, merely egoizing" (24). He is then ostracized from the group. As he makes his way out of the circle, he experiences a singing in his ears, which he eventually quells by turning his mind to the Square:

> It was made of numbers and numbers were always cool and solid; when he was at fault he could turn to them, for they had no fault. He had seen the Square in his mind a while ago, a design in space like the design music made in time: a square of the first nine integers with 5 in the center. However you added up the rows they came out the same, all inequality balanced out . . . if only he could make a group that liked to talk about things like that. (24–25)

He questions his impulse to talk about the rock and the tree, and he is confused about the rightness or wrongness of the director's decision to expel him from the group. His head aches. Then he "looked inward, inward to the calm patterns":

> If a book were written all in numbers, it would be true. It would be just. Nothing said in words ever came out quite even. Things in words got twisted and ran together, instead of staying straight and fitting together. But, underneath the words at the center, like the center of the Square, it all came out even. Everything could change yet nothing would be lost. If you saw the numbers you could see that, the balance, the pattern. You saw the foundations of the world. And they were solid. (25)

There is a great deal happening in the above two scenes. As an infant, Shevek is isolated from the group. His mother has departed: he knows this or feels it (later in the novel Takver explains the effect of the separation: "She left when he was two. . . . He feels that he lost something essential . . . the importance loyalty has for him, it goes back to that, I think" [293]). He is already creating another world to make up for what he has just lost; "the Square window, in a white wall. . . . In the center of the sky is the sun" (21). This square opening in a wall and a centered luminous body have become his new reality. His screaming repetition of "mine sun!" cannot simply be dismissed as an inability to share; it is something he has focused on, made part of himself, to make up for what he is lacking. The classroom scene is a variation on and extension of this. The rock and tree idea not only illustrates Shevek's precociousness: it is a unique way of portraying a transitional space. There is a place where a subject is always only halfway between its origin and its object. It can never reach its goal. It is a place, which is equated with time, that partakes of both its subject and object, just as, say, the space or gap between Urras and Anarres is neither one nor the other, but not quite both either. Following the logic of Zeno's paradox, Shevek can never arrive at Urras, nor can he ever return to Anarres: he is obliged to continually explore that space which Winnicott claims is the artist's territory. This has further ramifications, as we shall see, but the germ of the idea is here.

After withdrawing from the "object world" of his classroom, Shevek recreates his own inner reality. He initiates this by focusing on the Square, which stems from the window in the white wall. Here he can indulge in his private language which is made up of numbers; they are a reliable presence, always cool and solid, faultless. A book written in numbers would be true; there would be none of the deception of public language. They would fit together and form a center, like the center of the Square, which is simultaneously a symbol of creative activity—"a design in space like the design music made in time"[16]—and a symbol of sameness within change (autistic children are obsessed with maintaining sameness or continuity; and Lichtenstein's identity theory is rooted in sameness within change): "Everything could change, yet nothing would be lost." Finally, there is the desire for balance: he wishes he could make up a group, be part of a group, to talk about this inner landscape or vision, which has separated him from his circle and yet has provided him with solace. The 5 in the center illustrates this need for balance and for a centering figure or, perhaps, a desire to be the centering figure. And out of these private, creative ruminations arises, subtly, a social concern—"all inequality balanced out"—which increasingly preoccupies Shevek as he emerges from his shell to make connections with the world at large.

These childhood scenes portray Shevek's (and Le Guin's and *TD*'s) basic dilemma: how to be isolated—in a private world which nourishes continuity and creativity largely by way of a private language—without having to be insulated, from the Other, from the world of change and "progress" and people. His dilemma is heightened and elaborated on in chapter 4, where the identity theme is more clearly delineated and where the separation-individuation problem is poignantly depicted. Anything else that Shevek does in the novel, and Shevek *is* the novel, is a variation on the scenes in chapter 4 that arise directly out of the two childhood scenes.

Chapter 4 begins with Shevek entering Abbenay, the place his mother, Rulag, left for eighteen years before. He is in Abbenay to study physics under a man named Sabul. His first task is to learn Iotic, the language of the Urrasti, because they are much further advanced in physics than the Anarresti. Sabul gives him an Urrasti book to work from: Shevek "was holding it, the thing he wanted to see, the alien artifact, the message from another world." As he fondles it, he remembers "the book of numbers" (85). A connection is made between that world of numbers, which was the child's solace, and another private language, one that is not understood on Anarres. He begins to learn this language alone "because it came only too naturally to him to work alone." In fact, since "he was very young he had known that in certain ways he was unlike anyone else he knew" (86), and he often resents "this curse of difference" and his "inward isolation." Eventually he finds he is no longer "reading Iotic, he was reading physics" (87). His life grows more hermetic; his only contact with the outside world is with Gvarab—he never misses one of her lectures on Frequency and Cycle. She soon picks him out of the crowd as "her constant auditor. She began to lecture for him. . . . In his face she saw her joy" (87). This mirroring idea soon develops into a kind of symbiosis: "what no one had ever shared with her, he took, he shared. He was her brother, across the gulf of fifty years, and her redemption" (88). They almost become like each other, "for the old woman was as shy as the young man" (88).

Shevek has to meet periodically with Sabul. Sabul insists that Shevek "keep the new Urrasti physics *private*" (89). Shevek becomes haunted by the idea of privacy: private language, private physics, private room. He feels that this is perhaps too propertarian; yet he acknowledges that this privacy is necessary to his work. He concludes: "Privacy, in fact, was almost as desirable for physics as it was for sex" (90). Sex is union and Shevek's goal is a "unified Theory of Time. . . . He felt that he was in a locked room in the middle of a great open country: it was all around him, if he could find the way out, the way clear" (91). He gets out of the habit of sleeping; he survives on naps, two or three hours here and there and soon finds himself functioning somewhere in the middle of sleep and waking life, a world which is filled with dreams:

> He dreamed vividly, and the dreams were part of his work. He saw time turn back upon itself, a river flowing upward to the spring. He held the contemporaneity of two moments in his left and right hands; as he moved them apart he smiled to see the moments separate like dividing soap bubbles. He got up and scribbled down, without really waking, the mathematical formula that had been eluding him for days. He saw space shrink in upon him like the walls of a collapsing sphere driving in and in towards a central void, closing, closing, and he woke with a scream for help locked in his throat, struggling in silence to escape from the knowledge of his own eternal emptiness. (91)

The mathematical formula that Shevek has been searching for, that has been eluding him (similar to the way that Shevek eluded Le Guin—catch me if you can!), arises out of a dream state. J.-B. Pontalis argues that a dream is fundamentally a maternal body and that the "illusion given to us by the dreamt dream is that of being able to reach that mythical place where nothing is disjointed: Where the real is the imaginary and the imaginary real . . . where skin is pulp, depth surface—but all of this in a *narcissistic space.*"[17] Shevek creates out of and for this space where nothing is disjointed: dreams are waking life, time turns back upon itself, a river flows up to the spring, the contemporaneity of two moments can be held in one's hands. When he separates the two moments, creates a space between them, he is able to write, to create. Although this is done out of a mythical place, where things are fused but not quite, he is able to disjoint the fusion just enough to create. The second the writing is done, that is, as soon as he has created a version of his identity theme out of a state which is as close to symbiosis as can be without being quite separate, he finds himself in the void. This compact passage is perplexing because it melds the overwhelming feeling of dissolution caused by symbiosis anxiety with the feeling of being doomed to "total isolation, as if . . . suspended in the void."[18] This feeling of separateness, which Le Guin experienced after writing *TD,* has to do with walls, and, in this case, they can be the collapsing walls of the womb and vagina that enclose and eject the infant during birth, which is the initial separation, the initial wall.

    After this experience, overwhelmed by his emptiness and isolation, Shevek begins to feel a need for others or some Other. "He wished there was a letter from somebody that he knew, or maybe somebody in the physics office to say hello to at least. But nobody was there except Sabul" (92). He discovers that a paper of his has been published but with two authors' names: "Sabul, Shevek." Obviously "Shevek was to do the thinking, and Sabul would take the credit" (95). Much to his chagrin, he realizes that he needs Sabul in order to make contact with the Urrasti. He is Sabul's instrument, "Sabul's man," as Mitis had told him he would be. But Sabul needs Shevek to keep his own reputation intact and to help him settle old debts with the more progressive Urrasti. This instrumentality for another, supposedly useful to a maintenance of identity, is too much at variance with the kind of mutuality that Shevek needs and that his social system is supposed to foster. It was "not a relationship of mutual aid and solidarity, but an exploitative relationship" (95). So he is left to ponder the fact that much of the work he did for Sabul followed Gvarab's ideas in Simultaneity; and he thinks of Mitis and the days past: "It seemed very long ago now, and so childishly peaceful and secure that he could have wept in nostalgia" (95). At this very moment, he passes Takver on the street. He does not know her name but remembers her as the girl who ate too many fried cakes at his going away party in the Northwest. He stops, "but the girl was gone around the corner. . . . Gone, gone, everything gone" (95). He begins speaking to himself in Iotic and then goes home unable to stop shaking. He huddles up in his orange blanket and tries to sleep. But he cannot stop shaking because he is under "constant atomic bombardment from all sides." He thinks that he is "going insane. Fear of madness drove him to seek help" (96). At a clinic his insanity is diagnosed as pneumonia. Periodically a woman comes to take care of him. "Let me alone," he says, "Who are you?" He tries to explain to her the cornerstone of his theory of Simultaneity. He speaks partly in the Anarresti (public) language and partly in the (private) Iotic language. He writes formulas and equations on a piece of slate in an attempt to further communicate. "She touched his face and tied his hair back for him. Her hands were cool. He had never felt anything pleasanter in all his life than the touch of her hands. He reached out for her hand. She was not there, she had gone" (97). (This passage recalls the cool security of the numbers and square, and echoes the "gone, gone" of Takver's disappearance.) Eventually his fever breaks and the woman comes and sits by his cot. She says, "How do you feel?" He replies, "New born." He asks who she is and she responds, "The Mother." He babbles something about rebirth on Urras, so she touches his forehead: "No fever." "Her voice in saying those two words touched and struck something very deep in Shevek's being, a dark place, a place walled in. . . . He looked at the woman and said with terror, 'You are Rulag'" (97). He shrinks from her "as if she were not his mother but his death." Yet he finds that everything about her person was "harmonious and controlled. Her voice was low, pleasant in timbre" (98). She is struck by how much he looks like her. She expresses her regret that she had to leave him as an infant but with her the "work comes first." She attempts reconciliation—"But we are brother and sister, here and now" (100)—which he rejects. She gets up to leave, saying, "I don't suppose I'll be back."

> He did not speak. She said, "Goodbye, Shevek," and turned from him as she spoke. He had either a glimpse or a nightmare imagination of her face changing drastically as she spoke, breaking down, going all to pieces. It must have been imagination. . . .
> He gave way to that fear that had come with her, the sense of the breaking of promises, the incoherence of time. He broke. He began to cry. . . . One of the old men . . . patted his shoulder. "It's all right brother. It'll be all right little brother." . . . Even from the brother there is no comfort in the bad hour, in the dark at the foot of the wall. (101)

The bulk of chapter 4, then, traces Shevek's trancelike experience, after which he reaches out for connection, only to find Sabul, a kind of negative alter ego. (It "occurred to him that he was getting to be like Sabul" [223]). This is followed by strong feelings for Gvarab and Mitis, and childlike yearnings for peace and security—all of which coincide with his meeting Takver, who is no sooner seen than gone. The only mutuality he finds is with his orange blanket. His temporary insanity leads him to the original object of mutuality, his mother Rulag, to whom he babbles in a private and a public language. For the autistic child the wish to be reborn is everpresent but hidden in his secret language because, to him, this wish is something daring and frightening.[19] Shevek does communicate in his language of equations and finds himself seduced by Rulag's touch. Then, in a complete reversal, he pulls back from her in panic and feels that she is his death. This is a common feeling for those who experience the two contradictory tendencies of the desire to unite again with the mother and the effort to forestall complete reunion, which may "prevent loss of identity and the personal death involved in total reunion with her."[20] This is also related to the panic that the autistic child, who had previously treated the mother as nonexistent, feels when his shell is threatened by symbiotic fusion or intrusion. Nonetheless, despite the pain and the fear, Shevek is able to maintain the separation.

Le Guin thus portrays those experiences or trials that are the foundation of the human individual. Lacan tells us that one of the images that is "always bound up with the elucidation of the earliest problem of the ego" is the " 'image of the body in bits and pieces.' . . . Such typical images appear in dreams, as well as in fantasies. They may show, for example, the body of the mother as having a mosaic structure like that of a stained-glass window. More often, the resemblance is to a jigsaw puzzle."[21] Hence the "nightmare imagination" of Rulag's face falling to pieces. The uncanny quality of this image comes from the mirroring experience. Rulag remarks how much Shevek looks like her. Later, Shevek, looking at himself in the mirror while trying on his newly purchased "skin," is forced to admit that, thus clothed on Urras, "his resemblance to his mother Rulag was stronger than ever" (107). The mirroring effect is reflected in the fact of Anarres and Urras being mirrors or doubles of each other. Lacan writes of "mirror reversal" and the "dream images" that "represent the patient's ego in its characteristic role; that is, as dominated by the narcissistic conflict." He further notes how "mirror reversals have often been pointed out in Phantom Doubles."[22] Lichtenstein, commenting on the Narcissus myth, argues that the primary identity is always based on a mirroring experience—"mirroring reinforces the identity delineation through magnification and reduplication (echo)," which usually indicates a second birth.[23] Winnicott claims that the "precursor of the mirror is the mother's face" and that ordinarily what the baby sees when he looks at the mother's face is himself. A positive mirroring process is essentially the mother "giving back to the baby the baby's own self."[24] In a nutshell, this is what is happening in the crucial Rulag-Shevek scene that ends chapter 4, although the "sense of self" that Rulag "gives" to Shevek is not a particularly positive and complete one.

The separation from Rulag, however, would seem to be complete. It is a fact of existence as we know it that birth involves pain. The separation-individuation process is experienced as a second birth, and one of Shevek's tasks in the novel, as he is creating variations on his identity theme, is to learn to accept pain. It is questionable whether he is ever able to do this. The "bad hour, in the dark at the foot of the wall," that is, the pain, the fear, and the isolation caused by the wall that keeps self from Other will always be present as long as he courageously strives to unbuild walls. Walls will always remind him of birth, of separation, of his isolation. Bettelheim asserts that "to be born again . . . is not enough for a full human existence. What is still lacking is the ability to be active: to deliberately reach out to others for warmth and affection, to dare on one's own to close the gap between self and other."[25] The action of the novel is an attempt to close this gap and, consequently, is a consistent variation on the scheme of separation/autism, rebirth, action, symbiosis. Shevek wants to break down walls, but he is also afraid of either finding only more walls or of losing the self in the Other; he wants, therefore, in accordance with Le Guin's identity theme, simultaneous separation and symbiosis.

After Shevek returns home from the hospital, he considers his situation: "His illness had made him realize that if he tried to go on alone he would break down altogether. . . . He had been keeping himself for himself, against the ethical imperative of brotherhood" (126). Henceforth, "He volunteered. . . . He attended. . . . He went with groups of cheerful young people" (126-27). Working for his society and socializing gives him a sense of communality, but it doesn't last long. "His efforts to break out of his essential seclusion were, in fact, a failure. . . . Solitude was his fate; he was trapped in his heredity." Rulag had said it: "The work comes first" (128). No sooner is he convinced of this imprinted isolation and work motif than he makes "a point of getting to know Gvarab better," only to end up "evading Gvarab when he could" (128). So he spends his time writing letters, attempting to communicate with other physicists and scientists on Urras. When he receives a response, he is elated for days, only to come back to earth again, "to dry ground." Just as he comes to the conclusion that "nothing he did was understood . . . nothing he did was meaningful. . . . He had come up against the wall for good," he meets an old friend, Bedap: "Shevek was over-whelmed by love" (131). Although Shevek was "pretty definitely heterosexual" and Bedap "pretty definitely homosexual" they take up a room together as lovers. They become instruments for each other: the sexual pleasure is mostly for Bedap while Shevek needs the companionship and trust. Out of their union Shevek experiences another kind of rebirth. Bedap "had changed Shevek's life and Shevek knew it, knew that he was going on at last, and that it was Bedap who had enabled him to go on" (140). Shevek works through the bisexual conflict (the child's fusion with a condensation of mother and father images);[26] at the same time, he learns about the limitations of his society and how it subtly coerces an individual to stop thinking for himself. With Bedap's influence, he eventually becomes a leader of the subversive syndicate. It is also through his relationship with Bedap that he finds Takver—"Intimacy after long solitude" (148)—and forms "the bond." He and Takver become a unit independent of the social group: "the meetings and the friends were peripheral to them." Although Takver's "existence was necessary to Shevek her actual presence could be a distraction" (152) from his work; he needs her but also needs his work. Yet he finds himself withdrawing from her as his book becomes more important. When she is about to give birth to their first child, he goes to find a midwife. He is gone longer than he believes necessary and begins to feel anxiety: "He went home, and at every stride the panic in him grew, the terror, the certainty of the loss" (195). Shortly after the birth of a girl, Shevek receives, with a "wrench," a notice of his new work posting, away from Takver and Abbenay. When he returns home sixty days later, Takver and the child are gone, Takver having received a famine posting. There "in the dark, in the silence, all at once, he learned what separation was" (207). He roams around the room in a fury; again, he "had come up against the wall" (208).

It is no coincidence that from this point on Shevek becomes increasingly critical of the Anarresti social system. Although he believes these postings to be necessary, he finds that the complaints of a neighbor "voiced all his own most despicable fears": "They're against partnerships, you can see it all the time, they intentionally post partners apart" (209). Before long Sabul reprimands him because his teaching and behavior reflect a degree of privatism." After four years of working against the famine and drought, he is reunited with Takver: "They came together, holding on to each other fiercely" (257). Following this reunion, Shevek decides, along with Takver, Bedap, and friends, to go to Abbenay to start a printing syndicate. Realizing now that their idea of State is a myth, he is going to unbuild walls in an attempt to create a genuine reciprocity of society and individual. The mutuality or reciprocity, it seems, can be found by communicating with the mother planet. This felt imperative is actually a simulacrum of what has been happening on Anarres since its inception. Darko Suvin writes, "Le Guin's future is lonely for the past, as ascetic Anarres is for the promises (the plant and animal creation as well as the people) of Urras."[27] Indeed, the entire project of the Anarresti is to transform their bleak planet—to become like Urras.

Subsequently, Shevek becomes the "soul" and the "symbol" of the syndicate. The syndicate is in favor of communication, potential union with Urras, while the opposition is in favor of maintaining the separation. "It was like an argument among brothers, or among thoughts in an undecided mind" (284). The strongest "opponent" and "enemy" of the syndicate, a personification of the wall, is Rulag, the person who engendered the original wall for Shevek. "She opposed the Syndicate of Initiative on every issue, including its right to exist" (284). (Significantly, the precipitating factor in infantile autism is the parent's wish that her child should not exist.[28]) Although Rulag and her group are able to sustain the policy of "no mixing, no contact" with Urras, they cannot prevent Shevek from leaving Anarres for Urras. But, Rulag adds, "Anyone can leave Anarres. . . . He can't come back. . . . A person coming from Urras is an Urrasti" (287). Her concluding statement reveals the bedrock of the action in the novel, an action which increasingly blurs the distinction between private and public concerns: "You have no right to involve us all in a risk that private motives compel you to take" (289). Shevek's personal conflict extends into and has ramifications for two planets.

With Takver's prompting, Shevek decides to make the trip to Urras. Interestingly enough, his personal motives are scarcely concealed. He believes he could finish his theory there; "Here I'm walled in. I'm cramped, it's hard to work" (304). There is, however, no guarantee that he will be allowed to return to Anarres since Rulag and the others might prevent him from landing. Takver says of Rulag: "She only knows denial. How to deny the possibility of coming home." To which Shevek responds, "That is quite true. That says it completely" (303). If he is allowed back but Rulag and company are still hostile, "We'll go live in Lonesome. . . . We'll make a new community. . . . We'll go make an Anarres beyond Anarres, a new beginning" (304–5). So ends the "past" part of the novel, the Anarres part. It ends with a separation and the hope of a return (rebirth) and a welcome reunion. If not, action will be taken for another rebirth and a new sense of communality-mutuality.

The separation, rebirth, action, symbiosis scheme that is worked through the Anarres sections is also enacted in the Urras sections. Shevek leaves Anarres on the space freighter *Mindful*. As the ship takes off, Shevek watches the liftoff on a screen. He loses his breath and his "body" cries out *"Not now, not yet, wait!"* He recovers from "the autism of terror" and he becomes

> clearly aware of only one thing, his own total isolation. The world had fallen out from under him, and he was left alone.
>
> He had always feared that this would happen, more than he had ever feared death. To die is to lose the self and rejoin the rest. He had kept himself, and lost the rest. (5)

The coincident feeling of self, as an entity apart from the "rest," and of rebirth, is followed by a doctor speaking to him in a foreign language, Iotic. "The words made sense." The doctor keeps saying "something about throwing rocks. But the rocks will never hit, he thought" (5). This is a foreshadowing (or an echoing?) of the child Shevek's theory (Zeno's paradox). And like a child, he receives a "measles vaccine," with some resistance on his part. Shevek is very much a child at times on Urras. He wants to read "books for children" (60) because he feels he knows so little. The first time he sees a bird "he stood in wonder like a child" (62). He is called "a child among thieves" (111), and his greatest joy is to visit Oiie's family and play with the children in the snow. Although he confronts the expected walls, he is at first able to overlook (look over) them because he does have a sense of himself as entity. With his long hair and his height, he stands out among the Urrasti, who are all short and bald. And he is "a galactically famous scientist," the "first visitor from Anarres," the "man from the Moon," and the "greatest physicist alive."

Slusser claims that when "Shevek leaves for Urras then, he is both leaving home and going home."[29] This is underscored when he first meets the physicist Atro, who says, "Welcome to A-Io—welcome to Urras—welcome home!" (54). He feels at home. "Not lost, not alien, but at home. . . . This was home indeed, his race's world; and its beauty was his birthright" (62). He thinks that Urras is "Paradise" (102). Consequently, "I want walls down, I want solidarity, human solidarity. I want free exchange between Urras and Anarres" (112). "We're members of the same family. . . . The Cetians. You and I: Urras and Anarres" (115). But things sour as he realizes that no one shares his ambitions. He begins to refuse invitations and increases his isolation: "as always, he had cut himself off from them. He was lonely" (117). This is quickly alleviated when he goes to visit Oiie's family for a weekend. Talking to a woman and being with children "was like home" (123). That night, sleeping in their house, he dreams of Takver: "He dreamt that she was with him in his bed, and her arms were about him, her body against his body. . . . They were on the Moon together" (123). True to form, however, he encounters another wall when, back at the university, he receives a secret message from a revolutionary group. He is unable to get in touch with them and feels helpless, "he did not know how to break down the wall" (156). This frustration is relieved by another trip to Oiie's. There he meets Vea: "He clung to her rather thin voice and mincing manner as to a raft in deep water, and never knew it, never knew he was drowning" (158). That she is a maternal figure is underlined by her talk and laugh that "broke like a wave, a dark, smooth, powerful wave that washed out everything and left the sand empty" (159); and, "she studied him smiling. . . . People do not usually gaze at one another intently at very close range, unless they are mothers with infants" (174). Away from Vea and Oiie's family, out in the "real" world, he keeps running into walls: "There had to be a door open somewhere on this damned planet!" (166). He escapes from his retreat in the university to the city of Nio Esseia, but this only increases his alienation: there he felt "very much alone" (167). Confused and frustrated with having to deal with store clerks and the exchange of money for commodities, he realizes he "couldn't go on this way." He turns to Oiie's sister Vea.

After a day of eating and browsing, he accompanies Vea home to her "paradisal party" (as she puts it) which, for Shevek, "began to be like a party at home" (178). Subsequently, to be like the others, Shevek begins tossing back glasses of the "pleasant fizzy stuff" (alcohol is not an Anarresti beverage) and getting into involved conversations about Time. He becomes frustrated with the lack of understanding and sympathy shown for his Unified Theory of Time. "You can't assert two contradictory statements about the same thing" (180) is one man's response. Conversation about abstractions evolves into slightly more concrete matters such as industry and politics. Again, Shevek is at odds with the general feeling, which is the need for authoritarian structures. Something "dark" (reminding us of the dark at the foot of the wall) turns over in his mind, and he begins a monologue which compares Anarres with Urras. He ends by saying, "You are all in jail. Each alone, solitary, with a heap of what he owns. You live in prison, die in prison. It is all I can see in your eyes—the wall, the wall" (184). Feeling dizzy, he staggers with Vea into her bedroom, which is dimly lit by reflection. "A high white bed bulked against the wall; a looking-glass covered half another wall" (185). Thus enclosed, Shevek is overcome by Vea's seductiveness. They hug and kiss and Shevek is ready for copulation but Vea is not. Despite her resistance, he "gripped her to him, and his semen spurted out against the white silk of her dress" (185). Vea reacts with disgust and Shevek blunders out of the room only to double up and vomit all over the platter of tiny stuffed pastries.

The "ludicrous and abominable scene with Vea" (which is a representation of the "libidinal flow" between mother and child, as Loewald would have it) is the deciding factor: he realizes, the following morning, that he is too unlike the others on this planet, and that he has locked himself in jail and must somehow "act as a free man." Now, for "the first time he had let himself think of going home as a genuine possibility. The thought threatened to break down the gates and flood him with urgent yearning" (220). With this thought of reunion, he isolates himself for eight days in his "gracious prison cell" to work on his theory; before long it becomes plain: "It was a revelation. It was the way clear, the way home, the light" (225). He experiences a form of rebirth by means of this discovery: "The spirit in him was like a child running out in the sunlight" (225). He eventually falls into a deep sleep and is found by his servant Efor, "lying half-dressed on the bed, his eyes shut, talking in a foreign language" (227). This scene is analogous to the one where, as a young man of twenty on Anarres, he experiences the spurt of creativity that lands him in the hospital. Efor, a sort of sympathetic Rulag, diagnoses the fever and takes care of Shevek, locked in his room (he refuses to be taken to a hospital), for the next few days. During this period, they form a bond of trust and when Shevek learns about the world of the lower-class Urrasti, he decides to take action. He escapes to Old Town where the leaders of the radical movement reside. When he finds the leader, he tells him, "I can't go home. So I came here" (236). He becomes their Odo, the "proof," writes tracts for various newspapers, and gives a speech at their major demonstration, in their language: "But he never hesitated for words. He spoke their mind, their being, in their language, though he said no more than he had said out of his own isolation, out of the center of his own being, a long time ago" (241). His speech is terminated by the clattering of police helicopters, which swoop in and open fire on the mob. He escapes and hides in an abandoned basement.

He makes contact with the rebels again, and they smuggle him into the womblike Terran Embassy, housed in the "River Castle" that stands with its drawbridge down and gates open. Safe inside the embassy, Keng informs him that she is the ambassador. "Her voice had an odd, singsong quality, but it was husky, like Takver's voice. 'Takver,' he said, in his own language, 'I don't know what to do' " (272). Two days later they have a lengthy conversation that touches on most of the issues raised by the novel. They recognize that they "are both aliens" on Urras and agree on most matters, but Shevek concludes, "You don't believe in Anarres. You don't believe in me" (281). They do agree, however, that Shevek's Theory should be broadcast to all the known worlds and that he should be taken home to Anarres. So ends the Urras portion of the novel.

Clearly, the action on Urras follows the same kind of scheme that we observed on Anarres, that of separation (autism), rebirth, action, symbiosis, accompanied by Shevek's occasional sense of entity or identity. *TD*, therefore, characteristic of all Le Guin's novels, keeps constantly refining and reworking the same basic dilemma. The final task of the chapter is to further demonstrate that this dilemma is fundamentally an artistic one. Always allied with the artistic predicament is the role of language; in *TD,* the problem of time is closely bound with the artist and with language. Just as the plot of the entire novel is a macrocosm of chapter 4, so too the artistic dilemma in the novel is a variation on chapter 4, which stems from the childhood scenes in chapter 2.

The main attraction for Shevek, after the separation scene with Rulag in chapter 4, is art. For Shevek, as for Anarres, language and identity are aligned with art: "Art was not considered as having a place in life, but as being a basic technique in life, like speech"; and "only the theater stood wholly alone, and only the theater was ever called 'the Art'—a thing complete in itself" (127). The art of drama on Anarres provides the simultaneous separation and symbiosis that Le Guin and Shevek search for: it rises out of and embodies "the isolation and communality of the Anarresti spirit." Shevek, however, is slightly ambivalent about drama: "He liked the verbal splendor, but the whole idea of acting was uncongenial to him" (127). After two years in Abbenay, Shevek discovers that music is "his Art: the art that is made out of time. . . . The music was a more urgent need, a deeper satisfaction, than the companionship" (127). So he has his music, his Art, which is equated with time; the art is essentially a language, like speech. With these things, and his perhaps more private languages of Ioti and numbers, Shevek needs no companionship—none, that is, except for those physicists on Urras to whom he compulsively writes letters "in a language he could not speak" (130). This is typical of the autistic child who communicates "through private signals, valid only to those who have learned to understand their meaning."[30]

Shevek's signals to the mother planet have to do with language (private language: numbers, physics, Iotic) and time, all of which is allied with the art-music metaphor. The equation of time and music is significant. His Square as a child, which can express by way of numbers what words cannot, is described as "a design in space like the design music made in time" (24). This Square was his solace, his balance, which he created and used to offset his isolation. The music of time is one of the keystones of Shevek's identity theme. The maternal figures in the novel are associated with music—specifically, the music that comes out of their mouths. The lectures of Gvarab, who is perhaps the main influence on Shevek's work, portray the "universe as a giant harpstring, oscillating in and out of existence" (94); Shevek is attracted to Vea's "tinkling talk" (159); almost everything about Rulag is "harmonious and controlled. Her voice was low, pleasant in timbre" (98); Keng's voice "had an odd, singsong quality" (272); and Takver "did most of the talking, and he listened as he might have listened to music" (261). The implication of all this is that the original relating of mother and child, which is a process prior to time and is the prerequisite for the experience of temporality, represents for Le Guin a timeless relation beyond language: "preverbal." This is what the musical metaphor refers to; it is a process, an interaction that cannot be entirely expressed in words, but which affects the child for the duration of her life. Bedap says, "Music is a cooperative art, organic . . . and by its nature, by the nature of any art, it's a sharing. The artist shares, it's the essence of his art" (142). Lichtenstein, we know, maintains that man has no identity, that it is a creative act, and that this "thematic identity will be 'developed' in the course of life as an infinite variety of identity transformations, as a simple musical theme is developed into a symphony."[31] Time, music, language, sharing, identity—Le Guin intuits a relation between these and refashions them into works that she shares with us.

TD can be compared to a symphony, and Shevek–Le Guin is the conductor. That Shevek, the galactically famous scientist, represents the artist, is not at all incongruous. Herbert Read, for instance, writes: "The first perceptions of what is novel in any science tend to assume the form of metaphors—the first stages of science are poetic."[32] In Shevek's case the stages are actual stages, dramatic as well as poetic. Drama is *the* Art on Anarres, complete unto itself. The only dramatist in the novel is Tirin, and Tirin is one of the "satellites" of Shevek. As adolescents, Shevek and Tirin stage a kind of play, a prison scene, in which Kadagv is imprisoned and Shevek and Tirin enact the roles of guards. Tirin, "a born artist," is considered crazy by their society's standards. He's a creator, someone "who's got to turn everything upside down and inside out." Eventually he is ostracized and finds himself compulsively writing the same play over and over. "He wanted desperately to talk about it but he couldn't. . . . When a man feels himself alone against all the rest, he might well be frightened" (263). Shevek is enthralled by Tirin because "he could never build walls. He was a natural rebel." Speaking of Tirin, Takver says to Shevek, "No wonder he haunts you. . . . His play. Your book." To which Shevek replies, "But I'm luckier. A scientist can pretend that his work isn't himself. . . . An artist can't hide behind the truth. He can't hide anywhere" (265). When they start the printing syndicate to publish Shevek's *Principles,* he insists on publishing Tirin's play because Tirin taught him what prisons are. And when Shevek decides to go to Urras to complete his work, he says, "It would help keep the Revolution alive—on both sides—wouldn't it? . . . What a crazy idea! Like Tirin's play, only backwards" (302). On Urras, Shevek describes himself to Oiie's family as a "nuchnib," one who doesn't cooperate, so he keeps moving on. He tells them, "I am a sort of nuchnib. I am here evading my own work posting. I moved farther than most" (122). On Anarres there is a conversation about various nuchnibi (one of whom was a "nice composer") who all "told such lovely lies and stories" (264). Shevek is admired by Oiie's children because he "told very good stories about the Moon" and because he represents something they cannot find words for, "only words that held an echo of it; the word *voyager,* the *exile*" (157). Finally, in addition to his partly insane, feverish states during and following "his moments of highest creativity" (165), he is often inclined to give vent to "his suppressed verbal fantasies, what Takver called his crazy streak" (200).

Shevek is clearly the rebellious, alienated, slightly schizoid artist (dramatist, liar, storyteller) disguised as the creative scientist. Christopher Caudwell, in *Illusion and Reality,* can make no distinction between the artist, who wishes to cast his private experiences in such form that they will be incorporated in the social world of art (in order to lessen the discrepancy between his feeling and the current acceptable forms of expression of it) and the scientist, who wishes to contribute something of his own to the changing symbols of science.[33] Shevek's theory of time is something of his own—it is directly related to his own way of being—and it definitely contributes something to the changing symbols of science. It will potentially unite all the known worlds by leading to the creation of the ansible (which plays such an important part in *The Left Hand of Darkness*). This theory, which is in his head and nowhere else, will make possible communication between planets light years apart. However, his theory, which is the unification of Sequency theory and Simultaneity theory, amounts to little more than a resolution of Zeno's paradox, the ramifications of which had nurtured him during his periods of isolation and creativity since childhood. He explains the gist of his theory to the people at Vea's party:

> But Sequency thinking also has its dilemma. It is like this, to make a foolish little picture—you are throwing a rock at a tree, and if you are a Simultanist the rock has already hit the tree, and if you are a Sequentist it never can. So which do you choose? . . . I prefer to make things difficult and choose both. . . . After all, the rock does hit the tree. Neither pure sequency nor pure unity will explain it. . . . [It is a] complexity that includes not only duration but creation. (182)

Choosing both—separation and symbiosis, difference (change) and sameness, sequency and simultaneity—is Shevek-Le Guin's primary identity; the unification theory is a brilliant and crafty variation of this, and it represents the dynamic transformation of the personal into the social, philosophical, and political. Two critics claim that Shevek's quest is a "quest to unite the peoples of the Twin Planets as he would unite Sequency physics with Simultaneity physics."[34] Another critic argues that "Shevek's search for the unity between Sequency and Simultaneity in the temporal theory parallels his increasing understanding of the complex relationship between the individual and society."[35] For Le Guin, this relationship is a creative one: neither pure sequency nor pure unity can hope to explain the relationship—it is a "complexity that includes not only duration but creation." At one point Shevek compares the passage of time to "reading a book" (178). Later, he explains:

> It is only in consciousness, it seems, that we experience time at all. A little baby has no time. . . . He does not know time passes. . . . The unconscious mind of the adult is like that still. In dream there is no time. . . . In myth and legend there is no time. What past is it the tale means when it says "once upon a time?" (179)

Time, or rather the absence of time, timelessness, is equated with childhood, dreams, the unconscious, myths, legends, fairytales. Obsessive rumination about the passage or nonpassage of time, Bettelheim tells us, is characteristic of the autistic child; one of his greatest desires is to stop time in its tracks, because time is the destroyer of sameness.[36] Although Shevek's theory will, ideally, balance sameness and change or difference, the primary result will be to allow space travel "without traverse of space or lapse of time." Therefore, Keng, for instance, "could find out what's happening at home *now*, not eleven years ago" (276). Consequently, the theory can "leap the great gaps," the gap between present and past, self and other, male and female, child and mother. It is essentially a wish to stop time, a wish for a timeless at oneness with some other.

Winnicott has written about how creative scientific work, like artistic work, is an intense experience of the intermediate area that goes unchallenged in that it belongs to inner or external (shared) reality. That intermediate area or transitional space is, too, a way of communicating that is really a denial of separation. What Winnicott calls the transitional object is a symbol of the union of the baby and the mother. This symbol can be located

> at the place in space and time where and when the mother is in transition from being (in the baby's mind) merged with the infant and alternatively being experienced as an object to be perceived rather than conceived of. The use of an object symbolizes the union of two now separate beings, baby and mother, *at the point in time and space of the initiation of their state of separateness.*[37]

The space and the object that comes to symbolize it represent a separation that is also a form of union, just as a wall could be said to symbolize that which divides and that which brings together (this is especially evident in *The Left Hand of Darkness*). Probably the most conspicuous transitional object in *TD* is the spaceship; it is neatly connected with the "curious objects" made by Takver that come to symbolize the union (and separation) of her and Shevek. They were "complex concentric shapes made of wire, which moved and changed slowly and inwardly when suspended from the ceiling. She called them Occupations of Uninhabited Space" (148). The delicate mobiles are described as moving with "introverted precision, silence, mystery of the organs of the body or the processes of the reasoning mind" (151). (Winnicott affirms that the object must be able to "move, or to have texture, or to do something to show that it has vitality or reality of its own.")[38] When Shevek returns home to learn "what separation was. . . . Nothing was gone. . . . Only Sadik and Takver were gone. The Occupations of Uninhabited Space turned softly" (207). Later, the mobile is described as "a curious object," which "came alive" as it "turned silently seeking its balance" (260–61). When a second child, Pilun, is born, Takver makes another mobile: "two thin, clear bubbles of glass that moved with the oval wires in complexly interwoven ellipsoid orbits about the common center, never quite meeting, never entirely parting. Takver called it the Inhabitation of Time" (295). Never quite meeting and never entirely parting: another variation on the primary theme and an accurate description of the intermediate space and its symbol. The description connects it directly with the spaceship and thereby, once again, private experience is transformed into something larger: "From the outside it was as bizarre and fragile-looking as a sculpture in glass and wire . . . it never traveled through any atmosphere thicker than interplanetary space" (306).

One final example of what Winnicott calls the interplay between separateness and union is the "interplay between originality and the acceptance of tradition," which is the basis for "inventiveness."[39] This interplay manifests itself in Shevek's melding of the traditional theory of relativity ("Ainestain's") with his own original theory; it is also revealed by his acceptance of Odo's theory of anarchism, along with his recognition that her ideology, in practice, needs to find more room for the creative individual. Shevek's experiences, therefore, have much to do with what Winnicott calls "ego-relatedness, at the place where it can be said that *continuity* is giving place to *contiguity*."[40] Continuity and contiguity, sequency and simultaneity, symbiosis and separation: Le Guin and Shevek explore the space between these extremes, sometimes tending to widen the gap, but always attempting to narrow it, bridge it, or eliminate it altogether. The unity that would come with closing the gap completely or unbuilding all walls is illusory; and the structure of the novel implies as much. All of the action in the Anarres sections of the novel leads up to the voyage in space in the opening chapter; similarly, all of the action in the Urras sections of the novel leads up to the voyage in space in the final chapter. So whether one reads the novel from front to back or back to front, in the past (Anarres) or the present (Urras) or both simultaneously, one will always end up in that space between two worlds—there can never be total unity.

Several critics have touched on this peculiarity and its ramifications. Slusser remarks that "the end seems to turn back to the beginning, as in a circle," and Shevek is "between two worlds powerless to be born."[41] Another claim is that "Shevek cannot be completely at home in either society. To be true to himself, he must, in Camus' phrase, be 'in revolt' against both."[42] Hence the ambiguous, open-ended "ending"—Shevek could finally get home, only to be in revolt again, but he could also be destined, physically as well as emotionally, psychologically, or artistically, to continue to roam that space between self and other. Certainly, on one level, he is seeking a midpoint between the best of Anarres and the best Urras has to offer. As Kingsley Widmer puts it, "Shevek searches for yet a different freedom than the too-narrow negative one on Urras or the too-rigid communal one on Anarres."[43] This different freedom could be found in Lonesome, where they might be compelled to make a new beginning, a new Anarres. Given the logic of the novel and of Shevek's unified theory of time, however, sooner or later the new Anarres in Lonesome would have to come to terms with the mother Anarres—searching again for the fusion of separation and symbiosis. Even if

Shevek were to be accepted into Anarres with open arms by all, there is still a loose end, which would be the beginning of another story similar to Shevek's. This likelihood is embodied in Ketho, the tall young Hainishman who wants to land with Shevek. He has studied Odo's works and has learned some Pravic, but Shevek warns him, "If you land with me, even more gets broken loose" (309). And, contradictorily, he tells Ketho, "once you walk through the wall with me, then as I see it you are one of us;" however, "You would find yourself very much alone" (309–10). In their final exchange at the end of the novel, Shevek asks,

> "You're sure you want to walk through this wall with me, Ketho? You know, for me, it's easy. Whatever happens, I am coming home. But you are leaving home. 'True journey is return. . . .'"
> "I hope to return," Ketho said in his quiet voice. "In time." (311)

What we have, then, is another young Shevek beginning a quest that corresponds to the one at the "opening" of the novel. The idea of border is being blurred as well. Rulag said that anyone who comes from Urras is an Urrasti. So there is an Anarresti who is an Urrasti and a Hainishman who is an Urrasti, hoping to become an Anarresti, ostensibly crossing the border. This is the novel's final attempt at uniting sameness and difference. The novel does "end," the way it began, with the idea of the badness of walls and the need to remove them; but the conclusion we are forced to make is that no matter how bad walls are, they seem to be necessary. Just as the child cannot be one with the mother without risking dissolution, so Anarres could not be unified with Urras without losing its (social, political, economic, philosophic) identity. The same analogy applies for Shevek the rebel, when and if he returns to Anarres. If the Kropotkin principle of anarchism is "individual/social symbiosis"[44] and if "Anarchist sociology means struggle between unity and separation,"[45] then even in the best of worlds there will always have to be walls of some kind, or at least some space between self and other, so that the two can be apart, together. If complete unity is an illusion, the alliance between individual and society will forever be an uneasy one, especially for the artist. Much to their chagrin, perhaps, Shevek and Le Guin might have to concur with Robert Frost that good fences make good neighbors.

Always Coming Home:
The Art of Living

I'm producing too many stories at once because what I want is for you to feel, around the story, a saturation of other stories that I could tell and maybe will tell or who knows may already have told on some other occasion.

Italo Calvino
If on a winter's night a traveler

Man should not dispute or assert but whisper results to his neighbor, and thus by every germ of Spirit sucking the Sap from mould ethereal every human might become great, and Humanity instead of being a wide heath of Furse and Briars with here and there a remote Oak or Pine, would become a grand democracy of Forest Trees.

John Keats
The Letters

Could it be, then, that speaking another's tongue we cannot be ourselves, that the search for the lost self begins when we have been translated into another and will not end until there has been translation, transformation once again?

Eli Mandel
Another Time

Always Coming Home (1985) is like no other novel I have read. Still, it is patent Le Guin. Though the most "writerly" of her novels (to borrow Barthes's term), nonetheless, like her other major works, *ACH* goes rolling and bowling about what it's all about. "A First Note," for example, which appears before the narrative begins, would seem to be just that—a note to the reader as preparation for what is to come. But it is a kind of reversal in that it makes the reader even less ready to go on; it confuses and decenters. Yet, like the rest of the novel, it has the curious ability to encourage an identification as well as an alienation effect. Moreover, it condenses the central concerns of the work. The first sentence is, "The people in this book might be going to have lived a long, long time from now in Northern California." This peculiar construction is a typical Le Guin (con)fusion: the people are neither present nor absent. They are present in the book, the words on the pages, but they are absent from the real world—they might come to be or they might not. Perhaps they are somewhere in the gap between present and absent. Furthermore, the reader is disconcerted by the time shifts from future to past to present. Just as the first sentence decenters the reader, the second sentence, which begins the second paragraph, decenters the traditional authorial persona: "The main part of the book is their voices speaking for themselves in stories and life-stories, plays, poems, and songs." This plurivocity suggests that a great many artists, creative individuals, are represented here, so the focus is no longer on that one exceptional creative individual of her other major works. We are then told that the book is divided into the "narrative" and "The Back of the Book," which contains "explanations." This ostensible division is one of the novel's misleadings, for there are many "explanations," "facts," and "histories" spliced into the narrative part of the text. In fact, as we might expect, one main project of *ACH* is to blur boundaries: art/life; fiction/fact; inside/outside; child/parent; foreign language/familiar language; nonhuman/human—how do these, or should these, interact? A parallel thrust of *ACH* is a subtle invitation to transgression—breaking and reversing laws, particularly laws of genre and gender. As we shall see later in the chapter, it is significant, when we can recall the sea (mother) versus the land (father) conflict in *Wizard* and *Lathe,* that the second *Webster* definition of transgression is "the spread of the sea over land areas and the consequent unconformable deposit of sediment on older rocks."

The third and last paragraph of "A First Note" opens, "The difficulty of translation from a language that doesn't yet exist is considerable, but there's no need to exaggerate it." Then we are told that, for example, the *Tao teh ching* has often been translated into English and that the Chinese have to keep retranslating it into Chinese at every cycle of Cathay, "but no translation can give us the book that Lao Tze (who may not have existed) wrote." What precisely is the relationship between repeated translations and the questionable existence of an author? One answer is that the writer lives by seeking her identity with each writing, creating herself endlessly but never quite succeeding. Lichtenstein and Holland have documented the strong connection between repetition-compulsion and identity. Similarly, Lacan believes that "narrative" is the attempt to recapitulate retrospectively the traumatic separation (the moment when the body senses its split from the Real), "to tell this happening again and again, to re-count it: the narrative of the subject caught in the net of signifiers . . . the story of the repetition compulsion."[1]

ACH is a translation from the language of the matrilineal Kesh society into English. It is important to consider the nature of translation, remembering that there is no need to exaggerate. Translation is an attempt to capture meaning from one language and carry it over to another language; it is a desire for two different languages to imitate each other, perhaps even an attempt to become one. Walter Benjamin points to the symbiotic nature of translation when he says that the language of translation must let itself go, "so that it gives voice to the *intentio* of the original not as reproduction but as harmony, as a supplement to the language in which it expresses itself, as its own kind of *intentio.*" For Benjamin, it is not the highest praise of translation to say that it reads as if it had originally been written in that language, rather, "the significance of fidelity as ensured by literalness is that the work reflects the great longing for linguistic complementation. A real translation is transparent; it does not cover the original, does not block its light, but allows the pure language, as though reinforced by its own medium, to shine upon the original all the more fully."[2] Translation, then, does at least two things. It attempts to articulate the difference (the different light) of the original language, but it also wishes to articulate a complementary relationship (as in supplying each other's lack) between the two languages. Another insight into the nature of translation is supplied by Margaret Waller. In the preface to her translation of Kristeva's *Revolution in Poetic Language,* Waller says that the translator's preface usually begins by assessing what is "lost" in the translation, and she adds that in "representing what is textually 'other,' the translation inevitably appropriates the 'alien' through the familiar. Indeed, inasmuch as it replaces the previous work, a translation is not only a transformation of that text but also its elimination: the homage paid is a covert form of parricide."[3] Translation is therefore an act that makes something different, alien, become similar, familiar. But while transforming (and attempting not to lose) and elevating the original, it eliminates as well. Given the fact that the word parricide means murdering the father *or* the mother (as opposed to the more specific patricide and matricide), we might ask if Le Guin is murdering the father or the mother, or both? This is slightly complicated by the fact that Le Guin is translating the language of a matrilineal society that does not yet exist.

The either-or, both-and, absent-present nature of translation is also traced by Derrida:

> A text lives only if it lives on *[sur-vit]*, and it lives *on* only if it is *at once* translatable *and* untranslatable (always . . . at the "same" time). Totally translatable, it disappears as a text, as writing, as a body of language *[langue]*. Totally untranslatable, even within what is believed to be one language, it dies immediately. Thus triumphant translation is neither the life nor the death of the text, only or already its living *on,* its life after life, its life after death.[4]

According to this description (prescription?), *ACH* is a triumphant translation. The text is neither present (the language and people do not yet exist) nor absent (they exist in the book, in the created language). Also, as quoted above, "A First Note" points out that, as an example, "no translation can give us the book that Lao

Tze (who may not have existed) wrote," so that "all we ever have is here now." This denial or perpetual postponement of origins, of presence, underlines a notion that Le Guin (and Derrida, in this context at least) subscribes to: the text is always already in process; there is no beginning or end; it is simply living on. Also, Le Guin makes *ACH* even more *at once* translatable *and* untranslatable by providing a substantial, fourteen-page glossary. The word that most often appears untranslated from the original Kesh is "heyiya." It means

> sacred, holy, or important thing, place, time, or event; connection; spiral, gyre, or helix; hinge; center; change. To be sacred, holy, significant; to connect; to move in a spiral, to gyre; to be or be at the center; to change; to become. Praise; to praise.

Although one of the above definitions, "Center . . . to be or be at the center," would seem to slightly undermine the decentering movement of *ACH,* most of the other definitions at once undermine any notion of a stable center. Heyiya betrays a desire for a stable center, but there is constant movement, a spiralling out of a center and therefore a potential displacing of it, recognizing its simultaneous presence and absence. And heyiya is *both* a noun *and* a verb.

Here are the final sentences of "A First Note":

> The fact that it hasn't yet been written, the mere absence of a text to translate, doesn't make all that much difference. What was and what may be lie, like children whose faces we cannot see, in the arms of silence. All we ever have is here, now.

A key word is "arms." In the arms of silence lie both the past *and* the future and both the dead *and* unborn children. The paradox, the aporia, is that the children are in the arms but they aren't—they have no faces, no identity. The arms also remind us of (or foreshadow) the fact that the Kesh towns are laid out in the form of a double spiral, because all Kesh have two houses: "in the Left Arm your dwelling place," when one lives with the immediate family, and "in the Right Arm," "your house, the heyimas." (The Kesh word for house, significantly, is "ma.") More than a center for worship, the underground room of the heyimas is where all communal activity takes place—work, study, decision-making, ceremony. Every Kesh, then, has both a private dwelling and a public one. In the center of each dwelling, each arm of the double spiral, is the Hinge: "for the center is the Hinge."[5] Hinge is one of the definitions of heyiya, the center which changes. Derrida too plays with "The Hinge *[La Brisure]*" which means both joint and break, and which therefore points to a presence only to dismantle it.[6] *Webster* defines hinge first as a joint and second as a determining factor, a turning point. The hinge, that which is in the center of the arms, like the faceless children of the past and future, is both a joining and a separating; also significant, I think, is that identity (or nonidentity), sameness and difference, is a determining factor, a turning point. This potential identity may come out of a (retrospectively remembered) center (or at least a desire for a center), but it is a center that is always turning, spiralling, living on, now. Being in someone's or something's arms implies a symbiosis. The anthropologist, for instance, who narrates the next short section of the book, "Towards an Archaeology of the Future," ends with some advice: the only way to find the Kesh is to "take your child or grandchild in your arms, a young baby, not a year old yet, and go down into the wild oats. . . . Stand quietly. Perhaps the baby will see something, or hear a voice, or speak to somebody there, somebody from home" (5). Out of this symbiosis, with Nature and nurturer, out of these arms, the baby (Le Guin? the artist as god?) will perhaps be able to find or create a people, a world, which is somehow connected with home. Finally, the pun on arms cannot be ignored. (One antinuclear slogan is "Arms are for hugging.") If we can silence the arms of patriarchal aggression, Le Guin is implying, we can one day become what the gentle Kesh are or will be.

All of the elements that are hiding, absent yet present, in "A First Note"—foreign language/familiar language, private/public, fiction/fact, past/present, child/parent, nonhuman/human, continuity/change, difference/sameness, and the reversal and blurring of all these—are evident in the central narrative of *ACH*. "Stone Telling" spirals through the book. It is the autobiographical narrative of an elderly Kesh woman of the Blue Clay lodge, whose personal history interlinks with all phases of Kesh activity. Stone Telling looks back on her childhood, when she was called North Owl and lived with her mother and grandmother, learning the rituals that harmonize with nature and studying the habits of animals. She is not totally content however; she is somewhat alienated from her people, largely because her father is a member of the Condor people, a warrior race to the north.[7] After he returns for a time, she leaves with him to live in his land. There she feels even more alien and, with help from her father, eventually escapes and returns to the land of the Kesh, where she attempts to make peace with herself and her family. Even though Stone Telling rejects the Condor, who are a reflection of us, and returns to what many would call a Utopia, her life continues to be a struggle as she comes to terms with her difference; she attempts to learn to be her middle name, Woman Coming Home, before she takes on her last name, Stone Telling, in conjunction with her husband Alder's new name, Stone Listening.

One astute reviewer contends that "Stone Telling" is largely a "coming-of-age story as the narrator recalls how, when young, she walked the mountains alone, tried to understand her Kesh mother and absent warrior-Condor father."[8] This, in a nutshell, is what the narrative is all about (and what all of Le Guin's narratives are about): a relatively solitary creative individual withdrawing into another space to speculate on a world peopled by mothers and fathers and children. The result is a constant dedifferentiating and differentiating process—becoming one with, becoming distant from, but always betraying a desire for oneness. Stone Telling opens her narrative with a comment on naming and a simile that reveals this movement toward oneness:

> Stone Telling is my last name. It has come to me of my own choosing, because I have a story to tell of where I went when I was young; but now I go nowhere, sitting like a stone in this place, in this ground, in this Valley. I have come where I was going. (7)

By "last name" she means the final name she will take on in her life: this implies a kind of final product, but it also implies a process in that it may only be the last name she has taken to date. Although being able to tell a story goes along here with having the power to choose one's own name, it is important to recognize that naming is, for the Kesh, intimately allied with Nature. For example, "babies' names often come from birds" (7) and to "go back to a first name is to go against the earth" (173). Regarding animals, Stone Telling says, "I learned not to name them" (9). She doesn't explain this puzzling statement, but a passage from a recent Le Guin story can help us to understand it. In "She Unnames Them," Eve unnames the animals that Adam had named:

> None were left now to unname, and yet how close I felt to them when I saw one of them swim or fly or trot or crawl across my way or over my skin, or stalk me in the night, or go along beside me for awhile in the day. They seemed far closer than when their names had stood between myself and them like a clear barrier: so close that my fear of them and their fear of me became one same fear. And the attraction that many of us felt, the desire to smell one another's scales or skin or feathers or fur, taste one another's blood or flesh, keep one another warm—that attraction was now all one with the fear, and the hunter could not be told from the hunted, nor the eater from the food.[9]

On the subject of naming, chapter 2 of this study concluded that naming is *both* a union with the maternal order (and defiance of the paternal order) *and* a separation from the maternal order (and inscription into the paternal one). Although the rest of this book has shown that Le Guin recognizes the need for mediation, she tends to valorize the union. From the above unnaming passage, which Harold Bloom says "might serve as a coda for all Ursula Kroeber Le Guin's varied works to date,"[10] it is clear that names (at least the names that people confer on Nature) act as barrier or separation. There is also the suggestion that men (Adam) see identity, naming, and separation as roughly equivalent, whereas women (Eve) see identity, (un)naming, and connection as equivalent. In *ACH*, naming is, I think, somewhere between Adam and Eve. Among the Kesh, both men and women are frequently named after elements of Nature, and there is no sure way to distinguish a man's name from a woman's. Nonetheless, a name does distinguish and separate who one is from whom one is not, and it usually designates *how* and what that person is at a specific time in his or her life. For example, when North Owl travels to the land of the Condor, she is no longer a child of the Kesh, so her father, a high-ranking official, gives her the name Ayatyu, which means "woman born above others" (186). When she is in the process of coming home and settling into a home, she becomes Woman Coming Home. And when she is a writer, she is Stone Telling. Her "telling" has to do with how she made a choice between living at odds with Nature in Condor or living with Nature in the valley of the Kesh. So her telling comes from the place of the stone; as she puts the simile—"I go nowhere, sitting like a stone in this place, in this ground, in this Valley." Out of this fusion with the earth, she tells of her difference and of her sameness. In this respect, naming is closely allied with the significance attributed to naming by North American Indians, particularly the Laguna, for whom all "names embody stories and confer identity. . . . They form connection with others, ties with the past."[11]

The emphasis on connection with Nature in *ACH* parallels connection with the feminine-maternal. Dirt, for example, as Stone Telling puts it, is "the mother of my mothers" (19). House ("ma") is the place of the mother; it is the woman's privilege to accept a man into her house or to reject him: this is significant when we are told that "this valley is our house" (35). The place between the "spread legs of the mountain" that overlooks the valley is known as "Granny's Twat" (15). And in Condor society, "animals and women were contemptible and unimportant" (345). The land, particularly the valley of the Kesh, as a female/maternal body, links with the child-parent reversal and blurring when North Owl, still a child leaving the valley with her father, begins "to feel the valley behind me like a body, my own body" (189). Near the end of her stay with the Condor, while she considers having a child, she "kept thinking that a child would be like the valley. It would be a part of me and I part of it; it would be beloved home" (349).

Stone Telling's symbiotic relatedness with the mother-environment is one that has involved and will continue to involve—as many feminist discussions of mother-daughter bonds have pointed out—not only intense gratification but much anxiety as well. The perpetual journey back and forth between dedifferentiation and differentiation that each of Le Guin's protagonists makes is a demanding one, partly because the typical Le Guin protagonist is atypical of her society. Stone Telling is no exception. She is the only person in the valley born of a Kesh mother and a Condor father. "Some of the children, illmeaning or ignorant, called me Hwikmas, 'half-house.' I had also heard people say of me, 'she is half a person'" (9). Division is the condition of being for her in the valley, as it is in the land of the Condor, where she is "a half-animal" (199). Nonetheless, Stone Telling grapples with and gradually comes to qualified terms with her division and her difference. This begins when she and her mother and grandmother make a small journey to the hot springs to treat her grandmother's rheumatism. On the evening of their arrival, Stone Telling, frightened and tired from all the new and different things she had seen, begins to cry. Her grandmother takes off the silver crescent bracelet she always wore and slips it onto Stone Telling's right arm. "I stopped crying. In the lodging house by the hot springs that night I slept, but while I slept I knew all night that the moon was on my arm, under my head" (16). Her grandmother, a weaver, is the only mainstay throughout her life. In fact, her first memory "of being alive" is of her grandmother's fingers moving "across the warp of the loom, forth and back, a silver crescent shining on her wrist" (8). In a sense then, by giving Stone Telling her bracelet, she is forming a bond, instigating a way of being for her—a way that is closely allied with being an artist (weaver) and a mother (moon). This theme that Stone Telling is to follow had already been set in motion very early, as the first memory implies, and now it is reinforced in the giving of the bracelet. Indeed, the narrative ends with Stone Telling sitting amidst her husband and daughter and grandchildren; she has been made "the grandmother weaving at the loom" (376).

Out of the original union with the maternal unit, she is ostensibly equipped to live out and deal with her potential difference. She has yet to pit this relative difference against any patriarchal or symbolic order, and that is why, I think, Le Guin reaffirms the continuity with the maternal just before the crucial and peculiar scene in which Stone Telling, with mother and grandmother at her side, meets the Condor:

> On the next day I saw the Condor for the first time. Everything in Kastoha-na was strange to me, everything was new, everything was different from home; but as soon as I saw those men I knew that Sinshan and Kastoha were all one thing, the same thing, and this was a different thing.
>
> I was like a cat that scents a rattlesnake or a dog that sees a ghost. My legs got stiff, and I could feel the air on my head because my hair was trying to stand up. I stopped short and said in a whisper, "What are they?"
>
> My grandmother said, "Men of the Condor. Men of no House."
>
> My mother was beside me. She went forward very suddenly and spoke to the four tall men. They turned to her, beaked and winged, looking down at her. My legs went weak then and I wanted to piss. I saw black vultures stooping on my mother, stretching out their red necks, their pointed beaks, staring with eyes ringed with white. They pulled things out of her mouth and belly.
>
> She came back to us and we walked on towards the hot springs. (16)

Her mother had been speaking to these men about Stone Telling's father, who apparently will be returning to the valley. Since he is "an important person," the men listened intently: "'Did you see how they listened when I said his name?' My mother laughed. I had never heard her laugh that way." When her mother says, "I tell you he's coming back," Stone Telling saw "white sparkles crowding all around her face, like flies of light. I cried out, and then I began to vomit, and crouched down. 'I don't want it to eat you!' I kept saying" (16).

This memorable passage is a difficult one to sort out, mainly because it conflates many of the central concerns of the novel. First, the idea of difference: clearly, before this meeting with the Condor men, who are symbols of the father, difference, separation, patriarchy, domination, and so on, Stone Telling already had some notion of difference within the sameness of the maternal valley; but it is not the extreme kind that the Condor provide. Nonetheless, her sense of difference is more than enough, within the context of a Kesh society, which does not operate on the need for strong difference or separation—men and women share many qualities and duties, particularly when compared to the dramatic division of gender and labor that we later see in the land of the Condor. Second, when her grandmother describes them as men of no house, we make the connection that the Kesh make between house and Mother Nature. Much like our own society, the Condor's is one that is in constant warfare with Nature; they no longer feel of it, so they pit themselves against it, continually raping and mutilating it. Third, when Stone Telling's mother "went forward very suddenly," we witness (as Stone Telling witnesses, for she regularly reminds the reader that most of what she knows about her life she knows only retrospectively) an acute form of separation anxiety. The separation, though, is not only of the child from the mother, but also of the child from herself. The mother's move forward into the symbolic realm foreshadows Stone Telling's crossing into the land of the Condor with the father. What Stone Telling sees is her mother (herself) crossing over to the area where the other half of Stone Telling (half-house) resides. But this other half is as seen in a mirror; it is reversed: the Condor society is the reverse of the Kesh (the Kesh believe that the Condor have their heads on backwards).

Lacan's notion of the mirror stage is that it provides the key to the *division* of the Imaginary and the Symbolic, and that it designates the line of fiction in which the subject constructs herself. It also prefigures the whole dialectic between alienation and subjectivity. Although the infant normally displays great jubilation at the potential unity she sees (retrospectively), there is anxiety involved as well. This stems partly from her confusion of her own reflection with that of her adult companion, but more so from the (retrospective) fantasy of the "fragmented body"—fantasies of aggression, mutilation, castration, reduplications of the penis, congenital abnormalities, and being devoured. Lacan adds that it also "appears in the form of disjointed limbs, or of those organs represented in exoscopy, growing wings and taking up arms for intestinal persecutions."[12] This litany of horror helps explain Stone Telling's "overreaction." Kristeva's extension of Lacan's observations also assists us in understanding how the idea of reversal (rooted in the mirror stage), which is the overriding concern and movement of *ACH*, connects with Le Guin's ambitious invention of a new language:

> To rediscover the intonations, scansions and jubilant rhythms preceding the signifier's position as language's position is to discover the voiced breath that fastens us to an undifferentiated mother, to a mother who later, at the mirror stage, is altered into a *maternal language*. It is also to grasp this maternal language as well as to be free of it thanks to the subsequently rediscovered mother, who is at a *stroke* (a linguistic and logical *stroke*, mediated by the subject's position), pierced, stripped, signified, uncovered, castrated, and carried away into the symbolic.[13]

Jane Gallop asserts that the "mirror stage is a turning point" in the life of the subject.[14] Likewise, Stone Telling's narrative and *ACH* turn out of and around the hinge, the gyre—moving together and moving apart (changing)—and grow from the need to "grasp this maternal language as well as to be free of it." The import of this turning point, the mirror stage, then, is that the child is or will be separated from the maternal (Imaginary) but that the maternal will continue to live on in the form of its own language (a stripped, castrated language according to the Symbolic) that is carried off into the Symbolic but is nonetheless always already present. So, although the child may jubilantly "take on" her specular image, as Stone Telling eventually does, it is still just that, an illusion, a trick with mirrors—the child never does attain the unity or wholeness that she believes she has or will find, and that is why the image alienates her from herself. Although the goal of "reconciliation" remains latent in this relationship, from here on the subject's intrapsychic rivalry with herself, discovered in the "discord" of the mirror stage, is "projected into the 'aggressive interpsychic triad' of self, other, and mediating object."[15] The theme of reconciliation—that is, the desire to discover the missing complement, the half (house) that was divided from the whole—dominates Stone Telling's narrative, but this theme is intertwined with the aggressive interpsychic triad.

Immediately after Stone Telling repeatedly says "I don't want it to eat you," she is taken back to the lodge, and then she goes to the hot springs with her grandmother: "We lay a long time in the hot water. It was brownish-blue and full of mud and smelled of sulphur, very disagreeable at first, but once you were in it you began to feel like floating in it forever. . . . There were no walls. . . . All the people there had come there for healing, and talked only quietly, or lay alone in the water singing soft healing songs" (17). After her confrontation with the mirror, the image of things as they are and will be, Stone Telling retreats, thanks to Grandma, to fusion with and in the womb of Mother Nature. But it is a fusion that contains an element of separation or autism. The final line could serve as the coda for *ACH:* the people lay alone in the water singing soft healing songs; there is a sense of together-alone, a community of solitary "artists" creating works that heal. Her grandmother bathes in the waters every day, and her mother "went along up onto the mountain" to walk in the "tracks of the mountain lion." Stone Telling, afraid of the crowded, common places of the big town, spends time with an old man, who teaches her her first song, one that not many people knew: "It is in an old form, sung alone with a two note wooden drum, and most of the words are matrix, so it is no good for writing" (17). This "Earth song" that must be sung alone, corresponds to Kristeva's notion of the jubilant rhythms of the natural language that are rejuvenated, kept alive, after the mirror stage. Stone Telling says, "It was my first gift and I have given it to many" (17).

Returning home, Stone Telling finds that when "we got to the bridge across Sinshan Creek I was seeing everything backwards. . . . I went around all the places I knew finding everything turned around. It was strange, but I enjoyed the strangeness, though I hoped it would not remain." When she wakes up in the morning with the cat purring in her ear, everything was where it belonged, and "I have never seen the world backwards again, or only for a moment" (18). Although she may have passed the mirror stage, or crossed over (the bridge) to the other side of it, she never leaves it entirely; it is always present (always coming home) if only for a moment. Another "moment" comes when she leaves for part of her initiation into womanhood. As her grandmother puts it, "you are now in the middle" (18). For this part of her initiation, she decides (following the path of her mother) to walk in the tracks of the lion. She walks up into the mountains, where she finds "Sinshan mountains facing me from the wrong side" (20). Alone, at one with nature, Coyote allows her to come into her house. She sings *heya* to the different elements of the nonhuman world, and they reciprocate. Four days later, she returns home to find her grandmother "spinning in front of the house, by the hearth" (21).

Stone Telling's brief period of being apart from the human but a part of the nonhuman ends when she is compelled to assume the image and symbol of her difference. She finds a condor feather lying between her feet (we are reminded of her mother walking in the still air with a "blue feather in her hand" she had found at her feet [15]). "It was dark, stiff, thin, and long. I knew what it was: it was the word I must learn to speak" (25). She initially rejects the phallic signifier of patriarchy, the symbolic, the language of the dominator, but then recants, is almost jubilant: "I began to feel proud that it had come to me. If I had to be different from other people, then let my difference be notable, I thought" (25).

Her father appears on the "first day of the wine," during the dancing and celebrating and enacting of "the reversal," when everybody becomes somebody else. The carnival atmosphere is broken by the Condor: "black and red condor-heads in rows, legs and hooves of big horses, gunstocks, wheels" (26). She meets her father, "a beautiful man," who knew only "parts and pieces of our language" (27). She is unsure of her feelings for him, but his desire for her mother, and her mother's desire for him, soon become her own: "he looked at her, perhaps not understanding much of what she said, but with so much liking and warmth that my heart began to warm to him." That night her mother is "full of beauty" and "full of power" (28). Paradoxically, just as she had come to value her difference, Stone Telling now relishes her sameness. Sleeping on the balcony that night, she is "like those children" who sleep on balconies when their parents wish to be alone. But this is countered when she says, "Since we human beings have to learn what we do, we have to start out that way [wishing to be the same as others], but human mindfulness begins where that wish to be the same leaves off" (29). Then Stone Telling the writer inserts herself directly into the narrative (she is almost already there in the above statement) to tell us that about a year ago when she approached a story writer about how she should go about writing a story, she was told to try to be as she was at the time of which she is writing. Then she tells us, "This has been a good deal easier than I thought it would be, until now, this place now, where my father has come into the house" (29).

Even though her father is "entirely different from" the men in his camp in that he speaks some Kesh and is a "daughter's father" (30), he does not fit in, will not be allowed to fit into the Kesh society. People from outside the valley are simply not welcome for long. Further, her father has too many notions that are "reversals"—that a man should do one kind of work and a woman do another, that there should always be a boss, that bridges must be built where convenient, that wealth is having not giving. Nonetheless, sitting on her father's high horse (which is much larger than any valley horse) "in front of the big man with the condor helmet," Stone Telling feels as if she is "not a child but something quite different, something rarer than a human being" (32). She has difficulty, as does her mother, accepting the fact that he must leave one day, because he "was home, he was here, our family was whole; now everything was as it should be, balanced, complete; and so it would not change" (30). Despite the idealization of her father, Stone Telling is not blind to the fact that he will never quite fit in; and when he gives orders to his obedient men, she "felt the great energy of the power that originates in imbalance" (32). (Again, it is not entirely clear whether these observations are coming from Stone Telling the curious and questioning child or Stone Telling the grandmother; since it is related in retrospect, we should assume that it is both of them, together.) As her father is about to leave, promising to return, Stone Telling can see the "pulling two ways in her [mother's] body" (40). But her mother shuts the door on him and from then on reverts to her "first name," her baby name. Just as he leaves, he turns to Stone Telling: "Will you wait for me?" She begins crying and nods. The first portion of Stone Telling's narrative then ends, as it begins, with grandmother at her loom, weaving.

Although her father later returns, and Stone Telling leaves with him, it is important to recognize that he never is able to break her maternal attachment—keeping in mind that maternal means or includes mother, grandmother, and valley. It is a fact of the Western world, and Stone Telling and her ternary relationship portray this accurately, that the father is normally too distant, physically and emotionally, to sever the child's bond to the mother entirely. Nancy Chodorow explains the father's failure to break the attachment to the mother:

> This "failure" is because of a father's own emotional qualities; because he is not his daughter's primary caretaker, but comes on the scene after his daughter's relationship to this caretaker (her mother) is well established; and because he is not that involved with his children, however idealized and seductive he may be.[16]

The father most often represents the feelings of escape and freedom that accompany the child's ostensible separation from the mother. Although the ideal love of the child for the father reflects the child's desire to be recognized by a "powerful" other as being like him, this power and freedom are, according to Lacan, illusory as well, mainly because they are symbolic rather than real. For Lacan, the "real" father in our contemporary social system is "most often a discordant, deficient, or humiliated father . . . who is incapable of sustaining his symbolic function as the Other who is the locus of the Law (the prohibition of incest). Consequently, the oedipal relation is more often pathogenic than normalizing in its effects."[17] While focusing on the epigenesis of the subject in and through the preoedipal realm, Le Guin's works, at their most basic level, offer a description and critique of the oedipal realm. It should be apparent that in *ACH* in particular, and in Le Guin's other major works in general, despite some "cognitive estrangement" provided largely by the location of the novels in other worlds and times, she consistently allows us to identify with those worlds in order that we may understand that she is *describing* (as Freud and Lacan did) patriarchy while gently subverting it, hoping we will subscribe to a potential (dephallicized) alternative. Many feminists do not recognize her project, in much the same way that they do not wish to discern when Freud or Lacan are describing the system and when they are simply writing subjects caught up in, deluded by, the order they are trying to explicate. Jane Gallop's desire that feminism join hands with psychoanalysis, then, accords with my feeling that feminists who dismiss Le Guin should join hands with her instead. Gallop contends that when feminism

> complains about men in power, it endows them with the sort of unified, phallic sovereignty that characterizes an absolute monarch, and which little resembles actual power in our social economic structures. This monarchic model of power reproduces the daughter's view of the father. Perhaps . . . the encounter between psychoanalysis and feminism, by dephallicizing the father, can avoid the pitfall of familial thinking in order to have greater effect upon the much more complex power relations that structure our world.[18]

Stone Telling's image of the father is, to some extent, that he is a monarch. However, her strong link with the valley, its rhythms, intonations, philosophies, usually helps keep her aware—although the young child-old woman writer relation still complicates this—of the fallacy (phallusy?) of this view. Her father is pretty much incompetent in the valley, partly because the Kesh will not budge an inch on most issues and partly because he has an empathetic side to him that causes him to seek compromise. In his own land, although he is in a powerful position, he is still a few rungs from the top of the ladder and is therefore regularly scrutinized. Even "One," the absolute ruler and monarch of the Condor is not aware of what goes on outside his lands and is blind to rising discontent in his own country. He created, runs, and is the system ("the Mirror of One could do anything" [341]), but he is deluded by it. Because of her division, Stone Telling is privileged to enter the Condor society and see this all for herself. For the most part, she remains immune to its machinations because she carries the valley within her, because she is the valley. It seems moot whether her privileged position (in the sense that no Kesh has ever lived in Condor society) and concomitant separation from the valley are due more to her mother or her father. Had her mother not married her father against her society's will and had she agreed to take him back when he returned, Stone Telling would not have left. By the same token, if her father had not married an "animal" against the interdicts of his society, and if he had not insisted on leaving with his soldiers, Stone Telling would still be at home. This double transgression leaves Stone Telling in the middle, always coming home. As the title implies, she is always in process, never quite getting there, in the space (Winnicott's intermediate space) between home and not home. A split subject, she will perhaps always be the unconformable sediment left on older rocks when the sea spreads over the land. The remainder of the story, however, implies gradual victory by the mother, a true return home. But there is much in the narrative that deconstructs this movement.

Stone Telling opens the second section of her narrative by reminding us of her mother's withdrawal and of her own strong commitment to her father: "My loyalty to him made my difference from other people a virtue, and gave unhappiness both a reason and a term" (173). One of the social effects of the Condor's lengthy stay in the valley is that the Warrior Lodge is rejuvenated. The men begin doing more things like "making weapons, training people in the use of guns . . . and teaching various kinds of fighting" (175). The female equivalent is the Lamb Lodge, and they too increase their popularity and influence. Although Stone Telling is content with making pottery, "playing" stories, and talking to the animals, she does join the Lamb Lodge, largely due to the fact that a young man, Spear (formerly Hops), whom she loves, had joined the Warrior Lodge ("I blamed the Warrior Lodge for taking him away from me" [183]). The Lamb Lodge women, like the Warrior Lodge men, are duplicates of their counterparts in Condor society. The men are aggressive and power-hungry, and the women are "loving, serving, obeying, sacrificing" (184). Spear is a substitute for the absent father, and Stone Telling has difficulty writing about his role in her life, much as when her father came on the scene earlier: "I do not think I cared for or thought about anything that year except Spear, but I do not know how to write about it. To try to remember that kind of feeling is to try to remember being very drunk, or to try to go mad sanely" (183). (Going mad sanely is a neat description of the artistic state of mind.) Despite her fervent desire to be with and like Spear, Stone Telling, paradoxically but typically, is able to retain some distance. She confesses that the whole year she "lived in the Lamb Lodge was a lie" (184), and she is sensitive to the insights of her grandmother, who at one point scolds her own frequently absent Warrior husband:

"You're trying to be like those Condor men, who are so afraid of women they run a thousand miles away from their own women, so as to rape women they don't know!" (179).

Stone Telling's father soon returns, and she meets him at the bridge. She does not want him to visit her mother because, as she puts it, "It was as if I was trading myself for her. I did not understand this then, but I felt it" (186). He then names her Ayatyu—"I did not ask the meaning of the name then; to me it was my father's kindness, my own freedom" (186). During the journey to his land, he teaches her his language. She has some difficulty with it, partly because of her "stupidity" which was actually "that I did not want to understand" (191) and partly because of the "reversal." At one point she (the writer) interjects, "what to us is disaster to them is their glory. How am I to write all this story in reversal-words?" (192). She cannot leave the valley behind and, "not being entirely a person, I could not become a different person" (193).

So Stone Telling remains the same person, at odds with Condor society but living quietly inside the many walls of the city with the other women, observing the stupidities of a society, much like ours, where almost everyone believes "that to be a person at all is to be separate from and apart from everyone and everything" (200). Nonetheless, Stone Telling, regarded by many as "an animal person, dangerous and crazy" (346), marries a man from that society. Never "alone and therefore always lonely," she kept "thinking that a child would be like the valley. It would be a part of me and I part of it; it would be beloved home" (349). Because the child that she bears is female, it makes Stone Telling a "daughter's mother": "Whenever I saw her pink flower-cunt I said heya in my heart, for if she had decided to be a son, that son would have 'belonged' to my husband and been a Condor" (351). The Condor priest names the daughter Danaryu, which means Woman Given to One, but Stone Telling renames her Ekwerkwe, Watching Quail. Two years later, risking his safety and reputation, Stone Telling's father arranges for her return to the valley. The final scene with him reinforces the mother-daughter fusion in the narrative. "He spoke with his head bowed to the child's head, so that I do not know if he spoke to her or to me. 'Tell your mother not to wait, not to wait for me'" (355).

She returns to Sinshan, crosses over the bridge and remembers her father. She says to her daughter, "Passing this place we may have him in mind in the days to come," and adds that Ekwerkwe "saw what my memory saw" (363). Back with her people, she finds that she "had not been willing to think that any change had come to them" (364). Her grandmother has died and her mother is withdrawn totally into herself and is "crippled" (365). Stone Telling makes a living by weaving on her grandmother's loom. She meets a man, Alder, who had "a gift of healing but was somewhat lame from a boyhood fall" (372). She eventually decides to "marry" him. At one point an ill-natured person comments that Alder "hangs around the dying like a buzzard," to which Stone Telling responds, "my husbands are all condors and buzzards" (375). Sometimes, like her mother, she wants to go "away up in the hills away from human people," but she remains with her husband, listening to him "sing, almost under his breath, one of the songs of his art" (375). After she becomes Stone Telling, he becomes Stone Listening. The relationship is a symbiotic one, but there are more than two people involved here. Alder's lameness, for example, identifies him with the lame grandmother (and, to some extent, with the crippled mother near the end of the narrative), who is also Stone Telling; and the suggestion that he is a buzzard or condor connects him with the father. Stone Telling's relationship with Stone Listening, then, recalls what Mahler describes as the child's need to "maintain or restore the narcissistic fusion, the delusion of oneness with the mother and/or father" which is often a "hallucinated fusion with the condensation of father-mother images."[19] It also correlates with Kristeva's notion of an ideal self which is based on "a pre-oedipal 'father of individual pre-history' who combines maternal affection with masculine support."[20] This return to the preoedipal realm (which Stone Telling never really left) is a return to a phase of gender that is not rigidly defined. Jessica Benjamin describes this phase while calling for its renewal:

> The child is still interested in identifying with both parents, in being everything. My point is not that gender can or should be eliminated but that along with a conviction of gender identity, the individual ideally integrates and expresses male and female aspects of selfhood. This integration then allows flexibility in the expression of gender and one's own individual will. That could be called an argument for androgyny or bisexuality—not a rejection of gender but a vision of reconciling the gendered self with the self that is bi- or supra-, or nongendered.[21]

This could be Le Guin herself speaking. Indeed, she has described her works (especially *The Left Hand of Darkness*) as thought experiments about the meaning of sexuality and gender. However, just because the people in *The Left Hand of Darkness* are androgynous does not mean that we will be or should be androgynous. "I'm merely observing," she says, "that if you look at us at certain odd times of day in certain weathers, we already are."[22] The thrust of Stone Telling's narrative, indeed all of *ACH*, is towards a rejuvenation of a state that we all proceed through and that continues to be a part of or latent in us all. It is a positive variation on Lacan's Imaginary, Kristeva's Semiotic, or the preoedipal of the object-relationists. These realms, however, as described by their theorists, are not punctuated by illusions of oneness, wholeness, completeness, and paradise. And a "return" to (or reexpression of) that earlier state is not a return to the mother, although a partial reading of *ACH* might suggest as much. Marlene Barr, for example, believes that with the publication of *ACH*, Le Guin "can finally marry her own right (in the sense of 'correct') revolutionary views with the left views of feminism." She continues:

Always Coming Home strongly signals that she now intends to make women the crux, or center, of her writing. Stone Telling directly confronts her role as a woman in society as she chooses to leave her father's patriarchal culture and re-enter her mother's matriarchal culture. In addition to focusing on a female character, the work can be read as Le Guin's own rejection of the Father and her return to the Mother. . . . Le Guin is at the moment and appropriately embracing the feminist viewpoint. . . . [23]

I think this chapter has adequately demonstrated that Le Guin is not "saying" anything radically different in *ACH* than she has in her other major works. The same overriding concern with separation and symbiosis dictates the structure and meaning of this work; certainly she continues to work imaginative variations on this theme, but there is no dramatic movement from father to mother. Her continued wish is to bridge the mother-father gap, dissolve the polarity. My quarrel, however, is not so much with Barr as it is with readers, feminist or otherwise, who wish to perpetuate the kind of dualisms that Le Guin is attempting to deconstruct and with those readers (usually the same ones) who fail to recognize that the signifier "mother" does not necessarily mean the biological mother of western history. In the first case, the dualistic oppositions, the warring elements of our society that Le Guin sets up into a dialectic—male/female, parent/child, conscious/unconscious, public language/private language, capitalism/communism, and so on—are organized in such a (Derridean) way that neither pole can become the center and complete guarantor of presence. Although we have seen Le Guin leaning toward the "communal," "female" pole, it is mainly to suggest that the lean in our society, which is too far to one side, needs to be redressed.

Susan Gubar has criticized some feminists for assuming the "interchangeability of the term *man* with a host of evils that include sexual violence, hierarchy, dominance, ecological exploitation, and racism while *woman* is identified with freedom, nurturance, harmony, supportiveness, the ecological interdependence of nature and human nature, and the erasure of discrimination."[24] One might at first think that Stone Telling's narrative and *ACH* itself are endorsing this kind of model. In Stone Telling's narrative, the "host of evils" are situated in the land of the Condor—patriarchy, phallogocentrism. The alternative to this, the valley of the Kesh (the preoedipal, semiotic), is, however, not interchangeable with Gubar's list of good things. It is a society that, by its very existence, is pitted against the other. But it is a society of men and women who, although often close to being in harmony with everything, are still subject to the limitations of human nature: there is conflict, there is suffering, there is racism, and Mother Nature is not always a comfortable bed-mate. The Kesh society is definitely matrilineal, but only in that "mother" is a signifier of a process that continually undermines, dephallicizes, and poses alternatives. Even though Stone Telling is a female character, her basic problem and concerns are much the same as Shevek's or Genly Ai's or any of the other male or female signifiers.

One cannot deny that much of Le Guin's work appeals to the part of the reader that wishes to reject the symbolic reality for the sake of a relatively controllable and narcissistically enjoyable picture of self and its relationship to its human and nonhuman environment. This relationship, which informs *ACH,* at first seems to be endorsed by Stone Telling's narrative, particularly by the ending. But even though Stone Telling and Stone Listening are linked with the world, by the very fact of their stronger link to each other, they compose a unit apart from that world. Because of the parent-child reversal and fusion, inside two people (who are one) we have a grandmother, a father, a mother, and a daughter/granddaughter, in addition to a husband and wife. This split subject, which inhabits at least two worlds, the outer world of the present and the inner world of the past, is further split by the fact that Stone Telling's daughter is part Kesh and part Condor. The Condor (or Buzzard-Alder, or Symbolic) is always already present.

In a sense, then, the family unit of Stone Telling and Stone Listening (which will perpetuate the split subject) is a microcosm of Kesh society. Geographically, the valley is a kind of peninsula; it is apart from but a part of the world. It has set up psychological and philosophical boundaries between itself and the Condor types; the Condor and their way of thinking, however, are not about to disappear. Like the autistic child, the Kesh refuse the language of the oppressor, the foreign language; they have their own. But language, by its very nature, will not allow equality, community, symbiosis. Since there are more signifiers than signifieds, there will never be a system of equivalent exchanges. Therefore Stone Listening as artist-healer and Stone Telling as weaver-grandmother (together but alone singing soft healing songs) will always be coming home, never finding wholeness, completeness, presence, always operating in the gap that is somewhere between the origin and the object—this, according to Winnicott, is the artist's territory. The grandmother is the original artist, the weaver. She is the one who imprints Stone Telling's way of being on her. And just as the grandmother is at odds with, while participating in, Kesh society—she is the main critic of the "evils" that are constantly creeping into their world—so too is Stone Telling. But since art is a basic technique in Kesh society (there is the Milling Art, the Cloth Art, the Book Art, the Tanning Art), all the members are equally artists who will, ideally, continue to undermine the "language" of their society in the same fashion that the Kesh society, by its very survival, continues to undermine the language of the Condor. The dephallicization is a perpetual process, even in Utopia.

Nonetheless, the main point is that the language of the Kesh redresses the language of phallogocentrism, even if it does not completely reverse it. The Kesh grammar, for example, has no provision for a relationship of ownership between living beings, and it is a language in which wealth consists not in *things* but in an *act* of giving. It is a language that does not fear separation from the mother; like Kristeva's Semiotic, it relishes its continued connection. Nor does it fear the parallel separation from Nature. We must imagine new languages and new worlds, whether they are entirely possible or not, and we must move, as Alice Jardine puts it, beyond the fear of falling back into the original maternal abyss and toward a "new access to the feminine."

> This (re)union with the feminine is the endpoint of History—u-topia—where . . . God and his correlate the Subject are dead, money no longer circulates, and the phallus, as the ultimate metaphor in patriarchal culture, collapses into metonymic indifferentiation. . . . It would seem to be the beginning of the end of patriarchal history and its result, a situation characterized by Philippe Sollers as that of "Puppet-men, women struck with terror, with respect to the virtual one-woman who reaches toward the loneman seen as god who does not exist."[25]

Although the Kesh do have a history, which they can tap into by means of the Exchange, they pay little attention to it. They are who they are, of course, partly because the radiation and chemical pollution of a past "civilization" has left a legacy of uninhabitable land and genetic diseases, and earthquakes and continental drift have moved the valley to the coast. But their various activities are largely responses to and relationships with Nature rather than history. The attitude towards history in *ACH*, then, is that it is a destructive realm that challenges the wholeness that these creative valley people can imagine in their reciprocal relationship with Nature. The Kesh refusal to name elements of Nature, and the fact that no creature or thing or person has any more worth than another, contributes to the contention that the strongest movement of *ACH* is towards an ideal of undifferentiation, which corresponds to the stage of a magical and animistic thought mode when the "primitive" man and the young child have no sense of difference between self and other, subject and object worlds. The bonding of person with bio-regional place, which is a kind of imprinting of place after the model of the mother, has profound political-ecological ramifications. As the different boundaries are dissolved—between human/nonhuman, male/female, symbolic/imaginary, and so on—radical cultural transformation can take place. Yet, although Le Guin tries to create an image of wholeness, an undifferentiating Imaginary self-sufficiency, she cannot help but simultaneously represent the sense of our (and her characters') division through the gaps she is trying to close. With whatever principle of undifferentiation that exists in Le Guin's discourse, then, also enters the realization of the impossibility of undifferentiation, the inevitability of (often alienating) dedifferentiation as long as there is language. Nonetheless, an alternate, creative, healing language is always already at work.

I would like to end this discussion of *Always Coming Home* by briefly considering its notion of the interrelationship between art and life. This interrelationship, again, is not much different from that presented in Le Guin's earlier works; it is a slightly more sophisticated elaboration. By displacing aesthetic hierarchies and generic categories, Le Guin seems to be calling for a cultural renovation that is neither utopian nor apocalyptic. Modern technology has destroyed many parts of this future world, but the Kesh have been able to separate themselves from an aggressive, destructive, technologically justified progress that they believe is not compatible with creative intelligence. They are selective. They take one computer Exchange when they can have nine, and though they have electricity, they continue to plow with oxen. Although we might question their concern with sameness, their almost complacent isolation—"The rest of the world was not a matter of very urgent concern to most people of the Valley"(453); "They were mostly not very happy about travelling anywhere" (475)—we have to remember that it is this isolation that allows them to maintain a creative and symbiotic relationship with the land that gives them their identity.

The Kesh identity, like Le Guin's, is symbolized by the hinge *(iya)*, "the center of a spiral, the source of a gyring motion; hence a source of change, as well as a connection" (489). Life stories or autobiographies, like Stone Telling's, are common in the valley, and they partake of fiction and fact. They "were a 'hinge' or intersection of private, individual, historical lived-time with communal, impersonal, cyclical being-time" (263). And the hinge is the center of a word and process: it is the iya in "heyiya-if, two spirals centered upon the same (empty) space." It is an "inexhaustible metaphor . . . the visual form of an idea which pervaded the thought and culture of the Valley" (45). An entire culture, then, is created out of a kind of simultaneity—changing, connecting, turning, dividing, *determining*. The hinged spiral or heyiya-if "is connected with a fundamental grammatical maneuver of the language" (44), and it is inscribed everywhere in *ACH:* in the formation of the various stories and rituals, in the assembly of a theatrical stage, in the building of a town, and in the many line drawings by Margaret Chodos. This is the identity theme, wheeling and reeling, twirling and gyring, always the same but always moving, omnipresent. Any "change" that takes place in Kesh society, then, is always within and always only a variation on what already is. This correlates with a mode of thought that can be found in primitive (and therefore, to Le Guin, highly advanced) cultures (and often in healthy children of our own culture). For instance, Paul Radin says that for the primitive man, "a mountain is not thought of as a unified whole. It [Granny's Twat] is a continually changing entity." Such a man lives in a world that is dynamic and ever-changing; since "he sees the same objects changing in their appearance from day to day, the primitive man regards this phenomenon as definitely depriving them of immutability and self-subsistence."[26] The slightly more advanced Kesh, however, as represented by the heyiya-if, see change as involving continuity rather than complete discontinuity. But this notion is due to Le Guin the artist imposing herself, being the god of her world. And, like Pandora, she observes this world and then becomes it. The artist (and therefore all Kesh, all split-off fragments of Le Guin) explores and attempts to bridge that space between continuity and discontinuity. This is underlined by part of a poem in *ACH* entitled "Artists":

What do they do,
the singers, tale-writers, dancers, painters, shapers, makers?
They go there with empty hands,
into the gap between.
They come back with things in their hands.
They go silent and come back with words, with tunes.

. . . .

The ordinary artists
  . . . delight in tools,
delight, and with these as their way
they approach the gap, the hub,
approaching in circles, in gyres,

. . . .

they describe the center,
though they cannot live there. (74–75)

I do not think that Le Guin is questioning the ontological status of art and artist in society. She is quite simply saying that the artist is and can be (and become) all people, "a choir of Valley voices, men and women, old and young" (263); simultaneously, all people are ordinary artists—or at least they can be if they take technology into their own hands. This desire, this desperate political need perhaps, to reintegrate art and life is, of course, not a novel idea. Andreas Huyssen reminds us that the goal of the historical European avant-garde (Dada, early surrealism) was "to undermine, attack and transform the bourgeois institution art and its ideology of autonomy."[27] Given what we know of Le Guin, we can certainly see why the notion of taking a separate autonomous view of art and merging it with life would be so attractive to her. But we also know that she knows there will always be a gap between art and life.

8

The Personal *Is* the Political

What I'm experiencing cannot be called an identity-crisis. In order to experience an identity-crisis, one must first have enjoyed some sense of identity. The tradition of the mad genius in literature. The tradition of the double in literature. The tradition of the story within the story, the tradition of the mad editor of the text, the tradition of the unreliable narrator.

John Barth
Chimera

The way to deal with the problem of "subjectivity," that shocking business of being preoccupied with the tiny individual who is at the same time caught up in such an explosion of terrible and marvellous possibilities, is to see him as a microcosm and in this way to break through the personal, the subjective, making the personal general, as indeed life always does, transforming a private experience . . . into something larger.

Doris Lessing
The Golden Notebook

One of this study's initial propositions was that Le Guin's work is a serious and successful effort to stretch or break through older conventions and to probe areas of experience that are not approached by "realistic" fiction. Le Guin's fictions—along with those of Lem, Delany, Nabokov, Calvino, Barth, and others—register an effective attack on the categorical rigidities which are constantly being imposed on prose fiction. Because of this overcategorization, the fate of some writers who use approaches similar to Le Guin's (she regards science fiction as the "most flexible, adaptable, broad-range, imaginative, crazy form prose fiction has ever attained")[1] has been to be pigeonholed more often than read. What this kind of fiction has needed, therefore, is to be taken seriously, *text by text,* and analyzed in light of what we know of the human mind and the peculiar demands of prose fiction.

The ambiguous and problematical relationship of the self to models of all sorts—political, social, mythological, linguistic, psychological—is a major concern of contemporary fictionalists. This relationship can be boiled down to the paradox expressed by Whitman: how to combine the idea of flowing together, a loving "ensemble," with the "centripetal isolation of a human being in himself."[2] The paradox is that of identity (particularly as it is formed or not formed, by or against language): sameness and difference, symbiosis and separation. The dilemma and quest of the "hero" of the contemporary novel, it has been argued, are analogous to those of the author. This study has, in Le Guin's case at least, borne this out. Le Guin's protagonists are, typically, "lonely, isolated, out on the edge of things." Le Guin herself confesses, "I am pretty much a lone wolf, always have been." And she says that she was "a very unusual person," one who never quite fit in: "I wasn't—you know, I never—my sweaters were never quite the right length or color. I never could do it right."[3]

In her novels, the most prevalent phrase for the situation of her protagonists is "cut-off." Cut-off suggests a final separation, as if a limb were severed from the body. This connoted dismemberment begs the questions, what body? whose body? Two logical answers are the body politic and the mother's body. Yet, almost as typical as the isolation of Le Guin's protagonists is their periodic "involvement"—there is always a tether of some sort that connects them to the other. For example, Ged, in *A Wizard of Earthsea,* never feels a part of the human world at large, the world of trade and commerce. But he does have a close involvement with the nonhuman environment that nurtures and sustains him. As a wizard, his creative relationship with the nonhuman world, a relationship that few others have, makes him someone special; a wizard's staff gains him free room, board, and "passage" almost anywhere he goes. His personal struggle with the shadow can have public ramifications: although he wants to become one with the shadow, so that he can feel whole and free, this act of union concomitantly saves the human world at large from a potentially destructive creature. Genly Ai, in *The Left Hand of Darkness,* is a stranger on a foreign planet. Due to things such as language, color, body size and, most importantly, sex, he can never feel a part of the societies to which he is ostensibly committed. He comes to enjoy his isolation, however, when he unites with his double, Estraven. Ai, like Ged, is special; he is the Envoy, the Mobile, one who has a creative mission—to unite two countries on one planet with a larger body of planets. George Orr, in *The Lathe of Heaven,* is a nondescript milquetoast who only wants to be left alone. But his unique power to dream-create new worlds obliges him to become involved, or at least concerned, with his creations. He is finally compelled to *act,* to restore continuity to a world that is being torn asunder. Shevek, the galactically famous creative scientist in *The Dispossessed,* feels cut-off from both Anarres and Urras. He prefers his private world of numbers to the irritating world at large. However, his personal obsession—to unify the theories of Sequency and Simultaneity—becomes a public one: to unite the mother planet of Urras with the child planet Anarres. Stone Telling, the subject of the central narrative within *Always Coming Home,* is often called "half-house" because she is the only child, in her society, of a Kesh woman and a Condor man. She is painfully aware of her difference but eventually comes to consider it a virtue. When she moves to the land of the Condor she is regarded as half animal. But, like the rest of the women of that society, she is isolated inside the city walls with little to do. Her difference and relative isolation from each society, however, give her the perspective to clearly describe and criticize them both. Because she is the only person ever to have lived in the two worlds, she is required to write her life story, so that her society (and perhaps even the Condor society) will learn and benefit from her experience.

Each of Le Guin's protagonists, then, although cut-off from his or her respective society and often cherishing that isolation, is compelled to seek an antidote to this separation. The opposition to the isolation or separation manifests itself in a striving for union with some personal, private other (or mother)—shadow and Yarrow in *Wizard;* Estraven and Faxe in *LHD;* Heather and Alien in *Lathe;* Odo and Takver in *TD;* Alder and Valley in *ACH*—which ultimately transforms into a striving or yearning for social unity, communion with others. This antinomy is the foundation of the artist *engagé* who desires to change the world (or at the very least hopes her creations will have some effect on outward reality) into a collectivity of creative brothers and sisters, yet wants to remain detached, in her own private space, with some semblance of entity that would be lost or subsumed by the push and press of business and politics. To say, however, that the role of Le Guin's protagonists is a metaphor of the artist in the world is not enough. One needs evidence. In search of this evidence, I found that I was obliged to consider the dynamics involved in the artist's dilemma. This dynamics, which is essentially the conflict between separation/autism and symbiosis, and the attempt to establish boundaries between self and other, inside and outside, dictates the movement and structure of each novel. Characteristically, the movement is from union to separation and back again, and from barrier to barrier in an attempt to remove or blur boundary distinctions but with a reluctant recognition of their necessity. For example, in a novel not discussed in this study, *The Beginning Place* (1980), which I consider to be somewhere between her major and minor works, Hugh, an isolated young man, unites with Irena in order to move more freely across the border that separates the private (inner) world from the public one. In the private land, the language of which contains no word for border, he removes the "thing" that has divided the people. But at the end of the novel there is the implication that it is sometimes better that the gate to the other world be closed. Le Guin's novels go "rolling and bowling about what they're all about," constantly refining and reworking the same crucial dilemma.

The dilemma is a fundamentally human one—that of identity—but more specifically it is that of the identity of the artist, whose problems are analogous to those of the autistic child. To say that the artist is like the autistic child may sound ludicrous. Yet like the autistic child, the artist moves into her own private reality, largely to create; in her fantasy world she (the artist or "autist") can affect reality, influence the inner environment, away from the symbiotic unit. This fantasy world, moreover, is a re-creation of the experienced symbiosis with the mother-environment-community and the problems involved in allaying the threat of total dissolution. Indeed, Le Guin, in a recent article, asks, "Why do we tell tales, or tales about tales—why do we bear witness, true or false? We may ask Aneirin, or Primo Levi, we may ask Scheherazade, or Virginia Woolf. Is it because we are so organized as to take actions that prevent our dissolution into the surroundings?"[4] And Robert Kiely reminds us that "even Robinson Crusoe dealt with isolation by re-creating the conditions of the society from which he had been separated."[5] Furthermore, if George Steiner's strong argument that we, especially artists, are moving toward a kind of autism is valid, then there is a need to continue to investigate this term, particularly when Steiner contends that the "study of the evolution of language is the study of the human mind itself," and concludes that "the problem of Babel is quite simply, that of human individuation."[6] While we all pass through an autistic phase, some, such as the artist, experience this phase more intensely; and, in keeping with the solidarity of memory and imagination, the artist brilliantly integrates this very early phase of ego-reality into forms of higher organization. Although the descriptions of the autistic child and its mechanisms by various investigators (mainly psychoanalytic) are markedly akin to Le Guin's protagonists, I will merely suggest that, at the very least, there is a rough or graded analogue between the autistic child and the artist—not always a close similitude or total coincidence of characteristics.

The autistic operation, like the artistic operation, is essentially a linguistic one. This is one of the main thrusts of Le Guin's discourse. The juxtaposition of her discourse with that of contemporary psychoanalytic discourse reveals that, with amazing insight and accuracy, she is portraying the experiences and trials that are the foundation of the individual, particularly the creative individual in her relationship to language. Close scrutiny of Le Guin's texts, which are so preoccupied with balance or equilibrium, allows us to define, or redefine, autism as it relates to the artist and the Symbolic order of language. Autism is a form of separation from the potentially overwhelming mother-environment that is not the same kind of separation instigated by public language, which is abrupt and which fragments identity. The autistic operation, the movement of which appears to be toward isolation, is paradoxically an attempt at two kinds of balance. First, it questions public language—puts it on hold, keeping it in check or balance—and invents its own private, neologistic language (True Speech; mind-speech; dream language or Barsoomian bisyllable; the cool language of numbers; the language of the Kesh), which allows it some semblance of identity. Second, it spurns the potentially overwhelming world of the mother-environment but balances this by a re-creation of that symbiotic world of fusion and oneness in its own fantasy world—this is the world of each Le Guin novel, typified by its qualified search for union.

The autistic/artistic operation is a peculiarly beautiful but unique and puzzling sort of compromise: one is neither assimilated by the Symbolic order (public language, paternal discourse) nor by the Imaginary order (or oversymbiosis). It is a form of separation that is a *(created)* union, and it can have the same kind of potentially liberating force as Kristeva's Semiotic. Just as Kristeva takes pains to set up a dialogue between the preoedipal Semiotic and the Symbolic, Le Guin too interpenetrates the private realm with the public one. Her work consistently moves toward a union of opposites, of differences. I would, however, agree with Lacan that complete unity is an illusion, and Le Guin's protagonists, despite all appearances, never achieve the kind of unity for which they, and Le Guin, strive. Le Guin's texts operate in a kind of middle area: they imply that we are not helpless before some inevitable destiny, but that also we cannot engineer a perfect (communal) future. The longings of her characters, therefore, cannot be realized in life. The structure of her novels reveals or betrays this, and that is one reason why the novels avoid closure—another story needs to be told, another attempt at union begun. So a novel ends and is still not completed, not a product, not a separated object. Identity must be constantly created; that which is creative must create itself. When the struggle to realize the self is ended, so is one's life.

Le Guin's identity theme is probably "stated" as well as it can be in the preceding definition of autism, which was the result of a juxtaposition of her discourse with contemporary psychoanalytic discourse. It is Le Guin's way of portraying the artistic paradox: how to be isolated—in a private world which nourishes continuity and creativity mainly by way of a private language—without having to be insulated, from the other, from the world of pointless change, from people and potential "progress." Another way of putting it is to say that Le Guin portrays the desire for simultaneous separation and symbiosis; she creates out of this simultaneity, or at least out of the "potential space" that may exist before or after the union. Yeats once said, "I have often had the fancy that there is some one Myth for every man, which, if we but knew it, would make us understand all he did and thought."[7] Whatever work Le Guin does will be a variation on that one "Myth." The working of the identity theme through the novels proves to be the homologue for all the various concerns and devices of the novels. This theme constantly manifests itself, germinating and informing theme and structure, acting as the narrative within the narrative. All of the following are subsumed under the rubric of identity: the obsessive nature of her protagonists and their temporary bouts with insanity; doubling of characters; the use of boundaries and the distinction or lack of distinction between inside and outside, self and other; the ubiquitous oral imagery—images of food and eating as well as of being engulfed, devoured, or overwhelmed; omnipotence and the magic power of words; and the polarities from which each novel builds and rebuilds: dream-reality, rebirth-death, stasis-action, continuity-change, creativity-destructiveness, female-male, private communication/language-public communication/language.

A knowledge of the dynamics of identity in Le Guin's canon also helps us to understand her predilection for male protagonists, which has been questioned by some feminist critics. It is not, it seems to me, a simple matter of her being co-opted by male or paternal discourse. She creates according to the image that presents itself to her and insists on its elaboration. This image is intimately allied with her identity theme. With this in mind, there can be several reasons for the "choice" of male "heroes." 1) Because of the kind of woman-person-artist that she is, her way of symbolizing one of the things she is looking for—the principle of maleness and femaleness combined into a wholeness (most clearly evidenced by *The Left Hand of Darkness)*—is through males: the unity or wholeness is there at its inception, where she aligns herself with her protagonists; female-artist is at one with male-protagonist-artist. 2) This unsuccessful search for wholeness through male protagonists is also paradoxically a kind of distancing, which is ultimately a separation (the male is different, apart from the female) that is a form of union (the protagonist is a part of me). 3) Since her identity theme is instigated in the preverbal, preoedipal stage, where there is little or no gender distinction (the bisexual situation is particularly prominent in the symptomatology of the autistic-symbiotic antinomy), and since she is so insightfully recording that experience, it seems reasonable that gender will be flexible; indeed, her protagonists are hardly traditional male characters, and they invariably have many "female" characteristics. 4) A component of bisexuality—and the double paradigm of childhood schizophrenia, autistic and symbiotic—is the preoedipal child's condensation of the mother-father images. We have observed this throughout the study. This fusion-confusion is underscored by Le Guin, who, in a preface to her story "Winter's King," tries to explain why she used the feminine pronoun for all Gethenians, while preserving such masculine titles as King and Lord, "just to remind one of the ambiguity":

> The androgyny of the characters has little to do with the events of the story, but the pronoun change does make it clear that the central, paradoxical relationship of parent and child is not, as it may have seemed in the other version, a kind of reverse Oedipus twist, but something less familiar and more ambiguous. Evidently my unconscious mind knew about the Gethenians long before it saw fit to inform me. It's always doing things like that.[8]

This "something less familiar" is one reason why Le Guin's writing strikes such a deep chord in us (male and female). It is a chord tracing back to experiences in our own individual lives, preverbal experiences unformulatable directly in our memories, when we were struggling along a path towards our status as persons. A sophisticated revival of this early experience, in which there is little or no gender distinction, can, while recognizing some difference, break down walls between people and not allow the discourse of one to rule over the other. Jane Gallop writes, "This problem of dealing with difference without constituting an opposition may just be what feminism is all about (might even be what psychoanalysis is all about)."[9]

Nonetheless, many feminist readers of Le Guin will continue to oppose her unless she creates more female protagonists. Still, most feminists would agree with Rosalind Coward that woman-centered writings do not necessarily have any relationship to feminism nor is the description of experience typical of women "sufficient to justify calling that account 'feminist.'"[10] It may very well be that "Stone Telling" is a more effective narrative because the protagonist is female. But, by itself, "Stone Telling" is not one of Le Guin's better works. Although it is perhaps the "center" of *Always Coming Home,* the strength of that novel comes from the many different voices—male or female signs. Indeed, all the novels analyzed in this study are characterized by a doubling, a splintering of character. Le Guin, like Lacan and Derrida, has abandoned the traditional notion of the autonomous self—for them, self is always other (mother, father, child). This doubling is simultaneously a renewal of the nongendered state, which we often find in our own dreams at night, and a kind of utopian dream, one similar to Derrida's notion that we need to move

> beyond the binary difference that governs the decorum of all codes, beyond the opposition feminine/masculine, beyond bisexuality as well, beyond homosexuality and heterosexuality which come to the same thing. As I dream of saving the chance that this questions offers I would like to believe in the multiplicity of sexually marked voices.[11]

Le Guin, like Derrida in this context, does not see the "feminist enterprise" in terms of male versus female. The world(s) that her novels describe, dream of, move toward, are characterized by a reaching beyond such polarities. *The Left Hand of Darkness* and *Always Coming Home* are more obviously concerned with a kind of sexual plurality than are the others. Indeed, at times, *Always Coming Home* seems to be endorsing Sade's longing for a combination of species: his desire for "'a universal prostitution of all beings,' providing unity with nature in a state of perpetual motion."[12] Plural sexuality is a strange, difficult, and radical proposition. Its ramifications for our society are deeply subversive, even volcanic.

Yet Le Guin's works are often regarded as relatively docile. Rosemary Jackson, for example, believes that the "utopianism" of Le Guin's novels "does not directly engage with divisions or contradictions of subjects *inside* human culture: their harmony is established on a mystical cosmic level."[13] If there is one thing that Le Guin's novels do, this study evinces, it is definitely to describe the subject divided in and against language and culture; and if there is "harmony," it is always qualified. Jackson's limited reading of Le Guin is further underscored by her thesis that the most subversive speculative fictions, none of which are Le Guin's, "attempt to *transform* the relations of the imaginary and the symbolic."[14]

And yet we have witnessed this attempted transformation in each novel. Another critic, Carol McGuirk, believes that "Le Guin's limitations are simply those imposed by the optimism of the humanist ideology and its literary offspring, utopia."[15] If Le Guin is a humanist, a problematic term anyway, then so are Lacan, Derrida, and Kristeva. And I am not sure why optimism is necessarily a limitation. Certainly many of us would like to see Le Guin using her talents in a more aggressive way. We would like to see tougher, more strident and negative tones. But this, it seems to me, would be too much out of "character" for her, and this kind of literary machismo can constitute more of a giving in to phallogocentrism than a critique of it. Le Guin's manner includes description, quiet subversion, and, usually, subtle instruction. Perhaps more people will listen this way.

This is not to say that Le Guin does not have her limitations. She does have a tendency to create totalizing systems (although these systems are normally undermined as well). While her works give us a description and understanding of the unconscious processes that construct subjective identity, they do not, as far as I can tell, deal sufficiently with the fact that these same processes are also those through which class is lived and through which subjection is organized. This, however, could be one of the limitations of utopian-dystopian writing. Finally, the fine edge or the impact that her novels can have is buffered by her overreliance on the mysticism of Jung and Lao Tze. But these shortcomings hardly offset her achievement, which includes a significant contribution to our understanding of the nature of human beings and contemporary art and thought. Her strong sense of the need for personal continuity and connection with older (more ecologically advanced) societies parallels her insight into the discontinuity created by modern society. As Gerald Graff put it, "Consumer Society, in its destruction of continuity through the exploitation of fashion, ephemeral novelty, and planned obsolescence, effects a 'systematic derangement of the senses' that makes the disruptions and defamiliarizations of vanguard culture look puny by comparison."[16] Le Guin's movement away from the centrality of man himself and her celebration of creative individuals (those who speak alternity) are her recognition of our increasing distance from Nature and our declining creativity in late capitalist society. A part of but apart from this society, she will continue to have to create other worlds (endlessly creating herself) that contain strategies against the symbolic and where identity is multiple and paradoxical. Hopefully, her readers will reciprocate. To slightly alter Lautréamont in *Malador* ("May the reader become as fierce as what he is reading"), may Le Guin's readers become as imaginative, as fierce, and as gentle as what they are reading.

Notes

Chapter 1

1. Quoted by Carl Yoke, "Precious Metal in White Clay," *Extrapolation* 21 (Fall 1980): 198.

2. The first quotation is from *The Language of the Night,* ed. Susan Wood (New York: Putnam, 1979), p. 159; the second quotation is from *The Wind's Twelve Quarters* (New York: Harper and Row, 1975; reprint ed., New York: Bantam, 1976), p. 119.

3. *The Language of the Night,* p. 58.

4. *After Babel: Aspects of Language and Translation* (London: Oxford University Press, 1975), p. 217.

5. Ibid., p. 173.

6. Ibid., pp. 175–76.

7. Ibid., p. 225.

8. Ibid., p. 226.

9. Ibid., p. 35.

10. Brewster Ghiselin, ed., *The Creative Process* (New York: Signet, 1952), pp. 14–15.

11. Ibid., p. 124.

12. *The Language of the Night,* pp. 158, 163.

13. Ghiselin, p. 56.

14. *The Language of the Night,* pp. 124, 125, 197.

15. Ghiselin, pp. 64, 125.

16. T. S. Eliot, *The Use of Poetry and the Use of Criticism* (London: Faber and Faber, 1933), p. 148.

17. Greene as quoted in *The Sphinx* 3:1 (1979): 4.

18. Ghiselin, p. 65.

19. Ibid., p. 71.

20. *The Language of the Night,* p. 78.

21. "The Orbiting Self," *The Georgia Review* 37:2 (Summer 1983): 250.

22. *The Liberal Imagination* (New York: Doubleday, 1953), p. 170.

23. *The Language of the Night,* pp. 84, 157.

24. *The Left Hand of Darkness* (New York: Ace, 1969), p. 63.

25. *Mother Jones* 9:1 (January 1984): 23; *The Language of the Night,* p. 200.

26. Ghiselin, p. 193.

27. Aljean Harmetz, "Interview," *The Globe and Mail,* 25 April 1983, Sec. E, p. 17.

28. Percy, p. 251.

29. Ghiselin, p. 78.

30. Hyder Edward Rollins, ed., *The Letters of John Keats* 1814-1821, Vol. 1 (Cambridge: Harvard University Press, 1958), p. 374.

31. Ibid., pp. 386–87.

32. *City of Words* (New York: Harper and Row, 1971), p. 19.

Chapter 2

1. *Literary Theory: An Introduction* (Minneapolis: University of Minnesota Press, 1983), p. viii.

2. *The Liberal Imagination* (New York: Doubleday, 1953), p. 49.

3. "Opponents, Audiences, Constituencies, and Community," *Critical Inquiry* 9 (September 1982): 9.

4. "Psychoanalysis and the Polis," *Critical Inquiry* 9 (September 1982): 78.

5. Said, p. 13.

6. "Circumnavigating Ursula Le Guin: Literary Criticism and Approaches to Landing," *Science-Fiction Studies* 8 (March 1981): 96.

7. See, for example, *After Babel* (London: Oxford University Press, 1975), pp. 224–27.

8. *Saving the Text* (Baltimore: The Johns Hopkins University Press, 1981), p. 128.

9. *Of Grammatology,* trans. Gayatri Chakravorty Spivak (Baltimore: The John Hopkins University Press, 1976), p. 112.

10. Ibid., p. lxxxiv.

11. Jacques Lacan, *Ecrits: A Selection,* trans. Alan Sheridan (New York: W.W. Norton, 1977), p. 148. Throughout this chapter my summaries of aspects of Lacan's theories rely on my own struggles with *Ecrits;* Anthony Wilden's notes in *The Language of the Self* (Baltimore: The Johns Hopkins University Press, 1968); Anika Lemaire's *Jacques Lacan,* trans. David Macey (London: Routledge and Kegan Paul, 1977); and Sherry Turkle's *Psychoanalytic Politics: Freud's French Revolution* (New York: Basic Books, 1978).

12. Hartman, *Saving the Text,* p. 101.

13. Quoted and paraphrased by Carolyn Burke, "Irigaray through the Looking Glass," *Feminist Studies* 7 (Summer 1981): 299.

14. *Desire in Language,* trans., Thomas Gora, Alice Jardine, and Leon S. Roudiez (New York: Columbia University Press, 1980), p. 289.

15. Ibid., p. 290.

16. Ibid., p. 291.

17. Margaret Mahler et al., *The Psychological Birth of the Infant* (New York: Basic Books, 1975), pp. 101, 167–69.

18. *Aspects of Internalization* (New York: International Universities Press, 1968), p. 41.

19. Rafail Nudelman, "An Approach to the Structure of Le Guin's SF," *Science-Fiction Studies* 2 (1975): 216.

20. Heinz Lichtenstein, *The Dilemma of Human Identity* (New York: Jason Aronson, 1977), pp. 12, 13, 78. Lichtenstein's idea of an "imprinted" identity theme, through the interaction of mother and child, is not as idiosyncratic as it first appears. The whole subject of imprinting would seem to belong to ethology; however, whatever problems one may have here with the word imprinting are, it seems to me, largely semantic (it may even be a simple matter of diction). D.W. Winnicott is known to have reservations about the subject of imprinting and its relevance to the early object-relating of human infants. Nonetheless, he frequently describes the early mother-infant relationship in a fashion similar to Lichtenstein's. For example, in *Playing and Reality* (New York: Basic Books, 1971), p. 112, he writes:

> What does the baby see when he or she looks at the mother's face? I am suggesting that, ordinarily, what the baby sees is himself or herself. In other words the mother is looking at the baby and *what she looks like is related to what she sees there.* . . . I can make my point by going straight over to the case of the baby whose mother reflects her own mood or, worse still, the rigidity of her own defenses.

Or, in his *The Maturational Processes and the Facilitating Environment* (New York: International Universities Press, 1965), p. 54:

> With "the care that it receives from its mother" each infant is able to have a personal existence, and so begins to build up what might be called *a continuity of being*. On the basis of this continuity of being the inherited potential gradually develops into an individual infant.

The notion of imprinting is implicit in some of Lacan's important statements. In "Reflections on the Ego," *International Journal of Psychoanalysis* 34 (1953), p. 16, speaking of man's search for self-mastery through the "illusion" of the original unity, he remarks that it is the "gap separating man from nature that determines his lack of relationship to nature, and begets his narcissistic shield, with its nacreous covering on which is painted the world from which he is forever cut off, but this same structure is also the sight [*sic*] where his own milieu is grafted on to him." Louis Althusser, in an essay that summarizes Lacan's thought and attempts to ally it with historical processes, claims that the subject's "story" is not biological "since from its beginning it is completely dominated by the constraint of the sexed human order that each mother engraves on the small human animal in maternal 'love' or hatred, starting from its alimentary rhythm and training." See "Freud or Lacan," in *Lenin and Philosophy and Other Essays,* trans. Ben Brewster (London: New Left Books, 1971), p. 190.

Melitta Sperling writes about "Children's Interpretations and Reaction to the Unconscious of their Mothers," *International Journal of Psychoanalysis* 31 (1950): 36–41. And Julia Kristeva (in *Desire*, p. 283), while commenting on that early "threshold" of space that she labels the "chora," refers to it as the "imprint of an archaic moment."

Imprinting, therefore, is another way of saying that self, originally, is other; or, the ego is an object, built up from identifications in which self is fused with other—the original fusion, or the initial and most important and lasting interrelation is designated by Lichtenstein as imprinting, largely because of the receptiveness or impressionableness of the infant to both the conscious and unconscious feelings of the mother. So the notion of an imprinted theme or "unchanging essence" is not an essentialist one; it is not static and not necessarily adaptive—it is capable of all kinds of variations, dependent upon the nature of the self-other relationship(s), and the social context.

21. For an indication of some of these arguments see Arthur F. Marotti, "Countertransference, the Communication Process, and the Dimensions of Psychoanalytic Criticism," *Critical Inquiry* 4 (Spring 1978): 476–79.

22. D.W. Winnicott, *Playing and Reality,* pp. 2, 13, 96–97, 103.

23. Winnicott, *The Maturational Processes and the Facilitating Environment,* pp. 180, 185, 192.

24. Mahler, "On Child Psychosis and Schizophrenia: Autistic and Symbiotic Infantile Psychoses," *The Psychoanalytic Study of the Child* 7 (1952): 297, 297, 301.

25. Mahler, *Birth,* p. 224.

26. Bruno Bettelheim, *The Empty Fortress* (New York: The Free Press, 1967), pp. 52, 56–57, 68, 163.

27. It may appear that I am mixing Lacan with the wrong company because he is well-known for his attack on Anglo-American ego psychology. For example, in *Ecrits,* p. 306, he writes:

> I shall not return here to the function of my "mirror stage," the first strategic point that I developed in opposition to the favour accorded in psychoanalytic theory to the supposedly *autonomous ego.* The academic restoration of the "autonomous ego" justified my view that a misunderstanding was involved in any attempt to strengthen the ego in a type of analysis that took as its criterion of "success" a successful adaptation to society—a phenomenon of mental abdication that was bound up with the aging of the psychoanalytic group in the diaspora of the war, and the reduction of a distinguished practice to a label suitable to the "American way of life."

Lacan is just in his criticism of the domesticated brand of psychoanalysis. As we can see, his strongest objection is to the notion of the autonomous ego. For him the ego is the source of alienation, the bearer of neurosis, the center of all resistance to help, and it continually searches for substitutes for the object of "lost desire" buried in the unconscious. Above all, the ego and its vanity block our realization that the symbolic order has shaped us and lives through us. However, it is difficult to find in Lacan and his followers a sustained and explicit argument against ego-psychology; what we find is a radically different way of writing about the psyche—one which mistakenly identifies all Anglo-American psychoanalytic theory with ego-psychology. On this topic, see Jeffrey Mehlman, "The Floating Signifier: From Lévi-Strauss to Lacan," in *French Freud: Structural Studies in Psychoanalysis* (New Haven: Yale University Press, 1972), pp. 19–20. In addition, Jean Laplanche, in *Life and Death in Psychoanalysis,* trans., Jeffrey Mehlman (Baltimore: Johns Hopkins University Press, 1976), pp. 125–26, questions Lacan's valorization of the Symbolic to the detriment of the Imaginary. He contends that Lacanians have been so concerned with downgrading the ego and thus the Imaginary (the ego is the agency of the Imaginary), that they have overlooked the more positive side of the Imaginary. Julia Kristeva, however, focuses attention on the Imaginary to the extent that she is rewriting that crucial segment of Lacanian thought. It is significant that Kristeva frequently draws on the work of Winnicott and René Spitz since object-relations theory, largely because it sees mental life as originally undifferentiated and it integrates drives and social relations into a psychodynamic account of development, is quite compatible with Lacanian thought.

28. Lacan, "Reflections on the Ego," p. 12.

29. Lacan, *Ecrits,* p. 269.

30. Eagleton, *Literary Theory*, p. 166.

31. Dewdney, *Alter Sublime* (Toronto: The Coach House Press, 1980), pp. 76, 91.

32. Kristeva, *Desire*, p. 157.

33. Gallop, *The Daughter's Seduction: Feminism and Psychoanalysis* (Ithaca, New York: Cornell University Press, 1982), p. 124.

34. Eagleton, p. 189.

35. Others who will be of assistance from time to time throughout this study are Hans Loewald, J.-B. Pontalis, Harold Searles, J. Laplanche, Fredric Jameson, René Spitz, Marion Milner, and Norman N. Holland.

36. Lichtenstein, p. 78.

37. Winnicott, *Playing and Reality*, pp. 67, 112.

38. Frye, "Literary Criticism," in *The Aims and Methods of Scholarship in Modern Languages and Literature*, ed. James Thorpe (New York: MLA, 1963), p. 65.

39. Le Guin, "It Was a Dark and Stormy Night," p. 194. Strictly speaking the "absolute proof" of my contention that each work of Le Guin's is built around a preverbal image or intimation that is related to her identity theme, upon which she is compelled to *create* variations, could come only from examining every one of her works. The limits of this study, however (and the limits of my readers' time and patience), don't allow me to do this. I have therefore chosen what I consider to be Le Guin's best and most representative works: these novels, with the exception of the recent *Always Coming Home*, are also the ones that have received the most critical scrutiny.

Chapter 3

1. "Lagniappe: An Informal Dialogue with Ursula K. Le Guin" in *Selected Proceedings of the 1978 Science Fiction Research Association National Conference*, ed. Thomas J. Remington (Cedar Falls, Iowa: University of Northern Iowa, 1979), p. 271.

2. *The Language of the Night*, ed. Susan Wood (New York: Putnam, 1979), p. 53.

3. Ursula K. Le Guin, *A Wizard of Earthsea* (New York: Parnassus, 1968; reprint ed., New York: Puffin, 1980), p. 11. All subsequent quotations followed by a page number in parentheses are from this edition.

4. Harold F. Searles, *The Nonhuman Environment in Normal Development and in Schizophrenia* (New York: International Universities Press, 1960), p. 107.

5. Ibid., p. 171.

6. Ibid., p. 176.

7. "Feminine Guilt and the Oedipus Complex," in J. Chassequet-Smirgel, ed., *Female Sexuality* (Ann Arbor: University of Michigan Press, 1970), pp. 115–16. The notion of penis-envy is a controversial one and it always will be. I would prefer to avoid the phrase and its dynamics altogether, just as I would prefer to talk about "man" and "woman" as sign rather than as biological creature (I try to do this for the most part anyway). However, it is difficult to evade the issue; if we are attempting to see what value psychoanalysis has as an interpretative tool here, how can we not try to come to terms with the "great staffs" that all these wizards are wielding? What is at issue here, it seems to me, is not whether Le Guin or Ged or whoever is suffering from penis-envy, but what we can learn from the dialogue between psychoanalysis and Le Guin. It is

perhaps a matter of us *all* assuming our (linguistic) castration. Some very helpful critical discussions directed toward the problem of the phallus, penis-envy, and castration are: Jessica Benjamin, "A Desire of One's Own: Psychoanalytic Feminism and Intersubjective Space" in Teresa de Lauretis, ed., *Feminist Studies* (Bloomington: University of Indiana Press, 1986); Kaja Silverman, *The Subject of Semiotics* (New York: Oxford University Press, 1983), pp. 134–50; Jane Gallop, *Reading Lacan* (Ithaca, New York: Cornell University Press, 1985), pp. 142–49; Teresa de Lauretis, *Alice Doesn't* (Bloomington: University of Indiana Press, 1984), pp. 21–24; Jacqueline Rose, "Introduction II," in *Female Sexuality: Jacques Lacan and the École Freudienne*, eds. Juliet Mitchell and Jacqueline Rose, trans. Jacqueline Rose (New York: W. W. Norton, 1985). For a history of the literature on penis-envy see Hannah Lerman, *A Mote in Freud's Eye: From Psychoanalysis to the Psychology of Women* (New York: Springer, 1986), especially pp. 118–56.

8. Nancy Chodorow, *The Reproduction of Mothering* (Berkeley and Los Angeles: University of California Press, 1978), p. 123.

9. Ibid., p. 138.

10. Chodorow, "Mothering, Object-Relations, and the Female Oedipal Configuration," *Feminist Studies* 4:1 (February 1978): 154.

11. Jane Gallop, *The Daughter's Seduction: Feminism and Psychoanalysis* (Ithaca, New York: Cornell University Press, 1982), p. 124.

12. Julia Kristeva, "Women's Time," *Signs: Journal of Women in Culture and Society* 7:1 (1981): 31–32.

13. Margaret Mahler, "On Child Psychosis and Schizophrenia: Autistic and Symbiotic Infantile Psychoses," *The Psychoanalytical Study of the Child* 7 (1952): 297–98.

14. *The Empty Fortress* (New York: The Free Press, 1967), p. 163.

15. Roheim, *Magic and Schizophrenia* (Bloomington: Indiana University Press, 1955), pp. 46, 82.

16. Ibid., pp. 46, 53, 55.

17. *A Critical Dictionary of Psychoanalysis* (Middlesex, England: Penguin, 1972), p. 161.

18. J. LaPlanche and J.-B. Pontalis, *The Language of Psychoanalysis*, trans. Daniel Lagache (New York: W.W. Norton, 1973), pp. 436–37.

19. Roheim, p. 7.

20. Emilio Rodrigué, "The Analysis of a Three-year-old Mute Schizophrenic," in *New Directions in Psychoanalysis*, eds. Melanie Klein et al. (London: Tavistock, 1955; reprint ed., London: H. Karnac, 1977), pp. 176–77.

21. Mahler, p. 293.

22. Jacques Lacan, *Ecrits: A Selection*, trans. Alan Sheridan (New York: W.W. Norton, 1977), p. 306.

23. David Macey, "Jacques Lacan," *Ideology and Consciousness* 4 (1978): 115.

24. Lacan, *Ecrits*, p. 19.

Chapter 4

1. Fredric Jameson, "World-Reduction in Le Guin: The Emergence of Utopian Narrative," *Science-Fiction Studies* 2 (1975): 221.

2. Ursula K. Le Guin, *The Language of the Night,* ed. Susan Wood (New York: Putnam, 1979), p. 110.

3. Ibid., pp. 110–11, 159.

4. Ursula K. Le Guin, *The Left Hand of Darkness* (1969; rpt. New York: Ace, 1976), p. 11. All subsequent quotations followed by a page number in parentheses are from this edition.

5. David Ketterer, *"The Left Hand of Darkness:* Ursula K. Le Guin's Archetypal 'Winter-Journey,'" *Riverside Quarterly* 5 (1971): 295.

6. "Harth" is a blatant pun on "Hearth," which is a symbol of creative energy in the novel, mainly due to: (1) the universal equation of fire and creation, (2) its use in the novel, and (3) its definition in *Webster's* as "a vital creative center"; the example of usage is a phrase of Le Guin's father, A. L. Kroeber: "the central hearth of occidental civilization."

7. Hans W. Loewald, "Ego and Reality," *International Journal of Psychoanalysis* 32 (1951): 15.

8. Heinz Lichtenstein, *The Dilemma of Human Identity* (New York: Jason Aronson, 1977), pp. 76–77.

9. Loewald, p. 17.

10. Ketterer, p. 296.

11. Margaret S. Mahler et al., *The Psychological Birth of the Human Infant* (New York: Basic Books, 1975), p. 291.

12. Ibid., p. 289.

13. Ibid., p. 290.

14. Lichtenstein, p. 10.

15. Mahler, *Birth,* p. 11.

16. See Barbour's "Wholeness and Balance in the Hainish Novels of Ursula K. Le Guin," *Science-Fiction Studies* 1 (1974): 167.

17. Robert Plank, "Ursula K. Le Guin and the Decline of Romantic Love," *Science-Fiction Studies* 3 (1976): 42.

18. Mahler, "Child Psychosis," p. 292.

19. Mahler, *Birth,* p. 101.

20. Geoffrey H. Hartman, *Saving The Text* (Baltimore: Johns Hopkins University Press, 1981), p. 101.

21. Lichtenstein, p. 90.

22. In Mahler, *Birth,* p. 47.

23. Mahler, "Child Psychosis," p. 297.

24. Lichtenstein, pp. 12, 215.

25. See Hartman, p. 100.

26. Paul Kramer, "On Discovering One's Identity," *Psychoanalytic Study of the Child* 10 (1955): 70.

27. Robert J. Stoller, *Splitting: A Case of Female Masculinity* (London: Hogarth, 1973), p. 53.

28. D.W. Winnicott, *Playing and Reality* (New York: Basic Books, 1971), pp. 54–55.

29. Ursula K. Le Guin, "It Was a Dark and Stormy Night; or Why Are We Huddling about the Campfire?" *Critical Inquiry* 7:1 (Autumn 1980): 199.

30. Bruno Bettelheim, *The Empty Fortress* (New York: The Free Press, 1967), pp. 25, 46.

31. Sigmund Freud, "Formulations on the Two Principles of Mental Functioning," *Standard Edition*, Vol. 12 (London: Hogarth, 1958), p. 221.

32. Jameson, p. 229.

33. Erik H. Erikson, *Young Man Luther* (New York: W.W. Norton, 1958), p. 264.

34. Jacques Lacan, "Some Reflections on the Ego," *International Journal of Psychoanalysis* 34 (1953): 15.

35. Otto Rank, *Beyond Psychology* (New York: Dover, 1941), p. 66, 81.

36. Mahler, "Child Psychosis," p. 297.

Chapter 5

1. Ursula K. Le Guin, *The Lathe of Heaven* (1972; rpt. London: Granada, 1978), p. 7. All subsequent quotations followed by a page number in parentheses are from this edition.

2. Gerard Klein, "Le Guin's 'Aberrant' Opus: Escaping the Trap of Discontent," *Science-Fiction Studies* 4 (1977): 292.

3. J.-B. Pontalis, "Dream as an Object," *International Review of Psychoanalysis* 1 (1974): 128.

4. Ibid., p. 128.

5. "Transitional Objects and Transitional Phenomena," in *Playing and Reality* (New York: Basic Books, 1971), pp. 4, 5.

6. Ibid., p. 5.

7. Ibid., p. 9.

8. Margaret S. Mahler et al., *The Psychological Birth of the Human Infant* (New York: Basic Books, 1975), p. 44.

9. Ibid., p. 90.

10. Winnicott, p. 14.

11. Ibid., p. 14.

12. Bruno Bettelheim, *The Empty Fortress: Infantile Autism and the Birth of the Self* (New York: Free Press, 1967), p. 56.

13. Winnicott, pp. 5, 7.

14. "Communicating and Not Communicating Leading to a Study of Certain Opposites," in *The Maturational Process and the Facilitating Environment* (New York: International Universities Press, 1965), p. 180.

15. Ibid., p. 179.

16. Pontalis, pp. 131, 132.

17. Freud discusses the close relationship between the fantasy of murdering one's mother or mother surrogate and the fantasy of incest in *The Interpretation of Dreams,* trans. James Strachey (New York: Avon, 1965), pp. 289–91, 435. For an imaginative Lacanian rendering of this idea, see Pontalis, pp. 128–32.

18. Mahler, *Birth,* p. 10.

19. Bettelheim, p. 308.

20. Pontalis, p. 133.

21. Heinz Lichtenstein, *The Dilemma of Human Identity* (New York: Jason Aronson, 1977), pp. 9–10.

22. Ibid., p. 12.

23. Winnicott, "Communicating," p. 185.

24. Bettelheim, p. 458.

25. Mahler, "On Child Psychosis and Schizophrenia: Autistic and Symbiotic Infantile Psychoses," *The Psychoanalytic Study of the Child* 7 (1952): 297.

26. Bettelheim, p. 263.

27. Mahler, "Child Psychosis," p. 301.

28. Mahler, *Birth,* p. 11.

29. Mahler, "Child Psychosis," p. 324.

30. Sigmund Freud, "Formulations on the Two Principles of Mental Functioning," *Standard Edition,* Vol. 12 (London: Hogarth, 1958), p. 221.

31. *Webster's New Collegiate Dictionary* (Toronto: Thomas Allen & Son, 1976), p. 363.

32. "Discovering Worlds: The Fiction of Ursula K. Le Guin" in *Voices for the Future,* ed. Thomas D. Clareson (Bowling Green, Ohio: Bowling Green University Popular Press, 1979), p. 171.

33. Bettelheim, p. 37.

34. Ibid., p. 40.

35. Freud, "Splitting of the Ego in the Process of Defence," *Standard Edition,* Vol. 23 (London: Hogarth, 1964), pp. 275–76.

36. Hans Loewald, "Ego and Reality," *International Journal of Psychoanalysis* 32 (1951): 14.

37. Winnicott, "Transitional Objects," p. 14.

38. Lichtenstein, p. 12.

39. Ibid., p. 12.

40. Ibid., p. 78.

41. Winnicott, "Communicating," p. 192.

42. Winnicott, "Transitional Objects," p. 25.

Chapter 6

1. See, for example, Joe De Bolt, ed., *Ursula K. Le Guin: Voyager to Inner Lands and to Outer Space* (Port Washington, N.Y.: Kennikat Press, 1979); Joseph D. Olander and Martin Harry Greenberg, eds., *Ursula K. Le Guin* (New York: Taplinger, 1979); and Leonard M. Fleck, "Science Fiction as a Tool of Speculative Philosophy: A Philosophical Analysis of Selected Anarchistic and Utopian Themes in Le Guin's *The Dispossessed*," in *Selected Proceedings of the 1978 Science Fiction Research Association National Conference*, ed. Thomas J. Remington (Cedar Falls, Iowa: University of Northern Iowa, 1979), pp. 135–45. The most significant, extended critique of *The Dispossessed* is Samuel R. Delany's "To Read *The Dispossessed*" in his *The Jewel-Hinged Jaw* (New York: Berkley Windhover, 1978), pp. 218–83. This cannot be the time or space to attempt a detailed critique of Delany's influential article, which is sometimes brilliant and sometimes befuddling. The chapter that follows here, I think, enters into its own dialogue with Delany's piece. His main criticism is that Le Guin's novel does not live up to the high standards required of it by the science fiction genre. This is a fair criticism. But if one better understands *how* (and that) Le Guin writes from the *inside*, as I hope this study helps illustrate, and does not allow conventions to restrict her—she sees science fiction as freedom and not confinement—then it becomes apparent that she simply cannot, without sacrificing her own "artistic" integrity, write the way Delany would like her to. Her novels will always be somewhere between the "mundane" (descriptive) and "science fiction" (prescriptive). I also hope that this chapter will show that Le Guin's psychological insight regarding Shevek and his split-off fragments or satellites (such as Rulag, Bedap, and so on) is much more astute and acute than Delany gives her credit for.

2. Ursula K. Le Guin, *The Language of the Night*, ed. Susan Wood (New York: Putnam, 1979), pp. 111, 112.

3. Ibid., p. 102.

4. Ibid., p. 112.

5. "Lagniappe: An Informal Dialogue with Ursula K. Le Guin," in Remington, p. 280.

6. Ursula K. Le Guin, *The Dispossessed* (New York: Harper & Row, 1974; reprint ed., New York: Avon, 1975), p. 36. All subsequent quotations followed by a page number in parentheses are from this edition.

7. Hans Loewald, "Ego and Reality," *International Journal of Psychoanalysis* 32 (1951): 14.

8. Heinz Lichtenstein, *The Dilemma of Human Identity* (New York: Jason Aronson, 1977), p. 12.

9. Quoted in Lichtenstein, p. 69.

10. Ursula K. Le Guin, *The Wind's Twelve Quarters* (New York: Harper & Row, 1975; reprint ed., New York: Bantam, 1976), pp. 260, 271.

11. Lichtenstein, p. 96.

12. Loewald, p. 11.

13. Emilio Rodrigué, "The Analysis of a Three-year-old Mute Schizophrenic," in *New Directions in Psycho-Analysis*, eds. Melanie Klein et al. (London: Tavistock, 1955; reprint ed., London: H. Karnac, 1977), p. 177.

14. George Edgar Slusser, *The Farthest Shores of Ursula K. Le Guin* (San Bernardino, California: Borgo Press, 1976), p. 52.

15. Margaret Mahler, "Autism and Symbiosis, Two Extreme Disturbances of Identity," *International Journal of Psychoanalysis* 39 (1958): 82.

16. Rodrigué (p. 179) makes an interesting statement about the autistic child and his relationship with music: "Perhaps in the blissful emotional tie with the ideal object, feelings are phrased in a pattern akin to music. In other words, music may be the medium of expression, the language of love with an ideal object."

17. J.-B. Pontalis, "Dream as an Object," *International Review of Psychoanalysis* 1 (1974): 133.

18. Lichtenstein, p. 9.

19. Bettelheim, p. 308.

20. Paul Kramer, "On Discovering One's Identity," *Psychoanalytic Study of the Child* 10 (1958): 73.

21. Jacques Lacan, "Reflections on the Ego," *International Journal of Psychoanalysis* 34 (1953): 13.

22. Ibid., p. 15.

23. Lichtenstein, p. 218.

24. D.W. Winnicott, *Playing and Reality* (New York: Basic Books, 1971), pp. 111–12, 118.

25. Bettelheim, p. 329.

26. Mahler, "On Child Psychosis and Schizophrenia: Autistic and Symbiotic Infantile Psychoses," *The Psychoanalytic Study of the Child* 7 (1952): 293.

27. "Parables of De-Alienation: Le Guin's Widdershins Dance," *Science-Fiction Studies* 2 (1975): 271.

28. See Bettelheim, p. 125.

29. Slusser, p. 50.

30. Bettelheim, pp. 424–25.

31. Lichtenstein, p. 218.

32. Quoted by Marion Milner, "Aspects of Symbolism in Comprehension of the Not-Self," *International Journal of Psychoanalysis* 33 (1952): 182.

33. Quoted by Milner, pp. 190–91.

34. John P. Brennan and Michael C. Downs, "Anarchism and Utopian Tradition in *The Dispossessed,*" in Olander, p. 125.

35. Elizabeth Cummins Cogell, "Taoist Configurations: *The Dispossessed,*" in De Bolt, p. 178.

36. See Bettelheim, pp. 84, 388.

37. Winnicott, pp. 96–97.

38. Ibid., p. 5.

39. Ibid., p. 99.

40. Ibid., p. 101.

41. Slusser, p. 54.

42. Brennan and Downs, p. 146.

43. "Utopian, Dystopian, Diatopian Libertarianism: Le Guin's *The Dispossessed*," *The Sphinx* 4:1 (1981): 62.

44. Philip E. Smith II, "Unbuilding Walls: Human Nature and the Nature of Evolutionary and Political Theory in *The Dispossessed*," in Olander, p. 86.

45. Larry L. Tifft and Dennis C. Sullivan, "Possessed Sociology and Le Guin's Dispossessed: From Exile to Anarchism," in De Bolt, p. 192.

Chapter 7

1. Elizabeth Wright paraphrasing Lacan in her *Psychoanalytic Criticism* (New York: Methuen, 1984), p. 113.

2. *Illuminations*, trans. Harry Zohn (London: Collins/Fontana, 1973), p. 79.

3. *Revolution in Poetic Language* (New York: Columbia University Press, 1984), p. vii.

4. "Living On Border Lines," in Harold Bloom et al., *Deconstruction and Criticism* (New York: Continuum, 1979), pp. 102–3.

5. Ursula K. Le Guin, *Always Coming Home* (New York: Harper & Row, 1985), p. 3. All subsequent quotations followed by a page number in parentheses are from this edition.

6. *Of Grammatology*, trans. Gayatri Chakravorty Spivak (Baltimore: Johns Hopkins University Press, 1976), pp. 65–73.

7. We are told on page 193 of *ACH:* "We call them the Condor people; their name for themselves as distinct from all other people is Dayao, One-People."

8. Dick Allen, "Fire Burning in the Rain," *The Hudson Review* 34:1 (Spring 1986): 136.

9. Quoted by Harold Bloom in his Introduction to *Ursula K. Le Guin*, ed. Harold Bloom (New York: Chelsea House, 1986), p. 1.

10. Ibid., p. 1.

11. Kenneth Lincoln, *Native American Renaissance* (Berkeley: University of California Press, 1983), p. 237.

12. *Ecrits*, trans. Alan Sheridan (New York: W.W. Norton, 1977), p. 4. See also: Lacan's "Some Reflections on the Ego," *International Journal of Psychoanalysis* 34 (1952): 12–15; Anika Lemaire, *Jacques Lacan*, trans. David Macey (London: Routledge & Kegan Paul, 1977), pp. 80–82, 177–79.

13. *Desire in Language*, trans. Leon S. Roudiez, Thomas Gora, and Alice Jardine (New York: Columbia University Press, 1980), p. 195.

14. *Reading Lacan* (Ithaca, New York: Cornell University Press, 1985), p. 79.

15. Lacan, quoted by Anthony Wilden in Wilden's *System and Structure* (London: Tavistock, 1972), p. 469.

16. "Mothering, Object-Relations, and the Female Oedipal Configuration," *Feminist Studies* 4:1 (February 1978): 153.

17.   Wilden, paraphrasing Lacan, p. 468.

18.   *The Daughter's Seduction* (Ithaca, New York: Cornell University Press, 1982), p. xv.

19.   "On Child Psychosis and Schizophrenia: Autistic and Symbiotic Infantile Psychosis," *The Psychoanalytic Study of the Child* 7 (1952): 293.

20.   Ann Rosalind Jones, quoting and paraphrasing Kristeva in Jones' "Julia Kristeva on Femininity: The Limits of a Semiotic Politics," *Feminist Review* 18 (November 1984): 68.

21.   "A Desire of One's Own: Psychoanalytic Feminism and Intersubjective Space" in Teresa de Lauretis, ed., *Feminist Studies* (Bloomington, University of Indiana Press, 1986), p. 90.

22.   *The Language of the Night,* ed. Susan Wood (New York: Putnam, 1979), p. 158.

23.   "On the Other Hand," *Science-Fiction Studies* 14 (1987): 114.

24.   "Feminism and Utopia," *Science-Fiction Studies* 13 (1986): 80.

25.   *Gynesis* (Ithaca, New York: Cornell University Press, 1985), p. 33.

26.   *Primitive Man As Philosopher* (New York: Appleton, 1927), p. 200.

27.   *After the Great Divide* (Bloomington: Indiana University Press, 1986), p. 192.

Chapter 8

1.   *The Language of the Night,* ed. Susan Wood (New York: Putnam, 1979), p. 234.

2.   Quoted in Tony Tanner, *City of Words* (New York: Harper & Row, 1971), p. 19.

3.   "Lagniappe: An Informal Dialogue with Ursula K. Le Guin," *Selected Proceedings of the 1978 Science Fiction Research Association National Conference,* ed. Thomas J. Remington (Cedar Falls: University of Northern Iowa, 1979), p. 278; "Ursula K. Le Guin: In a World of Her Own," interviewed by Nora Gallagher, *Mother Jones* 9 (January 1984): 23.

4.   "It Was a Dark and Stormy Night; or Why Are We Huddling about the Campfire?" *Critical Inquiry* 7 (Autumn 1980): 198.

5.   *The Romantic Novel in England* (Cambridge, Massachusetts: Harvard University Press, 1972), p. 23.

6.   *After Babel* (London: Oxford University Press, 1975), pp. 75, 473.

7.   "At Stratford on Avon," in *Ideas of Good and Evil* (London: A.H. Bullen, 1903), pp. 161–62. Norman H. Holland is particularly fond of this quotation.

8.   *The Wind's Twelve Quarters* (New York: Harper & Row, 1975; reprint ed., New York: Bantam, 1976), pp. 85–86.

9.   *The Daughter's Seduction: Feminism and Psychoanalysis* (Ithaca, New York: Cornell University Press, 1982), p. 93.

10.   "Are Women's Novels Feminist Novels?" in *The New Feminist Criticism,* ed. Elaine Showalter (New York: Pantheon, 1985), p. 237.

11.   "Choreographies," interview with Christie V. McDonald, *Diacritics* 12:2 (Summer 1982): 76.

12.   Rosemary Jackson, *Fantasy: The Literature of Subversion* (New York and London: Methuen, 1981), p. 73.

13. Ibid., p. 154.

14. Ibid., p. 91.

15. "Optimism and the Limits of Subversion in *The Dispossessed* and *The Left Hand of Darkness*" in *Ursula K. Le Guin,* ed. Harold Bloom (New York: Chelsea House, 1986), p. 253.

16. *Literature against Itself* (Chicago: The University of Chicago Press, 1979), p. 92.

Selected Bibliography

Primary Sources

Le Guin, Ursula K. *Always Coming Home*. New York: Harper & Row, 1985.
———. *The Beginning Place*. New York: Harper & Row, 1980.
———. *The Dispossessed*. New York: Harper & Row, 1974; reprint ed., New York: Avon, 1975.
———. *Hard Words and Other Poems*. New York: Harper & Row, 1981.
———. *The Language of the Night*. Edited by Susan Wood. New York: Putnam, 1979.
———. *The Lathe of Heaven*. London: Victor Gollanz, 1972; reprint ed., London: Granada, 1978.
———. *The Left Hand of Darkness*. New York: Ace, 1969.
———. *A Wizard of Earthsea*. New York: Parnassus, 1968; reprint ed., New York: Puffin, 1980.

Secondary Sources—Books

Althusser, Louis. *Lenin and Philosophy and Other Essays*. Translated by Ben Brewster. London: New Left Books, 1971.
Attebury, Brian. *The Fantasy Tradition in American Literature*. Bloomington: Indiana University Press, 1980.
Bakhtin, M.M. *The Dialogic Imagination*. Translated by Caryl Emerson and Michael Holquist. Austin: University of Texas Press, 1981.
Barr, Marlene S., ed. *Future Females: A Critical Anthology*. Bowling Green, Ohio: Bowling Green State University Popular Press, 1981.
Barthes, Roland. *S/Z*. Translated by Richard Miller. New York: Hill and Wang, 1974.
Belsey, Catherine. *Critical Practice*. London and New York: Methuen, 1980.
Benjamin, Walter. *Illuminations*. Translated by Harry Zohn. London: Collins/Fontana, 1973.
Bettelheim, Bruno. *The Empty Fortress: Infantile Autism and the Birth of the Self*. New York: The Free Press, 1967.
Bittner, James W. *Approaches to Ursula K. Le Guin*. Ann Arbor: UMI Research Press, 1984.
Bloom, Harold, ed. *Deconstruction and Criticism*. New York: Continuum, 1979.
———. *Ursula K. Le Guin*. New York: Chelsea House, 1986.
Borges, Jorge Luis. *Labyrinths*. Preface by Andre Maurois. New York: New Directions, 1962.
Bowlby, John. *Attachment*. New York: Basic Books, 1969.
Bradbury, Malcolm, ed. *The Novel Today*. Glasgow: Fontana/Collins, 1977.
Bucknall, Barbara J. *Ursula K. Le Guin*. New York: Ungar, 1981.
Burrow, Trigant. *Preconscious Foundations of Human Experience*. New York: Basic Books, 1964.
Chassequet-Smirgel, Janine, ed. *Female Sexuality: New Psychoanalytic Views*. Ann Arbor: University of Michigan Press, 1970.

Chodorow, Nancy. *The Reproduction of Mothering*. Berkeley and Los Angeles: The University of California Press, 1978.

Cummins Cogell, Elizabeth. *Ursula K. Le Guin: A Primary and Secondary Bibliography*. Boston: G.K. Hall, 1983.

DeBolt, Joe, ed. *Ursula K. Le Guin: Voyager to Inner Lands and to Outer Space*. London: Kennikat Press, 1979.

Delany, Samuel R. *The Jewel-Hinged Jaw*. New York: Berkley Windhover, 1978.

De Lauretis, Teresa. *Alice Doesn't*. Bloomington: Indiana University Press, 1984.

————, ed. *Feminist Studies: Critical Studies*. Bloomington: Indiana University Press, 1986.

Derrida, Jacques. *Of Grammatology*. Translated by Gayatri Chakravorty Spivak. Baltimore and London: Johns Hopkins University Press, 1976.

————. *Writing and Difference*. Translated by Alan Bass. Chicago: University of Chicago Press, 1978.

Detweiler, Robert. *Story, Sign, and Self*. Philadelphia: Fortress Press, 1978.

Dewdney, Christopher. *Alter Sublime*. Toronto: Coach House, 1980.

Eagleton, Terry. *Literary Theory: An Introduction*. Minneapolis: University of Minnesota Press, 1983.

Ehrenzweig, Anton. *The Hidden Order of Art*. London: Weidenfeld & Nicolson, 1967, reprint ed., St. Albans: Granada, 1973.

Eisenstein, Hester, and Jardine, Alice, eds. *The Future of Difference*. Boston: G.K. Hall & Co., 1980.

Ellul, Jacques. *The Technological Society*. Translated by John Wilkinson. New York: Vintage, 1964.

Erikson, Erik H. *Childhood and Society*. New York: W.W. Norton, 1963.

————. *Young Man Luther*. New York: W.W. Norton, 1958.

Federman, Raymond, ed. *Surfiction: Fiction Now and Tomorrow*. Chicago: Swallow Press, 1981.

Fenichel, Otto. *The Psychoanalytic Theory of Neurosis*. New York: W.W. Norton, 1945.

Gallop, Jane. *The Daughter's Seduction: Feminism and Psychoanalysis*. Ithaca, New York: Cornell University Press, 1982.

————. *Reading Lacan*. Ithaca, New York: Cornell University Press, 1985.

Ghiselin, Brewster. *The Creative Process*. New York: New American Library, 1952.

Glover, Edward. *Freud or Jung*. Cleveland: World Publishing, 1956; reprint ed., Cleveland: Meridian, 1965.

Graff, Gerald. *Literature Against Itself*. Chicago: University of Chicago Press, 1979.

Greene, Gayle, and Kahn, Coppelia, eds. *Making a Difference*. London and New York: Methuen, 1985.

Guntrip, H.J.S. *Psychoanalytic Theory, Therapy, and the Self*. New York: Basic Books, 1971.

Halperin, John, ed. *The Theory of the Novel*. New York: Oxford University Press, 1974.

Harrari, Josue V., ed. *Textual Strategies*. Ithaca, New York: Cornell University Press, 1979.

Hartman, Geoffrey H. *Saving the Text*. Baltimore: The Johns Hopkins University Press, 1981.

Hawkes, Terence. *Structuralism and Semiotics*. Berkeley and Los Angeles: University of California Press, 1977.

Holland, Norman N. *The Dynamics of Literary Response*. New York: Oxford University Press, 1968.

————. *Poems in Persons*. New York: W.W. Norton, 1973.

Howe, Irving. *The Idea of the Modern*. New York: Horizon, 1967.

Huyssen, Andreas. *After The Great Divide*. Bloomington: University of Indiana Press, 1986.

Jackson, Rosemary. *Fantasy: The Literature of Subversion*. London and New York: Methuen, 1981.

Jacobson, Edith. *The Self and the Object World*. New York: International Universities Press, 1964.

Jacoby, Russell. *Social Amnesia*. Boston: Beacon Press, 1975.

Jameson, Fredric. *Marxism and Form*. Princeton, New Jersey: Princeton University Press, 1971.

————. *The Political Unconscious*. Ithaca, New York: Cornell University Press, 1981.

————. *The Prison-House of Language*. Princeton, New Jersey: Princeton University Press, 1972.

Jardine, Alice A. *Gynesis*. Ithaca and London: Cornell University Press, 1985.

Johnson, Barbara. *The Critical Difference*. Baltimore and London: Johns Hopkins University Press, 1980.

Jung, C.G. *The Spirit in Man, Art, and Literature*. Translated by R.F.C. Hull. Princeton, New Jersey: Princeton University Press, 1966.

Khan, M. Maud R. *The Privacy of the Self*. London: The Hogarth Press, 1974.

Kiely, Robert. *The Romantic Novel in England*. Cambridge, Massachusetts: Harvard University Press, 1972.

Klein, George S. *Psychoanalytic Theory: An Exploration of Essentials*. New York: International Universities Press, 1976.

Klein, Melanie; Heimann, Paula; Money-Kyrle, R.E., eds. *New Directions in Psychoanalysis*. London: Tavistock, 1955; reprint ed., London: H. Karnac, 1977.

Kris, Ernst. *Psychoanalytic Explorations in Art*. New York: International Universities Press, 1977.

Kristeva, Julia. *Desire in Language: A Semiotic Approach to Literature and Art*. Translated by Thomas Gora, Alice Jardine, and Leon S. Roudiez. New York: Columbia University Press, 1980.

———. *Powers of Horror*. Translated by Leon S. Roudiez. New York: Columbia University Press, 1982.

———. *Revolution in Poetic Language*. Translated by Margaret Waller. New York: Columbia University Press, 1984.

Kroeber, Theodora. *Alfred Kroeber*. Berkeley: University of California Press, 1970.

———. *The Inland Whale*. Berkeley: University of California Press, 1963.

———. *Ishi in Two Worlds*. Berkeley and Los Angeles: University of California Press, 1969.

Kuhn, Thomas S. *The Nature of Scientific Revolutions*. Chicago: The University of Chicago Press, 1962.

Lacan, Jacques. *Ecrits: A Selection*. Translated by Alan Sheridan. New York: W.W. Norton, 1977.

———. *Female Sexuality*. Translated by Jacqueline Rose. New York: W.W. Norton, 1982.

———. *The Four Fundamental Concepts of Psychoanalysis*. Translated by Alan Sheridan. New York: W.W. Norton, 1981.

———. *The Language of the Self*. Translated by Anthony Wilden. Baltimore: The Johns Hopkins Press, 1968.

Laing, R.D. *The Politics of Experience*. New York: Ballantine, 1967.

Laplanche, J. *Life and Death in Psychoanalysis*. Translated by Jeffrey Mehlman. Baltimore: Johns Hopkins University Press, 1976.

Laplanche, J., Pontalis, J.-B. *The Language of Psychoanalysis*. Translated by Donald Nicholson-Smith. New York: W.W. Norton, 1973.

Leites, Nathan. *The New Ego*. New York: Science House, 1971.

Lemaire, Anika. *Jacques Lacan*. Translated by David Macey. London: Routledge & Kegan Paul, 1977.

Lentricchia, Frank. *After the New Criticism*. Chicago: The University of Chicago Press, 1980.

Lerman, Hannah. *A Mote in Freud's Eye: From Psychoanalysis to the Psychology of Women*. New York: Springer, 1986.

Lichtenstein, Heinz. *The Dilemma of Human Identity*. New York: Jason Aronson, 1977.

Lincoln, Kenneth. *Native American Renaissance*. Berkeley: University of California Press, 1983.

Lipshitz, Susan, ed. *Tearing the Veil: Essays on Femininity*. London: Routledge and Kegan Paul, 1978.

Lodge, David. *The Modes of Modern Writing*. Ithaca, New York: Cornell University Press, 1977.

Macherey, Pierre. *A Theory of Literary Production*. Translated by Geoffrey Wall. London: Routledge and Kegan Paul, 1978.

Mahler, Margaret S. *On Human Symbiosis and the Vicissitudes of Individuation*. New York: International Universities Press, 1968.

Mahler, Margaret S. et al. *The Psychological Birth of the Human Infant*. New York: Basic Books, 1975.

Mandel, Eli. *Another Time*. Toronto: Porcépic, 1977.

Marks, Elaine, and de Courtivron, Isabelle, eds. *New French Feminisms*. New York: Schocken Books, 1981.

Miller, Jean Baker. *Psychoanalysis and Women*. Middlesex: Penguin, 1973.

——— . *Toward a New Psychology of Women*. Boston: Beacon Press, 1976.

Mitchell, Juliet. *Psychoanalysis and Feminism*. New York: Pantheon, 1974.

Moi, Toril. *Sexual/Textual Politics*. London and New York: Methuen, 1985.

Nicholls, Peter, ed. *Science Fiction at Large*. New York: Harper & Row, 1976.

Norris, Christopher. *Deconstruction: Theory & Practice*. London and New York: Methuen, 1982.

Olander, Joseph D., and Greenberg, Martin Harry, eds. *Ursula K. Le Guin*. New York: Taplinger, 1979.

Ong, Walter J. *The Presence of the Word*. New Haven: Yale University Press, 1976.

Ornstein, Robert E. *The Psychology of Consciousness*. 1972; reprint New York: Pelican, 1975.

Parrinder, Patrick. *Science Fiction: Its Criticism and Teaching*. London and New York: Methuen, 1980.

Percy, Walker. *The Message in the Bottle*. New York: Farrar, Straus and Giroux, 1975.

Philmus, Robert. *Into the Unknown: The Evolution of Science Fiction from Francis Godwin to H.G. Wells*. Berkeley: University of California Press, 1970.

Priestley, J.B. *Man and Time*. London: Aldus Books, 1964.

Remington, Thomas J., ed. *Selected Proceedings of the 1978 Science Fiction Research Association National Conference*. Cedar Falls: University of Northern Iowa, 1979.

Riley, Dick, ed. *Critical Encounters: Writers and Themes in Science Fiction*. New York: Ungar, 1978.

Roheim, Geza. *Magic and Schizophrenia*. New York: International Universities Press, 1955; reprint ed., Bloomington: Indiana University Press, 1962.

Roland, Alan, ed. *Psychoanalysis, Creativity and Literature*. New York: Columbia University Press, 1978.

Rose, Mark, ed. *Science Fiction: A Collection of Critical Essays*. New York: Prentice-Hall, 1976.

Rosinsky, Natalie M. *Feminist Futures*. Ann Arbor: UMI Research Press, 1984.

Rutter, Michael, ed. *Autism: A Reappraisal of Concepts and Treatment*. New York: Plenum Press, 1978.

Rutter, Michael, and Scholpler, Eric, eds. *Autism*. New York: Plenum Press, 1978.

Rycroft, Charles. *A Critical Dictionary of Psychoanalysis*. Middlesex: Penguin, 1972.

Schafer, Roy. *A New Language for Psychoanalysis*. New Haven and London: Yale University Press, 1976.

Schlueter, June. *Metafictional Characters in Modern Drama*. New York: Columbia University Press, 1979.

Schneiderman, Stuart. *Jacques Lacan: The Death of an Intellectual Hero*. Cambridge, Massachusetts: Harvard University Press, 1983.

Scholes, Robert. *Structural Fabulation*. Notre Dame and London: University of Notre Dame Press, 1975.

Scholes, Robert, and Rabkin, Eric S. *Science Fiction*. New York: Oxford University Press, 1977.

Searles, Harold F. *The Nonhuman Environment in Normal Development and in Schizophrenia*. New York: International Universities Press, 1960.

Silverman, Kaja. *The Subject of Semiotics*. New York: Oxford University Press, 1983.

Shapiro, Sue A. *Contemporary Theories of Schizophrenia*. New York: McGraw-Hill, 1981.

Showalter, Elaine, ed. *The New Feminist Criticism*. New York: Pantheon, 1985.

Slusser, George Edgar. *The Farthest Shores of Ursula K. Le Guin*. San Bernardino, California: Borgo Press, 1976.

Slusser, George E.; Rabkin, Eric S.; and Scholes, Robert, eds. *Bridges to Fantasy*. Carbondale and Edwardsville: Southern Illinois Press, 1982.

Slusser, George E.; Guffey, George R.; and Rose, Mark, eds. *Bridges to Science Fiction*. Carbondale and Edwardsville: Southern Illinois Press, 1980.

Spivack, Charlotte. *Ursula K. Le Guin*. Boston: Twayne, 1984.

Steiner, George. *After Babel: Aspects of Language and Translation*. London: Oxford University Press, 1975.

Stern, Daniel. *The First Relationship*. Cambridge, Massachusetts: Harvard University Press, 1977.

Stoller, Robert J. *Sex and Gender*. New York: Jason Aronson, 1975.

———. *A Case of Female Masculinity*. London: The Hogarth Press, 1973.

Storr, Anthony. *The Dynamics of Creation*. New York: Atheneum, 1972.

Strouse, Jean, ed. *Women and Analysis*. New York: Grossman Publishers, 1974.

Suvin, Darko. *Metamorphoses of Science Fiction*. New Haven and London: Yale University Press, 1979.

Tanner, Tony. *City of Words*. New York: Harper & Row, 1971.

Trilling, Lionel. *Beyond Culture*. New York: Harcourt Brace Jovanovich, 1965.

———. *The Liberal Imagination*. New York: Doubleday, 1953.

———. *The Opposing Self*. New York: Viking Press, 1959.

Turkle, Sherry. *Psychoanalytic Politics: Freud's French Revolution*. New York: Basic Books, 1978.

Wilden, Anthony. *System and Structure*. London: Tavistock, 1972.

Winnicott, D.W. *The Maturational Processes and the Facilitating Environment*. New York: International Universities Press, 1965.

———. *Playing and Reality*. New York: Basic Books, 1971.

Woolf, Virginia. *Contemporary Writers*. London: Hogarth, 1965.

———. *Women and Writing*. Introduced by Michele Barrett. London: The Women's Press, 1979.

Wright, Elizabeth. *Psychoanalytic Criticism*. London and New York: Methuen, 1984.

Yaker, Henri, ed. *The Future of Time*. Garden City, New York: Doubleday, 1971.

Yeats, W.B. *Ideas of Good and Evil*. London: A.H. Bullen, 1903.

Secondary Sources—Articles

Abend, Sander. "Problems of Identity." *Psychoanalytic Quarterly* 43 (1974): 606–37.

Adorno, Theodor. "Sociology and Psychology." *New Left Review* 46 (November-December 1967): 67–80 and 47 (January-February 1968): 79–97.

Allen, Dick. "Fire Burning in the Rain." *The Hudson Review* 34 (Spring 1986): 135–40.

Arbur, Rosemarie. "Beyond Feminism, the Self Intact: Woman's Place in the Work of Le Guin." In *Selected Proceedings of the 1978 Science Fiction Research Association National Conference*, pp. 146–63. Cedar Falls: University of Northern Iowa, 1979.

———. "Le Guin's 'Song' of Inmost Feminism." *Extrapolation* 21 (Fall 1980): 223–26.

Attebery, Brian. "On a Far Shore: The Myth of Earthsea." *Extrapolation* 21 (Fall 1980): 269–77.

Bailey, Edgar C. Jr. "Shadows in Earthsea: Le Guin's Use of a Jungian Archetype." *Extrapolation* 21 (Fall 1980): 254–61.

Bain, Dena C. "The *Tao Te Ching* as Background to the Novels of Ursula K. Le Guin." *Extrapolation* 21 (Fall, 1980): 209–22.

Barbour, Douglas. *"The Lathe of Heaven:* Taoist Dream." *Algol* 21 (November 1973): 22–24.

———. "On Ursula Le Guin's *A Wizard of Earthsea." Riverside Quarterly* 6 (April 1974): 119–23.

———. "Wholeness and Balance in the Hainish Novels of Ursula K. Le Guin." *Science-Fiction Studies* 1 (1974): 164–73.

———. "Wholeness and Balance: An Addendum." *Science-Fiction Studies* 2 (1975): 248–49.

Barr, Marlene. "On the Other Hand." *Science-Fiction Studies* 41:14 (March 1987): 111–15.

Barrow, Craig, and Barrow, Diana. *"The Left Hand of Darkness:* Feminism for Men." *Mosaic* 20:1 (Winter 1987): 83–96.

Benjamin, Jessica. "A Desire of One's Own: Psychoanalytic Feminism and Intersubjective Space." In *Feminist Studies: Critical Studies,* edited by Teresa de Lauretis. Bloomington: University of Indiana Press, 1986.

Bickman, Martin. "Le Guin's *The Left Hand of Darkness:* Form and Content." *Science-Fiction Studies* 4 (1977): 42–47.

Bowlby, John. "The Nature of the Child's Tie to His Mother." *International Journal of Psychoanalysis* 39 (1958): 350–73.

Brink, Andrew. "Samuel Beckett's *Endgame* and the Schizoid Ego." *The Sphinx* 4 (1982): 87–100.

Brown, Barbara. *"The Left Hand of Darkness:* Androgyny, Future, Present, and Past." *Extrapolation* 21 (Fall 1980): 227–35.

Bucknall, Barbara J. "Androgynes in Outer Space." *Critical Encounters: Writers and Themes in Science Fiction,* edited by Dick Riley, pp. 56–69. New York: Ungar, 1978.

Burke, Carolyn. "Irigaray through the Looking Glass." *Feminist Studies* 7 (Summer 1981): 288–306.

Butor, Michel. "Science Fiction: The Crisis of Its Growth." In *SF: The Other Side of Realism,* edited by Thomas D. Clareson, pp. 157–65. Bowling Green, Ohio: Bowling Green University Popular Press, 1971.

Chodorow, Nancy. "Mothering, Object-Relations, and the Female Oedipal Configuration." *Feminist Studies* 4 (February 1978): 137-58.

Cunneen, Sheila. "Earthseans and Earthteens." *English Journal* 74 (February 1985): 68–69.

Derrida, Jacques. "The Law of Genre." *Critical Inquiry* 7 (Autumn 1980): 55–82.

_____ . "Living on Border Lines." In *Deconstruction and Criticism,* edited by Harold Bloom, pp. 75–176. New York: Continuum, 1979.

Edel, Leon. "The Biographer and Psycho-Analysis." *International Journal of Psychoanalysis* 42 (1961): 458–66.

Erlich, Richard D. "On Barbour on Le Guin." *Science-Fiction Studies* 4 (1977): 317–18.

Farrelly, James P. "The Promised Land: Moses, Nearing, Skinner, and Le Guin." *Journal of General Education* 33:1 (Spring 1981): 15–23.

Fekete, John. "Circumnavigating Ursula Le Guin." *Science-Fiction Studies* 8 (1981): 91–98.

_____ . *"The Dispossessed* and *Triton:* Act and System in Utopian Science Fiction." *Science-Fiction Studies* 6 (1979): 129–43.

Feral, Josette. "Antigone or the Irony of the Tribe." *Diacritics* 8 (Fall 1978): 2–14.

Fleck, Leonard M. "Science Fiction as a Tool of Speculative Philosophy: A Philosophical Analysis of Selected Anarchistic and Utopian Themes in Le Guin's *The Dispossessed."* In *Selected Proceedings of the 1978 Science Fiction Research Association National Conference,* edited by Thomas J. Remington. Cedar Falls: University of Northern Iowa, 1979.

Galbreath, Robert. "Taoist Magic in the Earthsea Trilogy." *Extrapolation* 21 (Fall 1980): 262–68.

Gallagher, Nora. "Ursula K. Le Guin: In a World of Her Own." *Mother Jones* 9 (January 1984): 23–27, 51–52.

Gallop, Jane. *"Writing and Sexual Difference:* The Difference Within." *Critical Inquiry* 8 (Summer 1982): 797–804.

Gardiner, Judith Kegan. "On Female Identity and Writing by Women." *Critical Inquiry* 8 (Winter 1981): 347–62.

_____ . "The (US)es of (I)dentity: A Response to Abel on '(E)Merging Identities.'" *Signs* 6 (Spring 1981): 436–41.

Greenacre, Phyllis. "The Family Romance of the Artist." *Psychoanalytic Study of the Child* 13 (1958): 9–36.

Greenson, Ralph R. "On Homosexuality and Gender Identity." *International Journal of Psychoanalysis* 45 (1964): 217–19.

Gubar, Susan. "Feminism and Utopia." *Science-Fiction Studies* 13 (1986): 79–83.

_____ . "'The Blank Page' and the Issues of Female Creativity." *Critical Inquiry* 8 (Winter 1981): 243–64.

Hartman, Geoffrey H. "The Fulness and Nothingness of Literature." *Yale French Studies* 16 (1965): 63–78.

———. "Touching Compulsion: Wordsworth and the Problem of Literary Representation." *The Georgia Review* 31 (Summer 1977): 345–61.

Hayman, Anne. "Verbalization and Identity." *International Journal of Psychoanalysis* 46 (1965): 455–66.

Heilbrun, Carolyn G. "A Response to *Writing and Sexual Difference*." *Critical Inquiry* 8 (Summer 1981): 805–11.

Holland, Norman N. "Criticism as Transaction." *What is Criticism?* edited by Paul Hernadi, pp. 242–52. Bloomington: Indiana University Press, 1981.

———. "The Delphi Seminar." *College English* 36 (1975): 789–800.

———. "'English' and Identities." *The CEA Critic* 35 (1973): 4-11.

———. "Human Identity." *Critical Inquiry* 4 (Spring 1978): 451-69.

———. "Literary Theory and Three Phases of Psychoanalysis." *Critical Inquiry* 3 (Winter 1976): 221–33.

———. "Postmodern Psychoanalysis." *Innovational Renovation: New Perspectives on the Humanities,* edited by Ihab Hassan and Sally Sassan, pp. 291–309. Madison: University of Wisconsin Press, 1983.

———. "A Touching of Literary and Psychiatric Education." *Seminars in Psychiatry* 5 (1973): 287–99.

———. "Unity Identity Text Self." *PMLA* 90 (1975): 813–22.

———. "You, U.K. Le Guin." *Future Females,* edited by Marleen S. Barr, pp. 125–37. Bowling Green, Ohio: Bowling Green State University Popular Press, 1981.

Inglis, Fred. "Spellbinding and Anthropology: The Work of Richard Adams and Ursula Le Guin." *Good Writers for Young Readers,* edited by Dennis Butts, pp. 114–28. St. Albans, England: Hart-Davis Educational, 1977.

Irigaray, Luce. "And the One Doesn't Stir Without the Other." Translated by Helene Vivienne Wenzel. *Signs* 7 (Autumn 1981): 60-67.

———. "When Our Lips Speak Together." Translated by Carolyn Burke. *Signs* 6 (Autumn 1980): 69–79.

James, Martin. "Premature Ego Development: Some Observations on Disturbances in the First Three Months of Life." *International Journal of Psychoanalysis* 41 (1960): 288–94.

Jameson, Fredric. "Imaginary and Symbolic in Lacan: Marxism, Psychoanalytic Criticism, and the Problem of the Subject." *Yale French Studies* 55/56 (1977): 338–95.

———. "Progress Versus Utopia; or, Can We Imagine the Future?" *Science-Fiction Studies* 9 (1982): 147–58.

———. "Towards an Awareness of Genre." *Science-Fiction Studies* 9 (1982): 322–24.

———. "World-Reduction in Le Guin: The Emergence of Utopian Narrative." *Science-Fiction Studies* 2 (1975): 221–30.

Jones, Ann Rosalind. "Julia Kristeva on Femininity: The Limits of a Semiotic Politics." *Feminist Review* 18 (November 1984): 56–73.

———. "Writing the Body: Towards an Understanding of L'Ecriture Feminine." *Feminist Studies* 7 (Summer 1981): 247–63.

Kanner, L. "Problems of Nosology and Psychodynamics of Early Infantile Autism." *American Journal of Orthopsychiatry* 19 (1949): 416–26.

Katan, Anny. "Some Thoughts About the Role of Verbalization in Early Childhood." *The Psychoanalytic Study of the Child* 16 (1961): 184–88.

Kelly, Michael. "Louis Althusser and Marxist Theory." *Journal of European Studies* 7 (1977): 189–203.

Ketterer, David. "*The Left Hand of Darkness*: Ursula K. Le Guin's Archetypal Winter-Journey." *Riverside Quarterly* 5 (April 1973): 288–97.

Klein, Gerard. "Le Guin's 'Aberrant' Opus: Escaping the Trap of Discontent." *Science-Fiction Studies* 4 (1977): 287–95.

Kloss, Robert J. "Further Reflections on Plath's 'Mirror.'" *Hartford Studies in Literature* 14 (1982): 11–23.

Kolodny, Annette. "Turning the Lens on 'The Panther Captivity': A Feminist Exercise in Practical Criticism." *Critical Inquiry* 8 (Winter 1981): 329–46.

Kramer, Paul. "On Discovering One's Identity." *Psychoanalytic Study of the Child* 10 (1955): 47–74.

Kristeva, Julia. "Psychoanalysis and the Polis." Translated by Margaret Waller. *Critical Inquiry* 9 (September 1982): 77–92.

_____ . "Women's Time." *Signs: Journal of Women in Culture and Society* 7 (1981): 13–35.

Lacan, Jacques. "Reflections on the Ego." *International Journal of Psychoanalysis* 34 (1953): 11–17.

Lacan, Jacques, and Granoff, Wladimir. "Fetishism: The Symbol, the Imaginary and the Real." In *Perversions: Psychodynamics and Therapy*, edited by Sandor Lorand and Michael Balint, pp. 265–76. New York: Gramercy, 1956.

Lake, David J. "Le Guin's Twofold Vision: Contrary Image Sets in *The Left Hand of Darkness.*" *Science-Fiction Studies* 8 (July 1981): 156–64.

Leavy, Stanley A. "John Keats's Psychology of Creative Imagination." *Psychoanalytic Quarterly* 39 (1970): 173–97.

Le Guin, Ursula K. "It Was a Dark and Stormy Night; or Why Are We Huddling about the Campfire?" *Critical Inquiry* 7 (Autumn 1980): 191–200.

_____ . "On Writing Science Fiction." *The Writer's Handbook*, edited by Sylvia K. Burack, pp. 231–35. Boston: The Writer Inc., 1985.

_____ . "A Non-Euclidean View of California as a Cold Place to Be." *The Yale Review* 72 (Winter 1983): 161–80.

_____ . "The Space Crone." *The Co-Evolutionary Quarterly* 10 (Summer 1976): 108–11.

Loewald, Hans W. "Ego and Reality." *International Journal of Psychoanalysis* 32 (1951): 10–18.

_____ . "Internalization, Separation, Mourning, and the Superego." *Psychoanalytic Quarterly* 31 (1962): 483–504.

_____ . "Some Considerations on Repetition and Repetition Compulsion." *International Journal of Psychoanalysis* 52 (1971): 59–66.

Lubin, Albert J. "A Feminine Moses: A Bridge Between Childhood Identifications and Adult Identity." *International Journal of Psychoanalysis* 39 (1958): 535–46.

Macey, David. "Jacques Lacan." *Ideology and Consciousness* 4 (1978): 113–28.

Mahler, Margaret S. "On Child Psychosis and Schizophrenia: Autistic and Symbiotic Infantile Psychoses." *The Psychoanalytic Study of the Child* 7 (1952): 286–306.

_____ . "Autism and Symbiosis." *International Journal of Psychoanalysis* 39 (1958): 77–83.

Manlove, C.N. "Conservatism in the Fantasy of Le Guin." *Extrapolation* 21 (Fall 1980): 287–98.

Marotti, Arthur F. "Countertransference, the Communication Process, and the Dimensions of Psychoanalytic Criticism." *Critical Inquiry* 4 (Spring 1978): 471–89.

McGuirk, Carol. "Optimism and the Limits of Subversion in *The Dispossessed* and *The Left Hand of Darkness.*" In *Ursula K. Le Guin*, edited by Harold Bloom, pp. 243–58. New York: Chelsea House, 1986.

Miel, Jan. "Jacques Lacan and the Structure of the Unconscious." *Yale French Studies* 36/37 (1967): 104–11.

Milner, Marion. "Aspects of Symbolism in Comprehension of the Not-Self." *International Journal of Psychoanalysis* 33 (1952): 181–95.

Myers, Victoria. "Conversational Technique in Ursula Le Guin: A Speech-Act Analysis." *Science-Fiction Studies* 10 (1983): 306–16.

Nudelman, Rafail. "An Approach to the Structure of Le Guin's SF." *Science-Fiction Studies* 2 (1975): 210–20.

Percy, Walker. "The Orbiting Self." *The Georgia Review* 37 (Summer 1983): 249–62.

Plank, Robert. "Ursula K. Le Guin and the Decline of Romantic Love." *Science-Fiction Studies* 3 (1976): 36–43.

Pontalis, J.-B. "Dream as an Object." *International Review of Psychoanalysis* 1 (1974): 125–33.

Porter, David L. "The Politics of Le Guin's Opus." *Science-Fiction Studies* 2 (1975): 243–48.

Powers, Marla N. "Menstruation and Reproduction: On Oglala Case." *Signs* 6 (Autumn 1980): 54–56.

Remington, Thomas J. "A Time to Live and a Time to Die: Cyclical Renewal in the Earthsea Trilogy." *Extrapolation* 21 (Fall 1980): 278–86.

Remington, Thomas J., and Galbreath, Robert. "Lagniappe: An Informal Dialogue with Ursula K. Le Guin." In *Selected Proceedings of the 1978 Science Fiction Research Association National Conference*, edited by Thomas J. Remington, pp. 269–81. Cedar Falls: University of Northern Iowa, 1979.

Ricoeur, Paul. "Narrative Time." *Critical Inquiry* 7 (Autumn 1980): 169–90.

Rottensteiner, Franz. "Le Guin's Fantasy." *Science-Fiction Studies* 8 (1981): 87–90.

Rubinfine, David L. "Problems of Identity." *American Psychoanalytic Association Journal* 6 (1958): 131–42.

Said, Edward W. "Opponents, Audiences, Constituencies, and Community." *Critical Inquiry* 9 (September 1982): 1–26.

Sarlin, Charles N. "Feminine Identity." *Journal of the American Psychoanalytic Association* 11 (1963): 790–816.

Schafer, Roy. "Narration in the Psychoanalytic Dialogue." *Critical Inquiry* 7 (Autumn, 1980): 29–54.

Searles, Harold F. "Anxiety Concerning Change, as Seen in the Psychotherapy of Schizophrenic Patients, with Particular Reference to the Sense of Personal Identity." *International Journal of Psychoanalysis* 42 (1961): 74–85.

Sherman, Murray M. "Theodor Reik and Individualism in Psychoanalysis." *Psychoanalytic Review* 55 (1968): 172–86.

Showalter, Elaine. "Feminist Criticism in the Wilderness." *Critical Inquiry* 8 (Winter 1981): 179–206.

Sitterson, Joseph C. "Psychoanalytic Model and Literary Theory." *University of Toronto Quarterly* 51 (Fall 1981): 78–93.

Slethaug, Gordon E. "The Paradoxical Double in Le Guin's *A Wizard of Earthsea*." *Extrapolation* 27 (Winter 1986): 326–33.

Socarides, Charles W. et al. "Discussion of R. Stoller's 'Healthy Parental Influences on the Earliest Development of Masculinity in Baby Boys.'" *Psychoanalytic Forum* 5 (1974): 241–61.

Spivak, Gayatri Chakravorty. "'Draupadi' by Mahasveta Devi." *Critical Inquiry* 8 (Winter 1981): 381–402.

Stevenson, Lionel. "The Artistic Problem: Science Fiction as Romance." In *SF: The Other Side of Realism*, edited by Thomas D. Clareson, pp. 96–104. Bowling Green, Ohio: Bowling Green University Popular Press, 1971.

Stewart, Robert. "Crossings in Mist." *Starship* 17 (Summer 1980): 34–35.

Suvin, Darko. "Parables of De-Alienation: Le Guin's Widdershins Dance." *Science-Fiction Studies* 2 (1975): 265–73.

———. "The Science Fiction of Ursula K. Le Guin." *Science-Fiction Studies* 2 (1975): 203–4.

Theall, Donald F. "The Art of Social-Science Fiction: The Ambiguous Utopian Dialectics of Ursula K. Le Guin." *Science-Fiction Studies* 2 (1975): 256–64.

Trilling, Lionel. "Authenticity and the Modern Unconscious." *Commentary* 52 (September 1971): 39–50.

Watson, Ian. "The Forest as Metaphor for Mind: 'The Word for World Is Forest' and 'Vaster than Empires and More Slow.'" *Science-Fiction Studies* 2 (1975): 231–37.

———. "Le Guin's *Lathe of Heaven* and the Role of Dick: The False Reality as Mediator." *Science-Fiction Studies* 2 (1975): 67-75.

Walker, Jeanne. "Myth, Exchange, and History in *The Left Hand of Darkness.*" *Science-Fiction Studies* 6 (1979): 180–89.

Widmer, Kingsley. "Utopian, Dystopian, Diatopian Libertarianism: Le Guin's *The Dispossessed.*" *The Sphinx* 4 (1981): 55–67.

Williams, Raymond. "Utopia and Science Fiction." *Science-Fiction Studies* 5 (1978): 203–14.

Yoke, Carl. "Precious Metal in White Clay." *Extrapolation* 21 (Fall 1980): 197–208.

Index